The Form of Poetry

The Form of Poetry

THOMAS R. ARP

THE MACMILLAN COMPANY, NEW YORK

First Printing

Library of Congress catalog card number: 66–12345

THE MACMILLAN COMPANY, NEW YORK

COLLIER-MACMILLAN CANADA, LTD., TORONTO, ONTARIO

Printed in the United States of America

Designed by Andrew P. Zutis

Acknowledgments

W. H. AUDEN
  "September 1, 1939," "Musee des Beaux Arts" (ANOTHER TIME). Copyright 1940 by W. H. Auden. Reprinted from THE COLLECTED POETRY OF W. H. AUDEN by permission of Random House, Inc.
  Permission extended to Canada by Faber and Faber, Ltd.

ROBERT BRIDGES
  "Nightingales," "A Passer-By," "Low Barometer." Reprinted from THE POETICAL WORKS OF ROBERT BRIDGES by permission of The Clarendon Press, Oxford.

HART CRANE
  "Voyages I, II, III," "Repose of Rivers," "To Emily Dickinson." From THE COLLECTED POEMS OF HART CRANE. Reprinted by permission of Liveright, Publishers, N. Y. Copyright © R, 1961, by Liveright Publishing Corp.

J. V. CUNNINGHAM
  "Meditation on Statistical Method." Reprinted from THE EXCLUSIONS OF A RHYME: POEMS AND EPIGRAMS by J. V. Cunningham, by permission of the publisher, Alan Swallow. Copyright 1947, 1960 by J. V. Cunningham.

EMILY DICKINSON
  " 'Twas warm—at first—like Us," "And this of all my Hopes." From THE COMPLETE POEMS OF EMILY DICKINSON edited by Thomas H. Johnson, by permission of Little, Brown and Company. Copyright 1929, © 1957 by Mary L. Hampson. "These are the days when Birds come back," "There's a certain Slant of light," "I felt a Funeral, in my Brain," "After great pain, a formal feeling comes," "I heard a Fly buzz—when I died," " 'Twas warm— at first—like Us," "Because I could not stop for death," "And this of all my Hopes," "Further in Summer than the Birds," "The last Night that She lived," "A Route of Evanescence," "As imperceptibly as Grief." Reprinted by permission of the publishers and the Trustees of Amherst College from Thomas H. Johnson, Editor, THE POEMS OF EMILY DICKINSON, Cambridge, Mass.: The Belknap Press of Harvard University Press, Copyright 1951, 1955, by The President and Fellows of Harvard College.

T. S. ELIOT
  "Portrait of a Lady," "The Love Song of J. Alfred Prufrock," "Gerontion," "The Hollow Men." Reprinted by permission of the publishers from COLLECTED POEMS 1909–1962 by T. S. Eliot, copyright 1936 by Harcourt, Brace & World, Inc.; copyright © 1963, 1964 by T. S. Eliot.
  Permission extended to Canada by Faber and Faber, Ltd.

ACKNOWLEDGMENTS

WILLIAM EMPSON
"Missing Dates." Reprinted by permission of Harcourt, Brace & World, Inc., from COLLECTED POEMS OF WILLIAM EMPSON, copyright 1949 by William Empson.
Permission extended to Canada by Chatto and Windus, Ltd.

ROBERT FROST
"After Apple-Picking," "The Oven Bird," "Stopping by Woods on a Snowy Evening," "For Once, Then, Something," "Acquainted with the Night," "Desert Places," "Never Again Would Birds' Song Be the Same," "Come In," "Design," "Directive." From COMPLETE POEMS OF ROBERT FROST. Copyright 1916, 1923, 1928, 1930, 1939, 1947 by Holt, Rinehart and Winston, Inc. Copyright 1936, 1942, 1944, 1951, © 1956, 1958 by Robert Frost. Copyright © 1964 by Lesley Frost Ballantine. Reprinted by permission of Holt, Rinehart and Winston, Inc.

ROBERT GRAVES
"Recalling War." Reprinted from COLLECTED POEMS by Robert Graves, by permission of International Authors N. V. Copyright 1955, 1959 © International Authors N. V.

THOM GUNN
"On the Move," "The Unsettled Motorcyclist's Vision of His Death." Reprinted from THE SENSE OF MOVEMENT by Thom Gunn, copyright 1957. By permission of Faber and Faber, Ltd.

GERARD MANLEY HOPKINS
"The Windhover," "No Worst, There Is None," "I Wake and Feel the Fell of Dark," "In Honour of St. Alphonsus Rodriguez." From POEMS OF GERARD MANLEY HOPKINS, Third Edition, edited by W. H. Gardner. Copyright 1948 by Oxford University Press, Inc. Reprinted by permission.

A. E. HOUSMAN
"Epitaph on an Army of Mercenaries." From "A Shropshire Lad"—Authorised Edition—from THE COLLECTED POEMS OF A. E. HOUSMAN. Copyright 1940 by Holt, Rinehart and Winston, Inc. Reprinted by permission of Holt, Rinehart and Winston, Inc.
Permission extended to Canada by The Society of Authors as the literary representatives of the Estate of the late A. E. Housman, and Messrs. Jonathan Cape, Ltd., publishers of A. E. Housman's COLLECTED POEMS.

ELLEN KAY
"To a Blue Hippopotamus." Reprinted from A LOCAL HABITATION by Ellen Kay, by permission of the publisher, Alan Swallow. Copyright 1958 by Ellen Kay.

PHILIP LARKIN
"Church Going," "Toads." Reprinted from THE LESS DECEIVED by Philip Larkin © 1955, by permission of The Marvell Press, Hessle, Yorkshire, England.

ROBERT LOWELL
"As a Plane Tree by the Water." Reprinted by permission of Harcourt,

Brace & World, Inc., from LORD WEARY'S CASTLE by Robert Lowell, copyright 1944, 1946 by Robert Lowell. "My last Afternoon with Uncle Devereux Winslow." Reprinted from LIFE STUDIES by Robert Lowell, by permission of Farrar, Straus & Giroux, Inc. Copyright © 1959 by Robert Lowell.

MARIANNE MOORE
"A Grave." Reprinted with permission of The Macmillan Company from COLLECTED POEMS by Marianne Moore. Copyright 1935 by Marianne Moore, Renewed 1963 by Marianne Moore and T. S. Eliot. "What Are Years." Reprinted with permission of The Macmillan Company from COLLECTED POEMS by Marianne Moore. Copyright 1941 by Marianne Moore. "Nevertheless." Reprinted with permission of The Macmillan Company from COLLECTED POEMS by Marianne Moore. Copyright 1944 by Marianne Moore.

EZRA POUND
"Portrait d'une Femme," "An Immorality," "In a Station of the Metro." From PERSONAE by Ezra Pound. Copyright 1926, 1954 by Ezra Pound. Reprinted by permission of the publishers, New Directions.

JOHN CROWE RANSOM
"Here Lies a Lady." Copyright 1924 by Alfred A. Knopf, Inc. Renewed 1952 by John Crowe Ransom. Reprinted from SELECTED POEMS, Revised Edition, by John Crowe Ransom, by permission of Alfred A. Knopf, Inc. "Janet Waking." Copyright 1927 by Alfred A. Knopf, Inc. Renewed 1955 by John Crowe Ransom. Reprinted from SELECTED POEMS, Revised Edition, by John Crowe Ransom, by permission of Alfred A. Knopf, Inc.

EDWIN ARLINGTON ROBINSON
"Eros Turannos," "Bewick Finzer." Reprinted with permission of The Macmillan Company from COLLECTED POEMS by E. A. Robinson. Copyright 1916 by The Macmillan Company, Renewed 1944 by Ruth Nivison. "The Mill." Reprinted with permission of The Macmillan Company from COLLECTED POEMS by E. A. Robinson. Copyright 1920 by The Macmillan Company, Renewed 1948 by Ruth Nivison. "The Sheaves." Reprinted with permission of The Macmillan Company from COLLECTED POEMS by E. A. Robinson. Copyright 1925 by The Macmillan Company, Renewed 1952 by Ruth Nivison and Barbara R. Holt. "New England." Reprinted with permission of The Macmillan Company from COLLECTED POEMS by E. A. Robinson. Copyright 1925 by E. A. Robinson, Renewed 1952 by Ruth Nivison and Barbara R. Holt.
The following poems by Edwin Arlington Robinson are used by permission of Charles Scribner's Sons: "Miniver Cheevy" (Copyright 1907 Charles Scribner's Sons; renewal copyright 1935) and "For a Dead Lady" from THE TOWN DOWN THE RIVER. Copyright 1910 Charles Scribner's Sons; renewal copyright 1938 Ruth Nivison; "Luke Havergal" and "Richard Cory" from THE CHILDREN OF THE NIGHT (1897).

WALLACE STEVENS
"The Death of a Soldier," "Disillusionment of Ten O'Clock," "Peter Quince at the Clavier," "The Snow Man," "Sunday Morning." Copyright 1923; renewed 1951 by Wallace Stevens. Reprinted from THE COLLECTED

ACKNOWLEDGMENTS

POEMS OF WALLACE STEVENS, by permission of Alfred A. Knopf, Inc. "The Idea of Order at Key West." Copyright 1936 by Wallace Stevens. Renewed 1964 by Elsie Stevens and Holly Stevens. Reprinted from THE COLLECTED POEMS OF WALLACE STEVENS, by permission of Alfred A. Knopf, Inc. "The Course of a Particular." Copyright 1951 by Wallace Stevens. Reprinted from OPUS POSTHUMOUS, by Wallace Stevens, by permission of Alfred A. Knopf, Inc.

EDWARD TAYLOR
"Huswifery," "Meditation One." Reprinted from THE POETICAL WORKS OF EDWARD TAYLOR, edited by Thomas H. Johnson, by permission of Princeton University Press. Copyright © 1939 by Rocklands Editions. Copyright © 1943 by Princeton University Press.

RICHARD WILBUR
"The Death of a Toad." Reprinted by permission of Harcourt, Brace & World, Inc., from CEREMONY AND OTHER POEMS by Richard Wilbur, copyright 1948, 1949, 1950 by Richard Wilbur. "Mind." Reprinted by permission of Harcourt, Brace & World, Inc., from THINGS OF THIS WORLD by Richard Wilbur, © 1956 by Richard Wilbur.

WILLIAM CARLOS WILLIAMS
"Danse Russe," "The Widow's Lament in Springtime," "Spring and All," "The Red Wheelbarrow," "This Is Just to Say." From THE COLLECTED EARLIER POEMS OF WILLIAM CARLOS WILLIAMS. Copyright 1938, 1951 by William Carlos Williams. Reprinted by permission of the publishers, New Directions.

YVOR WINTERS
"The Slow Pacific Swell," "To the Holy Spirit," "At the San Francisco Airport." Reprinted from COLLECTED POEMS by Yvor Winters, by permission of the publisher, Alan Swallow. Copyright 1952, 1960 by Yvor Winters.

WILLIAM BUTLER YEATS
"To a Friend Whose Work Has Come to Nothing." Reprinted with permission of The Macmillan Company from COLLECTED POEMS by W. B. Yeats. Copyright 1916 by The Macmillan Company, Renewed 1944 by Bertha Georgie Yeats. "The Second Coming." Reprinted with permission of The Macmillan Company from COLLECTED POEMS by W. B. Yeats. Copyright 1924 by The Macmillan Company, Renewed 1952 by Bertha Georgie Yeats. "Sailing to Byzantium," "Among School Children." Reprinted with permission of The Macmillan Company from COLLECTED POEMS by W. B. Yeats. Copyright 1928 by The Macmillan Company, Renewed 1956 by Bertha Georgie Yeats. "For Anne Gregory." Reprinted with permission of The Macmillan Company from COLLECTED POEMS by W. B. Yeats. Copyright 1933 by The Macmillan Company, Renewed 1961 by Bertha Georgie Yeats. "Lapis Lazuli," "Long-Legged Fly." Reprinted with permission of The Macmillan Company from COLLECTED POEMS by W. B. Yeats. Copyright 1940 by Bertha Georgie Yeats.
Permission extended to Canada by Mrs. W. B. Yeats and The Macmillan Company of Canada, Ltd.

Preface

Except for the mechanical exclusion of very long poems, I have tried in this selection to avoid any criterion other than excellence. The poems are arranged only in the order of the birth dates of the poets.

The Introduction does not aim to convince the reader that poetry is exciting or important, trusting that he will have experienced these qualities in turning to the study of poetry. I have limited my discussion to formal and structural distinctions, presenting what I understand to be the rationale of verse forms. The practiced reader of poetry will realize immediately that I have avoided questions of what a poem means and how it means it. Because this book is chiefly designed for classroom use, I have left to the instructor the more pleasurable job of elucidating the contents of these poems. In a similar spirit, annotations have been limited to matters of information not readily available to the modern student, and there has been no attempt to offer explanations or interpretations.

For many of the ideas and attitudes expressed in the Introduction, I am indebted to the writing and teaching of Yvor Winters, to whom this book is dedicated.

T. R. A.

Contents

CONTENTS

XV

CONTENTS

xvi

1 day

Introduction

READERS OF POETRY, even those who are undertaking this experience for the first time, recognize that they are in a world in which language and thought and feeling are somehow different, somehow more rich and impressive. For their fullest enjoyment of the experience, they must wish to know exactly how and why this poetic world *is* different. They must ask themselves how this form of communication achieves things not available in other forms, what particular devices and attitudes are employed to open this new world to them, and why the poet has wanted to awaken this new response. For poetry is unique in its powers and its pleasures, and arouses not only our natural curiosity but also our desire to understand its ways.

The Limits of Poetry

Just to avoid attributing to poetic statements exclusive powers that they actually share with all forms of careful writing, it may be best to begin with negative definitions. There are many ways in which poetry is no different from other spoken and written communication, and there would be little point in making claims for it that would melt away the moment the eye leaves the page.

In the first place, poetry makes use of the language common to all of us. Words are arranged in sentences, sentences into larger units called stanzas or paragraphs, and these may in turn be organized into still larger wholes—chapters, cantos, books, and so forth. As we know, the words of our language possess a double power: they express concepts, point to things, reveal relationships and actions; and also, at the same time, they communicate emotional responses to the concepts, things, or actions they signify. "Fire" is not merely the name of a process but also a signal that, depending on its context, moves us to fear, or pleasure, or any of a number of other

I

responses. These two powers of language are commonly called denotation and connotation, the powers of words to point and to excite.

In a similar way, phrases and sentences not only share the powers of the individual words but also create a context and a forward motion, so that these larger organizations also express emotions and ideas. Not only that: by a kind of reflex action, the sentences and phrases restrict and alter the connotative and denotative qualities of the individual words. We may say with some justice that the syntactical whole is greater than the sum of its words, and that the words are actually transformed into new significations as they become parts of the whole.

The poet, then, like most writers, knows about the expressive powers of his language. And also like most writers, the poet takes full advantage of those powers, because he wishes to achieve a double purpose: he wants to make a statement to his readers, and he wants to excite their emotions. The emotions he arouses are the ones that he feels a reader *ought* to have about his statements, and therefore they reveal his judgment of the conditions or events he is writing about.

Finally, in this brief survey of the common ground that poetry shares with other expressive writing, we come to the quality that is probably the most obvious to readers: poets seem to pay a good deal of attention to the sounds that words represent, arranging their statements and choosing their words to create patterns in sound. In this matter, too, poetry is not unique, though the intensity of its effects may be greater, and the kinds of patterns it achieves are out of the ordinary. Writers of prose, nonfiction as well as fiction, are aware of the power of sonal qualities such as alliteration, consonance, assonance, and even rhyme. Accomplished prose writers know how to make their words clash and clang, or chime melodiously, as well as poets do.

Although it might be possible to distinguish poetry from other kinds of communication by its intention or its subjects, it is chiefly distinguished by its form. Poetry differs from the better kinds of prose primarily in its greater attention to measure; that is, to regular and recognizable patterns of words. The poet thus limits himself to relatively strict patterns in order to concentrate his ideas and effects, to intensify them and clarify them. He desires to heighten his details and restrict the attention of his readers, as if to isolate his remarks and thus to reveal their relationships in the clearest possible way. Like the scientist, the poet not only delights in orderliness but also recognizes that order helps to define his ideas and feelings precisely. And also like the scientist, the poet knows that an isolated definition never refers to itself alone, but in some sense represents other definition—a definition of the world as he sees it and feels it. One grain of sand or drop of water reveals to the scientist the general properties of any amount of the same substance; and one murder, or one daffodil, may reveal to the poet all knowledge and all experience.

In addition to the intellectual advantages of great clarity and precision in patterned language, there are also emotional advantages to be gained, even beyond the inherent expressiveness of rhythmic repetition. The actual phrases and the sounds they signal are placed by the poet against an ideal pattern of regularity. The poet impresses his reader with the ideal, unheard pattern, and then he proceeds to depart from the regularity that the pattern implies. He thus provokes his reader to respond emotionally to the congruence or departure from the norms he has established. Manipulating the reader's response through all the varieties of fulfillment or frustration of a desire to hear the sound patterns match the ideal patterns, the poet adjusts the reader's emotions. In this way he increases the reader's awareness of the importance of key words or phrases, and intensifies his emotional response both to the rational statement being communicated and to the emotional power of language and context. And not least of his interests, like the sportsman he recognizes the pleasure a spectator takes simply from witnessing an example of fine technique gracefully displayed, for pleasure and power are the ends his poetry serves.

Meter and Rhythm

Poets in English have traditionally employed two kinds of measure in constructing their verses: they have set up a regular number of syllables per line, and they have arranged these syllables in regular patterns, alternating syllables of heavier and lighter stress. These two sources of regularity might seem to imply inflexibility and rigidity, because, for example, a line of ten syllables in which every other syllable is stressed appears to have the invariability of the ticktock of a clock. But though the *pattern* may be rigid, as patterns and blueprints generally are, it takes only the audible reading of a few lines to see that no two ten-syllable lines are exactly alike, either in the amount of stress we place upon the individual syllables or even in the impression we have of the comparable lengths of lines. The fact is that only lines that exist in isolation from other lines, and that repeat the same sounds identically, are ever as invariable as the clock. Only if we say "ticktock, ticktock, ticktock, ticktock, ticktock" can we achieve the kind of rigidity that the pattern seems to suggest. And furthermore, we must say this line fully intending to make it seem rigid, and without the context of other less regular lines, to get that kind of rigidity. For example, if we are paying too much attention to reaching the end of the line, we will probably give a little more emphasis to that last "tick" than we gave to any of the others; and if the line occurs in the context of other lines in which, say, the third pair of syllables has been more heavily stressed, we may find ourselves stressing the third "ticktock" perceptibly more heavily.

The basic patterns of measure in English poetry depend upon a few simple forms. Lines are divided into units, called *feet*, which consist of a stressed syllable and its attendant unstressed syllables. There are only four feet of any major importance, and they exist in two groups, the "rising" and the "falling" feet. Rising feet are those in which the stressed syllable comes last, and the commonest ones are *iambic* (comprising one unstressed syllable followed by a stressed one) and *anapestic* (two unstressed, one stressed). For purposes of example, we may take two single words following these patterns: *bĕcáuse* is pronounced as an iamb, and *ĭncŏrréct* an anapest. The major falling feet are the *trochaic* (*únděr*) and *dactyllic* (*yésterdăy*). Poems are usually composed entirely of a single type of foot, with occasional variations introduced by substituting another type or by dropping one or more syllables in the pattern, though very occasion-

4

ally a poet will choose to combine, in different lines, patterns alternately iambic and trochaic.

Feet are combined into lines named according to the number of feet they contain: a one-foot line is called *monometer,* two feet *dimeter,* three *trimeter,* four *tetrameter,* five *pentameter,* six *hexameter,* and seven *heptameter.* The most common line in English is iambic pentameter, a five-foot line of iambics (thus ten syllables).

These patterns are the *metrical* form of the verse, or what we have been calling simply "pattern." As we have seen, they are subject to occasional variation in their regularity by *substitution,* the introduction of a different kind of foot into a line whose norm has been established. But substitution is only the most obvious means at the poet's disposal for modifying the regularity of his line. Much more important are those variations that depend not upon altering the ideal metrical patterns but refer instead to the actual sounds of the words in their contexts: what we call *rhythm.* As has been said, the patterns exist to provide for the poet the necessary scope to manipulate his effects, playing the actual (rhythm) against the ideal (meter). The only possible perfectly regular line is one that repeats identical syllables. In all other cases, the fact that words are arranged in sentences necessarily alters the relative stress or emphasis placed upon them. The rhythm of lines depends not on the metrical form, though this may slightly modify the way in which we say them, but upon the "natural" pronunciation of words in their sentences.

The difference between meter and rhythm is analogous to that between a blueprint plan of a house and the house itself, with all its textures of materials, its landscaping, and the effects of sunlight and shade and artificial lighting. As in architecture and the other arts, it is essential to the reader of poetry that he recognize the ideal form that underlies the actuality for him to appreciate it fully. The actual pronunciation of a line of poetry determines its rhythm, and this actuality is the real embodiment of the ideal pattern, the meter. It is the failure to make this distinction that leads some inexperienced readers to suppose that a line that is metrically regular is "monotonous" or even "singsong" or "jingling." Monotony is of course possible in poetry, but it results when the lines are not only without metrical variation (the substitution of different feet) but achieve no rhythmical variation either. That is, monotony occurs when all the stressed syllables are given approximately the same amount of stress in "natural" pronunciation, and when all unstressed syllables seem equally light.

But good poetry takes its cue from effective speech. When we speak, we do not accentuate all stressed syllables equally; we recognize that important words, key phrases, or turns of thought require us to emphasize disproportionately so that the relative importance of these words is recognized. So too in poetry, "normal" or "natural" speech rhythms, based on the sense we make in our statements, determine the relative stress placed on syllables. We may take as an example the first line of Ben Jonson's "Song: To Celia" (page 46):

> Drink to me, only, with thine eyes,
> And I will pledge with mine;
> Or leave a kiss but in the cup,
> And I'll not look for wine. . . .

It is clear that varying the relative emphasis given to certain words in the first line will alter the meaning of the statement. For example, were we to stress *drink* and *eyes,* the line would imply "do not drink to me with your glass but with your eyes," or perhaps "do not do anything else to me with your eyes except drink." If instead we were to accentuate *me,* the line would imply "do not drink to others with your eyes," and if *thine* were stressed the implication would be "do not drink to me with anyone else's eyes." We could go on with various other hypotheses, but the point seems clear: the proper rhythm of the line depends upon the meaning of the sentence in its context. The last possibility cited above is plainly not available to us, because it makes no sense at all, particularly in the context of the whole poem—and it is the context that finally determines the sense of the line. This exercise in possible pronunciations might be called the "rhetorical test," for it consists of examining the rhetoric of the spoken sentence, the effective emphasis given to words because of their plain, prosy meaning. It is incidentally also the highest test that we can apply to the rhythm of a line, for in almost no case can the rhythm of a line be other than that which satisfies our sense of the spoken statement.

The scansion of Jonson's line reveals another quality of the rhythm, an important one in understanding the way in which metrical patterns are manipulated for the poet's purposes. (Scansion consists simply of marking off the feet and indicating the relative stresses within the feet; that is, it only indicates meter and metrical variation, not rhythm.) Using the customary marks, the line would be scanned thus:

Drĭnk tŏ / me ón / lў wĭth / thĭne eýes.

So marked, the line reveals one example of metrical substitution, a trochee in the first position. This substitution is important not only because it alters the rhythm of the line (as metrical variation always does), and thus throws emphasis onto the word *drink,* thereby suggesting its importance to the meaning of the statement; but also, more subtly, because this trochee is echoed by the word *only,* which is naturally a trochaic word. But notice that in the marked scansion, *only* actually occurs in a pair of perfectly regular iambic feet, *me ón / lў wĭth.* Thus, although the metrical form in this pair of feet is regular, the rhythmic form is counter to the prevailing iambic, and the effect is to suggest that *Drink to* and *only* are to be emphasized in their importance to the statement.

But the scansion of the line suggests another problem: can we really say that *with* is a stressed syllable when *thine* is marked unstressed? Yes, because the terms *stress* and *unstress* are purely relative, referring only to the quality of the syllable within its own foot—not to its quality with respect to other feet in the line. *With* is more heavily stressed than *-ly,* and *thine* is less heavily stressed than *eyes.* In actual fact, in the pronunciation of the line, *thine* does indeed receive more stress than *with,* but that is a fact pertaining to the rhythm, not the meter, and we have no means for indicating such rhythmic facts other than describing them. No marking system exists that can capture every nuance of relative stress in pronunciation, simply because such stress depends upon the context of words in sentences. Discussions of rhythm must inevitably, and very early, rely on the descriptive power of the analyst, who would here have to resort to some such phrase as "four increasing degrees of accentuation." Two metrically regular iambic feet are thus seen to comprise a rhythmic unit that does not mirror the inherent qualities of the iambic foot but presents instead an increasing emphasis, in a more or less straight line from the syllable *-ly*.

Such degrees of accentuation are only one part of the rhythm of a poetic line, however. Another very significant aspect of the pronunciation of the English language is also involved, and again we may refer to natural speech rhythms as an example. In conversation we find ourselves emphasizing important words and phrases not only by stressing them more distinctly—by speaking them more loudly, that is—but also by extending their duration in time. This amount of time that it takes us to pronounce various units of sound is called *quantity*. Because of rhetorical emphasis, and also because of the necessity of altering the shape of the mouth, moving the tongue or lips or teeth or all of them, simultaneously either using or not using the vocal cords, some sounds simply take longer to say than others. The poet selects his words with an ear to quantity as well as *quality* (the relative accents). In Ben Jonson's line, each of those last four syllables also takes progressively longer to pronounce because they are intrinsically "longer" syllables. That is, both the physiological fact of pronunciation and the rhetorical fact of emphasis combine to make *eyes* the most important of these syllables. It might be noticed too that *eyes* is in some part a longer syllable *because* it is rhetorically accented; although we might debate about the natural relative length of *thine* and *eyes* in isolation, if we realize that to stress *thine* we would achieve a nonsensical statement ("do not drink to me with anyone else's eyes"), we are in little danger of making that error in pronunciation.

Syllable length, then, as well as accentuation, leads us to conclude that Jonson intends *eyes* to be the word of importance at the end of the line, a fact we can verify by examining the rest of the stanza. For other reasons—primarily because it is the accented syllable in a trochaic substitution, as we have seen, but also because of its grating, guttural *k*—the word *drink* is also a very important word. It might take the ear and wisdom of Solomon to determine whether *drink* or *eyes* is the more important, but if we merely think of them both as outstripping all other words, and if we recall the relative importance of *only* because of its effect of echoing the initial trochee, we will recognize that the rhythmic form of the line parallels the meaning that the rest of the poem supports, "drink to me not with your glass, but with your eyes."

We have seen that the quantity of separate syllables alters the length of time taken to pronounce each and thus increases or decreases the relative length of the line. So too the amount of time when no sounds are made will affect the total length of a line. That is, we are required to make certain pauses, of varying duration, either by the physiological fact of altering the shape of the vocal apparatus or, more important, by the pauses required to make sense of a statement. Such pauses within lines are called *caesuras,* and occur either as the result of punctuation marks—commas, periods, and the like— which enforce a pause, or as the result of the rhetoric of the line. Some of the variety possible in the employment of caesuras may be illustrated with the following lines from Tennyson's "Ulysses" (page 168):

> I am a part // of all that I have met;
> Yet all experience // is an arch wherethrough
> Gleams that untraveled world // whose margin fades
> For ever and for ever // when I move.
> How dull it is to pause, // to make an end,   5
> To rust unburnished, // not to shine in use!
> As though to breathe were life! // Life piled on life
> Were all too little, // and of one to me
> Little remains; . . .

Through the first four lines, the caesuras are the result of natural rhetorical stress, the common division of speech into rhythmic units in order to impress their meaning upon a hearer. They are extremely faint, occasioning very little pause, and produce the effect of steady and regular movement from the beginning of the second line to the end of the fourth. But beginning in the fifth line, Tennyson writes in short, appositive phrases, exclamatory and abrupt, increasing the emotional intensity of phrases that are already intense in their meaning. The contrast in sound patterns between the two groups of lines is as striking, we may say, as the contrast between the kinds of statements that they comprise. Lines two through four present a meditative, defining image of experience as an *arch*, a studied and thoughtful remark; and from line five to the end of the passage, the statement consists of an outburst directed against inutility and lethargy, an emotional outpouring in short and explosive phrases.

These lines display, too, another of the advantages of metric arrangements into lines: the line itself functions as a unit in verse, and may be ruptured or foreshortened in its rhythmic effect by the poet's treatment of the syntax. He may precisely match his sentence units to the line length, as in the first line, which completes a thought in the full length of the one line. Or he may choose to continue the sense of his sentences over the end of the line and on into the next, as in the second and third lines. This effect of carrying the statement over beyond the end of the single line is called *enjambement*, or *run-on lines*, and it functions in a way analogous to the relationship between the metrical foot and the rhythmic unit. That is, although we have before us an established ideal norm, the length of the line, we are also presented with the requirement to read the sentences as their syntax demands. The second line of the Tennyson passage ends with a subordinating conjunction, and to pause after it would destroy the sense of the statement: "Yet all experience is an arch wherethrough" is fragmentary and more or less meaningless. We cannot pause at this point but must hurry on to the completion of the idea. There are various degrees of urgency in such cases, ranging from the simple need to get on to a parallel phrase, all the way to the more essential requirement that would spring from the poet's placing an article or preposition at the end of a line, as is the practice of some modern poets.

The same question of the matching of line and phrase arises in the other lines quoted from "Ulysses," from the fifth line onward. Here Tennyson employs the pauses, signaled by punctuation, to break the normal ten-syllable line into smaller units and to create sense and rhetorical units smaller than the lines. Knowing as we do the basic unit to be the line, these two forms of disruption based on sentence structure accentuate for us the tone of voice and meaning in this passage. Such disruptions are not themselves a form of communication, of course; their relevance is in the reader's awareness of the disturbance of a prevailing norm. The subtle agitation caused by this disturbance adjusts the emotional response to the statements. Here, as in the rhythmic means that the poet employs to enforce our attention on his manipulation of an ideal standard of regularity, the purpose is to reinforce the communication. As always, we must remember that the formal adjustment is meaningful and expressive to the extent that it depends upon the primary means of communication, the words and the statements they convey.

This, then, is the rationale of the sound patterns we call rhythm: they help us to understand the lines, and to respond to them emotionally, while at the same time they provide the emotional communication inherent in all rhythm. The reader recognizes the ideal metric pattern; he hears the rhythm that actually exists against this pattern; and he is therefore aware of the slightest nuances of alteration from regularity. He will detect in these the reinforcement of the emotional tone communicated by the statements and by the connotative qualities of the words.

Rhyme and Stanzaic Forms

Similarity (or marked dissimilarity) of sounds is much more important and more effective in poetry than in prose, because poetry employs regularity as the source of some of its effects. The existence of patterns heightens the reader's awareness of all the qualities of sound. Such effects as alliteration, rhyme, and contrasting sounds are given more attention by the reader because he is conditioned to respond to the careful and detailed arrangements of words and sounds. Prose writers must count on a less full response to their sonal effects, simply because they have not "trained" their readers to be conscious of them. In *Moby-Dick,* for example, Herman Melville employs the following series of *s* alliterations:

> It was while gliding through these latter waters that one serene and moonlight night, when all the waves rolled by like scrolls of silver; and, by their soft, suffusing seethings, made what seemed a silvery silence, not a solitude: on such a silent night a silvery jet was seen far in advance of the white bubbles at the bow.
>
> (Chapter LI, "The Spirit-Spout")

Hart Crane, in "Voyages: II" (page 285), consciously echoing Melville, achieves the effect much more easily, with far fewer examples of the sound required:

> Take this Sea, whose diapason knells
> On scrolls of silver snowy sentences,
> The sceptred terror of whose sessions rends . . .

Because he cannot rely on the closeness of his reader's attention to his phonetic effects, Melville feels it necessary to make his intention very clear by what may seem to some readers an excessive use of the device. Crane, writing verse, can expect reaction to such details, not only because this particular poem reveals his care with the effects of sound but also because it *is* a poem, and readers of poetry have learned to respond to alliteration.

Rhyme, of course, is the most obvious source of patterns in sound. (It is so obvious, in fact, that many poets have refused to use it on the grounds that it is not "natural" to the spoken language.) Like those patterns that are based on meter, rhyme seems to have as its chief purpose the creation of regular form within which the poet can manipulate his effects. Rhyme is, after all, a pattern of expectation and fulfillment, and satisfies (or frustrates) the reader's natural desire to witness a completion or filling out of the formal arrangement. The poet establishes rhyme as a formalizing element, and constructs his patterns so as to capitalize on a known and accepted pattern. He offers the reader the satisfaction of anticipation and completion, or he teases and frustrates him by withholding the full sound linkage he expects, always with an eye to the appropriateness of such manipulations to the material of the poem. Such effects may even seem at times to augment the sense of the lines themselves, as when such a poet as Emily Dickinson employs words in the position of rhyme sounds that do not fully rhyme but only echo slightly the vowel or consonant sounds of each other. Her apparent purpose is to represent uncertainty, or anguish, or deprivation, or some other emotion related to incompleteness. In the following stanza from Miss Dickinson's "I Felt a Funeral in My Brain" (page 208), for example, the second and fourth lines share little more than the consonant sound *n*, but in the four preceding stanzas of the poem the second and fourth lines have rhymed:

> And then a Plank in Reason, broke,
> And I dropped down, and down—
> And hit a World, at every plunge,
> And Finished knowing—then—

By contrasting the rhyme effect with the pattern she has followed in the poem, the poet seems to reflect in her rhymes the loss of consciousness or control, which is the subject of this final stanza.

As the example from Emily Dickinson demonstrates, the varieties of effects under the general name of "rhyme" are not limited to the simple repetition of identical sounds. Her practice in such a stanza has been called "slant rhyme" or "half rhyme," though neither term is completely useful, because they imply a measurable quantity of rhyming. But the degrees of rhyme are probably as undefinable in their variety as the degrees of stress in a line, and as little subject to a strict system.

Rhyme, like rhythm, does not exist only for the sake of our sense of order and completeness, though this pleasure is involved. Its first function may be to arouse the reader's emotional response, but it also has what may be called a more intellectual purpose. It necessarily tends to emphasize and link the words that rhyme. It displays them for our closer scrutiny, and perhaps reveals connections between them that we have customarily overlooked, so that we are satisfied with the sense of fitness that makes two words that sound alike also have some real link of meaning. For example, Wordsworth ends the fourth stanza of the "Ode: Intimations of Immortality" (page 124) with the famous couplet

> Whither is fled the visionary gleam?
> Where is it now, the glory and the dream?

The *gleam-dream* rhyme is stated in the lines as an equivalence: the gleam *is* a dream. (And notice too that the *gleam* is the *glory,* the alliterative link and the rhyme link suggesting exactly what the lines claim: the gleam is *both* glory and dream. It is almost as if Wordsworth were insisting that *gleam* is etymologically composed of elements from the two words he identifies with it.)

The relationship of equivalence is far from being the only one a rhyme may suggest. As the study of most rhyming poems will indicate, the range of relatedness that rhyme can imply is almost as wide as the power of the mind to sense relationships between qualities, events, actions, or ideas. One of the functions a poet undertakes is the broadening of our awareness of the physical and psychological world we inhabit, so that this peculiar capability of rhyme has a significant value in suggesting the kinds of meanings he perceives. Even the old *moon-June* rhyme of popular love songs reveals the interesting relationship between the ideas and the lucky fact that these ideas are implied by two words of similar sound. What may seem at first a merely decorative and accidental similarity thus invites us to recognize an almost magical rightness.

Rhyme is also the foundation of the larger patterns many poems display: the stanzaic forms. There are many varieties of stanzas in English poetry, but they all serve approximately the same end: they organize the lines into repeating patterns, and thus produce effects similar to those of meter and rhythm. Usually those poems that are arranged in stanzas (and many are not) remain faithful to the form they establish, though there are also poems composed of varied stanzas. These display within the separate stanzas a pattern of rhymes, but they do not offer the recurrence of identical rhyme schemes from stanza to stanza.

Many stanza forms in English have special names of their own, though those that occur more rarely, or even uniquely, must be designated only by naming the number of lines, the length and meter of the lines, and the rhyme patterns. The most common stanzas include the *couplet* (a pair of rhymed lines of any uniform length), and the *heroic couplet* (a pair of rhymed, iambic pentameter lines, normally closed or stopped by punctuation after the second). The *quatrain* is a four-line stanza of any of a number of metrical and rhyming patterns. The commonest quatrain forms are the *ballad stanza* (alternate lines of iambic tetrameter and trimeter rhyming *abcb*); the *heroic quatrain* (iambic pentameter lines rhyming *abab*); and the *In Memoriam stanza,* named for Tennyson's lengthy elegy, though not invented by him (iambic tetrameter lines rhyming *abba*). Less common among the short stanzas is the *tercet,* a three-lined stanza most often rhyming with a single sound, of uniform line lengths. One form that resembles the tercet has had wider use, the Italian rhyme form called *terza rima,* in which three-line units are interlinked by the recurrence of a rhyme, in this pattern: *aba, bcb, cdc,* and so on.

The larger the number of lines that comprise a stanza, the greater the possibilities for variety, of course. There have been many stanza forms ranging from five to fourteen lines, of which the following are the most important: *rime royal,* a seven-line iambic pentameter stanza rhyming *ababbcc; ottava rima,* eight lines of iambic pentameter rhyming *abababcc;* the *Spenserian stanza,* named for Spenser's *The Faerie Queene,* a nine-line stanza of which the first eight lines are iambic pentameter, the last iambic hexameter (called an "alexandrine"), rhyming *ababbcbcc;* and the *sonnet,* usually occurring as a single poem but occasionally employed as a recurring stanza form. The sonnet always contains fourteen lines of iambic pentameter, but there have been several rhyme schemes devised for it. The two most common are the *Petrarchan* or *Italian sonnet,* which often divides into an octave and a sestet (units of eight and six lines), rhymed *abba abba cde cde;* and the *English* or *Shakespearean sonnet,* a series of three heroic quatrains and a concluding couplet, *abab cdcd efef gg.* One of the more interesting stanzas invented by a poet to fulfill his special requirements is the ten-line stanza devised by John Keats for his series of "Odes," a stanza Keats felt combined the particular qualities of both the Shakespearean and Petrarchan sonnets. He rhymed his iambic pentameter lines *abab cdecde,* thus linking one of the quatrains of the Shakespearean form to the sestet of the Petrarchan.

As Keats's invention of this stanza suggests, the older forms may come to have an abstract quality or a traditional use associated with them, to the extent that poets have felt themselves able to judge the appropriateness of a stanza form to their subjects. Such appropriateness has rested usually on one of two qualities attached to the form. Either it has been customarily used in a particular kind of poem or for a particular subject matter (as for several centuries the sonnet was commonly considered to be appropriate for a love poem addressed to the beloved, and therefore to be the proper form for any deeply felt, personal emotion). Or a stanza form might be judged on the rhetoric it seems to dictate, because the development of idea and image is limited by the number of lines the poet allots to it, and its characteristic turns of thought are determined by the rhyme words. Thus, for example, in the Shakespearean sonnet form, the fact that the poem is broken into three four-line units with parallel rhyme schemes suggests the use of three parallel four-line images, capped by a closing couplet that contains a closing thought. Similarly, the longer final line of the Spenserian stanza lends itself to a climactic, closing statement (a tendency Lord Byron uses for comic purposes in his long satiric poem *Don Juan,* in which this last line often contains an ironic counterstatement undercutting the seriousness of the first eight lines).

The reader's awareness of the traditional uses of the various stanza forms, and of the traditional manner of fitting the statement rhetorically to the number and length of the lines, leads to possibilities of variation parallel to those afforded by the recognized norm of the metrical line. Thus a poet may feel it unnecessary to reveal bluntly the quality of his subject if he is writing in a form customarily associated with that subject. Or he may profit from the reader's satisfaction with the manner in which a traditional subject is handled in the form associated with it, knowing that some of the reader's pleasure will be derived from a sense of the fitness of matter to form. He may also choose to write in a traditional form, such as the Petrarchan sonnet, but select a nontraditional subject for it, relying on the familiarity of the rhetorical patterns (in the case of the Petrarchan sonnet, which so readily divides into eight and six line sections, ideas are often developed to conform to this division, with the octave presenting a problem to be solved in the sestet). And he may also choose to write in a traditional form but in a manner, or with a subject, that differs markedly from the traditional usage. Byron's *Don Juan* affords an example of this as well, for the poet elects the Spenserian stanza *not* to write a Spenserian romance but to write a narrative that presents many of the elements of romance ironically. In any of these cases, and there are others possible, we may sense the poet's conscious employment of his chosen form in order to play upon his reader's perception of the form.

Blank Verse and Free Verse

Not all poetry, of course, is written in rhymed stanza forms, nor is it even all metric. Perhaps the most significant departure from the tighter formal patterns in English verse is the use of *blank verse,* unrhymed lines of iambic pentameter. The form is particularly significant because it has been employed so successfully by several of the greatest poets in the language—Shakespeare, Milton, Wordsworth, Tennyson, Robert Frost, and Wallace Stevens. One of the chief advantages that poets have found in blank verse is its closer resemblance to natural speech (which does not, obviously, include rhyme in any regular way). But the avoidance of rhyme does not lessen the effects of any of the other available sources of tight formal control the poet relies upon. The example of the lines from Tennyson's "Ulysses," which is a blank verse poem, will suggest how completely the poet insists upon an awareness of his metrical form to achieve the heightened effects of a formal statement, and how thoroughly he requires his reader to recognize the prevailing metrical norm even when his rhythms are opposed to his meter. The effect of conversation and of extended thought is achieved when Tennyson seems to ignore the ends of his lines, and the effect of explosive, emotional outbursts is the result of his using shorter units marked off by caesural pauses within the end-stopped lines. No serious poet is really interested in imitating conversational speech exactly, for he wishes to profit from the closer attention poetry demands. But he may often wish to suggest or represent a conversational or casual form of speech patterns, as Robert Frost frequently does, and blank verse is apparently uniquely capable of suggesting and representing these. It seems almost to afford the advantages of formalized discourse—heightened emotional response and tighter intellectual control—without the sense of artifice that may be one of the pleasures given by more rigid poetic forms.

It remains to say that there is one form of poetry that seems to ignore all regular formal design: *free verse*. Poets who write in this form have chosen to discard meter and often rhyme and to rely apparently only upon rhetorical emphasis to determine such things as stress, quantity, and line length. Free verse itself takes several forms, depending on the extent to which the poet "frees" himself from the restrictions of regularity. Thus Marianne Moore, although rejecting metrical regularity, does often employ rhyme and retains set patterns of syllable count per line. Other poets, such as Wallace Stevens in some of his verse, retain only a regularity of syllable count (the form is then called "syllabics"), whereas William Carlos Williams rejects meter, rhyme, and syllable counting.

But these forms, which seem so anarchic and counter to all the notions of the exactness of versification, do nevertheless have form. Most often, they stay fairly close to a regularity of the number of *rhetorically* stressed syllables per line, regardless of the number of unstressed syllables. What is most important to those poets who choose to write free verse, however, is the reader's knowledge that they are doing so. That is, free verse poetry depends on the existence of a tradition of more formal regularity for its effect. It is as if whole poems were written in conscious variation of the ideal of metrical precision. These poets do not write merely formless lines but consciously avoid traditional forms, just as in a single line of verse a more traditional poet will introduce a metric substitution or otherwise deploy the resources of rhythm to counter the metrical norm. Free verse, then, requires of the reader an even greater experience with older forms, for it demands the reader's awareness of the point of departure from standard meters.

Free verse does not, of course, give up the whole battery of resources not specifically concerned with metrical organization—euphony, precision of statement, imagery, metaphor, suggestiveness, and the rest. As a matter of fact, these nonformal aspects assume an even greater importance in free verse, for the poet has consciously resorted to them as his only means of achieving poetic quality. So it is that free verse often seems to us more subtle, more delicate, and more concentrated in its effects; or, on the other hand, more blatant, more violent, more prophetic. For the free verse poet, in turning away from established formal standards—we might almost say, in choosing to write in another poetic language—is forced to emphasize and increase those qualities that do remain to him. If Walt Whitman seems to us one of the most insistently bardic poets, so at the other extreme Marianne Moore and William Carlos Williams may seem the most subtly delicate.

But whether written in the more traditional metrical forms, or in free verse, poetry remains essentially a formal art. Its essential quality rests on the control that the poet exerts over his language and syntax, in order to state and express his ideas with greater intensity and clarity than prose permits, and in order to give us the rare pleasure of higher understanding and finer feeling.

Anonymous

WESTERN WIND,
WHEN WILT THOU BLOW

Western wind, when wilt thou blow,
The small rain down can rain?
Christ, if my love were in my arms
And I in my bed again!

Anonymous

LORD RANDALL

"Oh where ha'e ye been, Lord Randall my son?
O where ha'e ye been, my handsome young man?"
  "I ha'e been to the wild wood: mother, make my bed soon,
  For I'm weary wi' hunting, and fain wald lie down."

"Where gat ye your dinner, Lord Randall my son?   5
Where gat ye your dinner, my handsome young man?"
  "I dined wi' my true love; mother, make my bed soon,
  For I'm weary wi' hunting, and fain wald lie down."

"What gat ye to your dinner, Lord Randall my son?
What gat ye to your dinner, my handsome young man?"   10
  "I gat eels boiled in broo: mother, make my bed soon,
  For I'm weary wi' hunting and fain wald lie down."

"What became of your bloodhounds, Lord Randall my son?
What became of your bloodhounds, my handsome young man?"
  "O they swelled and they died: mother, make my bed soon,   15
  For I'm weary wi' hunting and fain wald lie down."

2. *small:* gentle.
11. *broo:* broth.

"O I fear ye are poisoned, Lord Randall my son!
O I fear ye are poisoned, my handsome young man!"
  "O yes, I am poisoned: mother, make my bed soon,
  For I'm sick at the heart, and I fain wald lie down."   20

Anonymous

BARBARA ALLAN

It was in and about the Martinmas time,
  When the green leaves were a-fallin',
That Sir John Graeme in the West Country
  Fell in love with Barbara Allan.

He sent his man down through the town   5
  To the place where she was dwellin':
"O haste and come to my master dear,
  Gin ye be Barbara Allan."

O slowly, slowly rase she up,
  To the place where he was lyin',   10
And when she drew the curtain by:
  "Young man, I think you're dyin'."

"O it's I'm sick, and very, very sick,
  And 'tis a' for Barbara Allan."
"O the better for me ye sal never be,   15
  Though your heart's blood were a-spillin'.

"O dinna ye mind, young man," said she,
  "When ye the cups were fillin',
That ye made the healths gae round and round,
  And slighted Barbara Allan?"   20

He turned his face unto the wall,
  And death with him was dealin':
"Adieu, adieu, my dear friends all,
  And be kind to Barbara Allan."

1. *Martinmas:* November 11.
8. *Gin:* if.

And slowly, slowly, rase she up,   25
   And slowly, slowly left him;
And sighing said she could not stay,
   Since death of life had reft him.

She had not gane a mile but twa,
   When she heard the dead-bell knellin',   30
And every jow that the dead-bell ga'ed
   It cried, "Woe to Barbara Allan!"

"O mother, mother, make my bed,
   O make it soft and narrow:
Since my love died for me today,   35
   I'll die for him tomorrow."

31. *jow:* stroke.

Anonymous

SIR PATRICK SPENS

The king sits in Dumferline town,
   Drinking the blude-reid wine:
"O whar will I get a guid sailor
   To sail this ship of mine?"

Up and spak an eldern knicht,   5
   Sat at the king's richt knee:
"Sir Patrick Spens is the best sailor
   That sails upon the sea."

The king has written a braid letter
   And signed it wi' his hand,   10
And sent it to Sir Patrick Spens,
   Was walking on the sand.

The first line that Sir Patrick read,
   A loud lauch lauched he;

2. *blude-reid:* blood-red.
9. *braid:* broad.
14. *lauch:* laugh.

The next line that Sir Patrick read,   15
    The tear blinded his ee.

"O wha is this has done this deed,
    This ill deed done to me,
To send me out this time o' the year,
    To sail upon the sea?   20

"Make haste, make haste, my mirry men all,
    Our guid ships sails the morn."
"O say na sae, my master dear,
    For I fear a deadly storm.

"Late late yestre'en I saw the new moon   25
    Wi' the auld moon in her arm,
And I fear, I fear, my dear master,
    That we will come to harm."

O our Scots nobles were richt laith
    To weet their cork-heeled shoon,   30
But lang owre a' the play were played
    Their hats they swam aboon.

O lang, lang may their ladies sit,
    Wi' their fans into their hand,
Or e'er they see Sir Patrick Spens   35
    Come sailing to the land.

O lang, lang may the ladies stand,
    Wi' their gold kembs in their hair,
Waiting for their ain dear lords,
    For they'll see thame na mair.   40

Half o'er, half o'er to Aberdour
    It's fifty fadom deep,
And there lies guid Sir Patrick Spens,
    Wi' the Scots lords at his feet.

23. *na sae*: not so.
30. *weet*: wet; *shoon*: shoes.
31. *owre a'*: before all.
32. *aboon*: above.
38. *kembs*: combs.
41. *Half o'er*: halfway over.

Sir Thomas Wyatt

WHO SO LIST TO HUNT

Who so list to hunt, I know where is an hind;
But as for me, alas, I may no more.
The vain travail hath wearied me so sore,
I am of them that farthest come behind.
Yet may I by no means my wearied mind   5
Draw from the Deer; but as she fleeth afore
Fainting I follow. I leave off, therefore,
Since in a net I seek to hold the wind.
Who list her hunt, I put him out of doubt,
As well as I may spend his time in vain.   10
And graven with diamonds in letters plain
There is written, her fair neck round about,
Noli me tangere for Caesar's I am
And wild for to hold, though I seem tame.

1. *list:* wishes.
13. *Noli me tangere:* touch me not.

THEY FLEE FROM ME

They flee from me, that sometime did me seek,
With naked foot stalking in my chamber.
I have seen them, gentle, tame, and meek,
That now are wild, and do not remember
That sometime they put themselves in danger   5
To take bread at my hand; and now they range,
Busily seeking with a continual change.

Thankèd be Fortune it hath been otherwise,
Twenty times better; but once in special,
In thin array, after a pleasant guise,   10
When her loose gown from her shoulders did fall,
And she me caught in her arms long and small,
And therewith all sweetly did me kiss
And softly said, "Dear heart, how like you this?"

12. *small:* slender.

25

It was no dream, I lay broad waking.   15
But all is turned, thorough my gentleness,
Into a strange fashion of forsaking;
And I have leave to go, of her goodness,
And she also to use newfangleness.
But since that I so kindely am served,   20
I fain would know what she hath deserved.

Barnabe Googe

OF MONEY

Give money me, take friendship whoso list,
For friends are gone come once adversity,
When money yet remaineth safe in chest,
That quickly can thee bring from misery.
Fair face show friends, when riches do abound;   5
Come time of proof, farewell they must away.
Believe me well, they are not to be found,
If God but send thee once a low'ring day.
Gold never starts aside, but in distress,
Finds ways enough to ease thine heaviness.   10

Henry Howard, Earl of Surrey

MY FRIEND,
THE THINGS THAT DO ATTAIN

My friend, the things that do attain
The happy life be these, I find:
The riches left, not got with pain;
The fruitful ground; the quiet mind;

26

The equal friend; no grudge, no strife;   5
No charge of rule, nor governance;
Without disease, the healthy life;
The household of continuance;

The mean diet, no dainty fare;
Wisdom joined with simpleness;   10
The night dischargèd of all care,
Where wine the wit may not oppress;

The faithful wife, without debate;
Such sleeps as may beguile the night;
Content thyself with thine estate,   15
Neither wish death nor fear his might.

SET ME WHEREAS THE SUN DOTH PARCH THE GREEN

Set me whereas the sun doth parch the green,
Or where his beams may not dissolve the ice,
In temperate heat, where he is felt and seen;
With proud people, in presence sad and wise,
Set me in base, or yet in high degree;   5
In the long night, or in the shortest day;
In clear weather, or where mists thickest be;
In lusty youth, or when my hairs be gray;
Set me in earth, in heaven, or yet in hell;
In hill, in dale, or in the foaming flood;   10
Thrall, or at large—alive whereso I dwell;
Sick or in health, in ill fame or in good;
Yours I will be, and with that only thought
Comfort myself when that my hap is naught.

Edmund Spenser

LIKE AS A HUNTSMAN

Like as a huntsman after weary chase,
  Seeing the game from him escape away,
Sits down to rest him in some shady place,
  With panting hounds beguilèd of their prey;
  So after long pursuit and vain assay,   5
When I all weary had the chase forsook,
  The gentle deer return'd the self-same way,
Thinking to quench her thirst at the next brook;
There she beholding me with milder look,
  Sought not to fly, but fearless still did bide,   10
Till I in hand her yet half trembling took,
  And with her own goodwill her firmly tied.
    Strange thing, me seem'd to see a beast so wild
    So goodly won, with her own will beguil'd.

WHAT GUILE IS THIS

What guile is this, that those her golden tresses,
She doth attire under a net of gold;
And with sly skill so cunningly them dresses,
That which is gold or hair, may scarce be told?
Is it that men's frail eyes, which gaze too bold,   5
She may entangle in that golden snare;
And being caught may craftily enfold,
Their weaker hearts, which are not well aware?
Take heed therefore, mine eyes, how ye do stare
Henceforth too rashly on that guileful net,   10
In which if ever ye entrappèd are,
Out of her bands ye by no means shall get.
Fondness it were for any being free,
To covet fetters, though they golden be.

ONE DAY I WROTE HER NAME

One day I wrote her name upon the strand,
But came the waves and washèd it away:
Again I wrote it with a second hand,
But came the tide, and made my pains his prey.
"Vain man," said she, "that dost in vain assay,   5
A mortal thing so to immortalize,
For I my self shall like to this decay,
And eek my name be wipèd out likewise."
"Not so," quod I, "let baser things devise
To die in dust, but you shall live by fame: 10
My verse your virtues rare shall eternize,
And in the heavens write your glorious name.
Where whenas death shall all the world subdue,
Our love shall live, and later life renew."

8. *eek:* also.

Sir Walter Ralegh

WHAT IS OUR LIFE?

What is our life? A play of passion,
Our mirth the music of division.
Our mothers' wombs the tiring-houses be,
Where we are dressed for this short comedy.
Heaven the judicious sharp spectator is,   5
That sits and marks still who doth act amiss.
Our graves that hide us from the searching sun
Are like drawn curtains when the play is done.
Thus march we, playing, to our latest rest,
Only we die in earnest, that's no jest.   10

EVEN SUCH IS TIME

Even such is time, that takes in trust
   Our youth, our joys, our all we have,
And pays us but with earth and dust;
   Who, in the dark and silent grave,
When we have wandered all our ways,   5
Shuts up the story of our days.
But from this earth, this grave, this dust,
My God shall raise me up, I trust.

THE LIE

Go, soul, the body's guest,
Upon a thankless errand;
Fear not to touch the best;
The truth shall be thy warrant.
Go, since I needs must die,   5
And give the world the lie.

Say to the court, it glows
And shines like rotten wood;
Say to the church, it shows
What's good, and doth no good.   10
If church and court reply,
Then give them both the lie.

Tell potentates, they live
Acting by others' action;
Not loved unless they give,   15
Not strong but by a faction.
If potentates reply,
Give potentates the lie.

Tell men of high condition,
That manage the estate,   20
Their purpose is ambition,
Their practice only hate.
And if they once reply,
Then give them all the lie.

Tell them that brave it most,   25
They beg for more by spending,
Who, in their greatest cost,
Seek nothing but commending.
And if they make reply,
Then give them all the lie.   30

Tell zeal it wants devotion;
Tell love it is but lust;
Tell time it is but motion;
Tell flesh it is but dust.
And wish them not reply,   35
For thou must give the lie.

Tell age it daily wasteth;
Tell honor how it alters;
Tell beauty how she blasteth;
Tell favor how it falters.   40
And as they shall reply,
Give every one the lie.

Tell wit how much it wrangles
In tickle points of niceness;
Tell wisdom she entangles   45
Herself in overwiseness.
And when they do reply,
Straight give them both the lie.

Tell physic of her boldness;
Tell skill it is pretension;   50
Tell charity of coldness;
Tell law it is contention.
And as they do reply,
So give them still the lie.

Tell fortune of her blindness;   55
Tell nature of decay;
Tell friendship of unkindness;
Tell justice of delay.

25. *brave it*: wear expensive clothes.
44. *tickle*: small.

And if they will reply,
Then give them all the lie.   60

Tell arts they have no soundness,
But vary by esteeming;
Tell schools they want profoundness,
And stand too much on seeming.
If arts and schools reply,   65
Give arts and schools the lie.

Tell faith it's fled the city;
Tell how the country erreth;
Tell manhood shakes off pity;
Tell virtue least preferreth.   70
And if they do reply,
Spare not to give the lie.

So when thou hast, as I
Commanded thee, done blabbing—
Although to give the lie   75
Deserves no less than stabbing—
Stab at thee he that will,
No stab the soul can kill.

Sir Philip Sidney

LOVING IN TRUTH

Loving in truth, and fain in verse my love to show,
That she, dear she, might take some pleasure of my pain,
Pleasure might cause her read, reading might make her know,
Knowledge might pity win, and pity grace obtain,
I sought fit words to paint the blackest face of woe: 5
Studying inventions fine, her wits to entertain,
Oft turning others' leaves, to see if thence would flow
Some fresh and fruitful showers upon my sunburnt brain.
But words came halting forth, wanting invention's stay;

Invention, nature's child, fled stepdame study's blows;   10
And others' feet still seemed but strangers in my way.
Thus, great with child to speak, and helpless in my throes,
Biting my truant pen, beating myself for spite:
"Fool," said my Muse to me, "look in thy heart, and write!"

WITH HOW SAD STEPS, O MOON

With how sad steps, O Moon, thou climb'st the skies!
How silently, and with how wan a face!
What, may it be that even in heavenly place
That busy archer his sharp arrows tries?
Sure, if that long-with-love-acquainted eyes   5
Can judge of love, thou feel'st a lover's case,
I read it in thy looks; thy languished grace,
To me, that feel the like, thy state descries.
Then, even of fellowship, O Moon, tell me,
Is constant love deemed there but want of wit?   10
Are beauties there as proud as here they be?
Do they above love to be loved, and yet
Those lovers scorn whom that love doth possess?
Do they call virtue there ungratefulness?

COME SLEEP!

Come sleep! O sleep, the certain knot of peace,
The baiting place of wit, the balm of woe,
The poor man's wealth, the prisoner's release,
The indifferent judge between the high and low;
With shield of proof shield me from out the prease   5
Of those fierce darts despair at me doth throw;
O make in me those civil wars to cease;
I will good tribute pay, if thou do so.
Take thou of me smooth pillows, sweetest bed,
A chamber deaf to noise and blind to light,   10
A rosy garland and a weary head;

2. *baiting place:* resting place, on a journey.
5. *prease:* press, crowd.

And if these things, as being thine by right,
Move not thy heavy grace, thou shalt in me,
Livelier than elsewhere, Stella's image see.

LEAVE ME, O LOVE

Leave me, O love which reachest but to dust;
And thou, my mind, aspire to higher things;
Grow rich in that which never taketh rust,
Whatever fades but fading pleasure brings.
Draw in thy beams, and humble all thy might   5
To that sweet yoke where lasting freedoms be;
Which breaks the clouds and opens forth the light,
That doth both shine and give us sight to see.
O take fast hold; let that light be thy guide
In this small course which birth draws out to death,   10
And think how evil becometh him to slide,
Who seeketh heav'n, and comes of heav'nly breath.
Then farewell, world; thy uttermost I see;
Eternal love, maintain thy life in me.

Fulke Greville, Lord Brooke

WRAPT UP, O LORD, IN
MAN'S DEGENERATION

Wrapt up, O Lord, in man's degeneration,
The glories of thy truth, thy joys eternal,
Reflect upon my soul dark desolation,
And ugly prospects o'er the sprites infernal.
  Lord, I have sinn'd, and mine iniquity
  Deserves this hell; yet Lord deliver me.   5

Thy power and mercy never comprehended,
Rest lively imag'd in my conscience wounded;

Mercy to grace, and power to fear extended,
Both infinite, and I in both confounded;   10
   Lord, I have sinn'd, and mine iniquity
   Deserves this hell, yet Lord deliver me.

If from this depth of sin, this hellish grave,
And fatal absence from my Saviour's glory,
I could implore his mercy, who can save,   15
And for my sins, not pains of sin, be sorry:
   Lord, from this horror of iniquity,
   And hellish grave, thou wouldst deliver me.

DOWN IN THE DEPTH OF MINE INIQUITY

Down in the depth of mine iniquity,
That ugly center of infernal spirits;
Where each sin feels her own deformity,
In these peculiar torments she inherits,
   Depriv'd of human graces, and divine,   5
   Even there appears this saving God of mine.

And in this fatal mirror of transgression,
Shows man as fruit of his degeneration,
The error's ugly infinite impression,
Which bears the faithless down to desperation;   10
   Depriv'd of human graces and divine,
   Even there appears this saving God of mine.

In power and truth, almighty and eternal,
Which on the sin reflects strange desolation,
With glory scourging all the sprites infernal,   15
And uncreated hell with unprivation;
   Depriv'd of human graces, not divine,
   Even there appears this saving God of mine.

For on this sp'ritual cross condemned lying,
To pains infernal by eternal doom,   20

I see my Saviour for the same sins dying,
And from that hell I fear'd, to free me, come;
  Depriv'd of human graces, not divine,
  Thus hath his death rais'd up this soul of mine.

Chidiock Tichborne

TICHBORNE'S ELEGY

WRITTEN WITH HIS OWN HAND IN THE TOWER
BEFORE HIS EXECUTION

My prime of youth is but a frost of cares,
My feast of joy is but a dish of pain,
My crop of corn is but a field of tares,
And all my good is but vain hope of gain;
The day is past, and yet I saw no sun,   5
And now I live, and now my life is done.

My tale was heard and yet it was not told,
My fruit is fallen and yet my leaves are green,
My youth is spent and yet I am not old,
I saw the world and yet I was not seen;   10
My thread is cut and yet it is not spun,
And now I live, and now my life is done.

I sought my death and found it in my womb,
I looked for life and saw it was a shade,
I trod the earth and knew it was my tomb,   15
And now I die, and now I was but made;
My glass is full, and now my glass is run,
And now I live, and now my life is done.

Samuel Daniel

CARE-CHARMER SLEEP

Care-charmer sleep, son of the sable night,
Brother to death, in silent darkness born,
Relieve my languish and restore the light;
With dark forgetting of my cares, return.
And let the day be time enough to mourn   5
The shipwreck of my ill-adventured youth;
Let waking eyes suffice to wail their scorn
Without the torment of the night's untruth.
Cease, dreams, th' imagery of our day desires,
To model forth the passions of the morrow;   10
Never let rising sun approve you liars,
    To add more grief to aggravate my sorrow.
Still let me sleep, embracing clouds in vain,
And never wake to feel the day's disdain.

Michael Drayton

SINCE THERE'S NO HELP

Since there's no help, come let us kiss and part;
Nay, I have done, you get no more of me,
And I am glad, yea glad with all my heart
That thus so cleanly I myself can free;
Shake hands forever, cancel all our vows,   5
And when we meet at any time again,
Be it not seen in either of our brows
That we one jot of former love retain.
Now at the last gasp of love's latest breath,
When, his pulse failing, passion speechless lies, 10

When faith is kneeling by his bed of death,
And innocence is closing up his eyes,
Now if thou wouldst, when all have given him over,
From death to life thou mightst him yet recover.

William Shakespeare

SONGS FROM THE PLAYS

TAKE, OH, TAKE THOSE LIPS AWAY

Take, oh, take those lips away,
  That so sweetly were forsworn;
And those eyes, the break of day,
  Lights that do mislead the morn:
But my kisses bring again, bring again;   5
Seals of love, but sealed in vain, sealed in vain.
                       Measure for Measure, IV, 1

FEAR NO MORE THE HEAT O' THE SUN

Fear no more the heat o' the sun,
  Nor the furious winter's rages;
Thou thy worldly task hast done,
  Home art gone, and ta'en thy wages;
Golden lads and girls all must,   5
As chimney-sweepers, come to dust.

Fear no more the frown o' the great,
  Thou art past the tyrant's stroke.
Care no more to clothe and eat;
  To thee the reed is as the oak.   10
The scepter, learning, physic, must
All follow this, and come to dust.

Fear no more the lightning-flash,
  Nor th' all-dreaded thunder-stone;
Fear not slander, censure rash;   15
  Thou hast finish'd joy and moan.

All lovers young, all lovers must
Consign to thee, and come to dust.

No exorciser harm thee!
   Nor no witchcraft charm thee!   20
Ghost unlaid forbear thee!
   Nothing ill come near thee!
Quiet consummation have;
And renowned be thy grave!

Cymbeline, IV, 2

FULL FATHOM FIVE

Full fathom five thy father lies;
   Of his bones are coral made;
Those are pearls that were his eyes:
   Nothing of him that doth fade,
But doth suffer a sea change   5
Into something rich and strange.
Sea nymphs hourly ring his knell:
   Ding-dong.
Hark! now I hear them—Ding-dong, bell.

The Tempest, I, 2

FROM THE SONNETS

55. NOT MARBLE NOR THE GILDED MONUMENTS

Not marble nor the gilded monuments
Of princes shall outlive this pow'rful rime,
But you shall shine more bright in these contents
Than unswept stone, besmeared with sluttish time.
When wasteful war shall statues overturn,   5
And broils root out the work of masonry,
Nor Mars his sword nor war's quick fire shall burn
The living record of your memory.
'Gainst death and all oblivious enmity
Shall you pace forth; your praise shall still find room   10
Even in the eyes of all posterity
That wear this world out to the ending doom.
   So, till the judgment that yourself arise,
   You live in this, and dwell in lovers' eyes.

tracery

WILLIAM SHAKESPEARE

73. THAT TIME OF YEAR THOU MAYST IN ME BEHOLD

That time of year thou mayst in me behold
When yellow leaves, or none, or few, do hang
Upon those boughs which shake against the cold,
Bare ruined choirs where late the sweet birds sang.
In me thou seest the twilight of such day   5
As after sunset fadeth in the west,
Which by and by black night doth take away,
Death's second self that seals up all in rest.
In me thou seest the glowing of such fire
That on the ashes of his youth doth lie,   *Time*   10
As the deathbed whereon it must expire,
Consumed with that which it was nourished by.
   This thou perceiv'st, which makes thy love more strong,
   To love that well which thou must leave ere long.

129. TH' EXPENSE OF SPIRIT IN A WASTE OF SHAME

Th' expense of spirit in a waste of shame
Is lust in action; and, till action, lust
Is perjured, murd'rous, bloody, full of blame,
Savage, extreme, rude, cruel, not to trust;
Enjoyed no sooner but despisèd straight;   5
Past reason hunted, and no sooner had,
Past reason hated as a swallowed bait
On purpose laid to make the taker mad:
Mad in pursuit, and in possession so;
Had, having, and in quest to have, extreme;   10
A bliss in proof, and proved, a very woe;
Before, a joy proposed; behind, a dream.
   All this the world well knows; yet none knows well
   To shun the heaven that leads men to this hell.

146. POOR SOUL, THE CENTER OF MY SINFUL EARTH

Poor soul, the center of my sinful earth,
Foiled by these rebel pow'rs that thee array,
Why dost thou pine within and suffer dearth,

2. *Foiled by:* an error in the first edition; two popular emendations are "Lord of" and "Fooled by."

Painting thy outward walls so costly gay?
Why so large cost, having so short a lease,   5
Dost thou upon thy fading mansion spend?
Shall worms, inheritors of this excess,
Eat up thy charge? Is this thy body's end?
Then, soul, live thou upon thy servant's loss,
And let that pine to aggravate thy store;   10
Buy terms divine in selling hours of dross;
Within be fed, without be rich no more:
   So shalt thou feed on Death, that feeds on men,
   And Death once dead, there's no more dying then.

10. *aggravate:* increase, enlarge.

Thomas Nashe

A LITANY IN TIME OF PLAGUE

Adieu, farewell, earth's bliss;
This world uncertain is;
Fond are life's lustful joys;
Death proves them all but toys;
None from his darts can fly;   5
I am sick, I must die.
   Lord, have mercy on us!

Rich men, trust not in wealth,
Gold cannot buy you health;
Physic himself must fade.   10
All things to end are made,
The plague full swift goes by;
I am sick, I must die.
   Lord, have mercy on us!

Beauty is but a flower   15
Which wrinkles will devour;
Brightness falls from the hair;
Queens have died young and fair;

Dust hath closed Helen's eye.
I am sick, I must die.   20
   Lord, have mercy on us!

Strength stoops unto the grave,
Worms feed on Hector brave;
Swords may not fight with fate,
Earth still holds ope her gate.   25
"Come, come!" the bells do cry.
I am sick, I must die.
   Lord, have mercy on us.

Wit with his wantonness
Tasteth death's bitterness;   30
Hell's executioner
Hath no ears for to hear
What vain art can reply.
I am sick, I must die.
   Lord, have mercy on us.   35

Haste, therefore, each degree,
To welcome destiny;
Heaven is our heritage,
Earth but a player's stage;
Mount we unto the sky.   40
I am sick, I must die.
   Lord, have mercy on us.

Thomas Campion

THERE IS A GARDEN IN HER FACE

There is a garden in her face,
Where roses and white lilies grow,
A heavenly paradise is that place,
Wherein all pleasant fruits do flow.

There cherries grow, which none may buy   5
Till "Cherry ripe!" themselves do cry.

Those cherries fairly do enclose
Of orient pearl a double row;
Which when her lovely laughter shows,
They look like rosebuds filled with snow.   10
Yet them nor peer nor prince can buy,
Till "Cherry ripe!" themselves do cry.

Her eyes like angels watch them still;
Her brows like bended bows do stand,
Threatening with piercing frowns to kill   15
All that attempt with eye or hand
Those sacred cherries to come nigh,
Till "Cherry ripe!" themselves do cry.

6. *"Cherry ripe!"*: the cry of street vendors of fruits.

FOLLOW YOUR SAINT

Follow your saint, follow with accents sweet;
Haste you, sad notes, fall at her flying feet.
There, wrapped in cloud of sorrow, pity move,
And tell the ravisher of my soul I perish for her love.
But if she scorns my never-ceasing pain,   5
Then burst with sighing in her sight, and ne'er return again.

All that I sung still to her praise did tend.
Still she was first, still she my songs did end.
Yet she my love and music both doth fly,
The music that her echo is, and beauty's sympathy.   10
Then let my notes pursue her scornful flight;
It shall suffice that they were breathed, and died for her delight.

43

Anonymous

WEEP YOU NO MORE,
SAD FOUNTAINS

Weep you no more, sad fountains;
    What need you flow so fast?
Look how the snowy mountains
    Heaven's sun doth gently waste.
      But my sun's heavenly eyes   5
        View not your weeping,
        That now lie sleeping
    Softly, now softly lies
        Sleeping.

Sleep is a reconciling,   10
    A rest that peace begets.
Doth not the sun rise smiling
    When fair at even he sets?
      Rest you then, rest, sad eyes,
        Melt not in weeping   15
        While she lies sleeping
    Softly, now softly lies
        Sleeping.

Anonymous

FINE KNACKS FOR LADIES

Fine knacks for ladies, cheap, choice, brave and new!
    Good pennyworths! but money cannot move.
I keep a fair but for the fair to view;
    A beggar may be liberal of love.
Though all my wares be trash, the heart is true.   5

Great gifts are guiles and look for gifts again;
   My trifles come as treasures from my mind.
It is a precious jewel to be plain;
   Sometimes in shell the Orient's pearls we find.
Of others take a sheaf, of me a grain.   10

Within this pack, pins, points, laces, and gloves,
   And divers toys, fitting a country fair.
But my heart lives where duty serves and loves,
   Turtles and twins, court's brood, a heavenly pair.
Happy the heart that thinks of no removes.   15

Ben Jonson

ON MY FIRST SON

Farewell, thou child of my right hand, and joy;
My sin was too much hope of thee, loved boy:
Seven years thou wert lent to me, and I thee pay,
Exacted by thy fate, on the just day.
O could I lose all father now! for why   5
Will man lament the state he should envy,
To have so soon 'scaped world's and flesh's rage,
And, if no other misery, yet age?
Rest in soft peace, and asked, say, "Here doth lie
Ben Jonson his best piece of poetry."   10
For whose sake henceforth all his vows be such
As what he loves may never like too much.

EPITAPH ON ELIZABETH, L. H.

Wouldst thou hear what man can say
In a little? Reader, stay.
Underneath this stone doth lie
As much beauty as could die;

Which in life did harbor give   5
To more virtue than doth live.
If at all she had a fault,
Leave it buried in this vault.
One name was Elizabeth;
Th' other, let it sleep with death: 10
Fitter, where it died, to tell,
Than that it lived at all. Farewell!

SONG: TO CELIA

Drink to me, only, with thine eyes,
  And I will pledge with mine;
Or leave a kiss but in the cup,
  And I'll not look for wine.
The thirst, that from the soul doth rise,   5
  Doth ask a drink divine:
But might I of Jove's nectar sup,
  I would not change for thine.
I sent thee, late, a rosy wreath,
  Not so much honoring thee,   10
As giving it a hope, that there
  It could not withered be.
But thou thereon did'st only breathe,
  And sent'st it back to me:
Since when it grows, and smells, I swear,   15
  Not of itself, but thee.

TO HEAVEN

Good, and great God, can I not think of thee,
  But it must, straight, my melancholy be?
Is it interpreted in me disease,
  That, laden with my sins, I seek for ease?
O, be thou witness, that the reins dost know,   5
  And hearts of all, if I be sad for show,

5. *reins*: kidneys or loins; thought to be the seat of feelings or affections.

And judge me after: if I dare pretend
  To aught but grace, or aim at other end.
As thou art all, so be thou all to me,
  First, midst, and last, converted one, and three;   10
My faith, my hope, my love: and in this state,
  My judge, my witness, and my advocate.
Where have I been this while exil'd from thee?
  And whither rap'd, now thou but stoop'st to me?
Dwell, dwell here still: O, being everywhere,   15
  How can I doubt to find thee ever, here?
I know my state, both full of shame, and scorn,
  Conceiv'd in sin, and unto labor born,
Standing with fear, and must with horror fall,
  And destin'd unto judgment, after all.   20
I feel my griefs too, and there scarce is ground,
  Upon my flesh t'inflict another wound.
Yet dare I not complain, or wish for death
  With holy Paul, lest it be thought the breath
Of discontent; or that these prayers be   25
  For weariness of life, not love of thee.

24. *holy Paul:* Romans 7:24, "O wretched man that I am: who shall deliver me from the body of this death."

MY PICTURE LEFT IN SCOTLAND

I now think Love is rather deaf than blind,
  For else it could not be,
    That she,
Whom I adore so much, should so slight me,
  And cast my love behind: 5
I'm sure my language to her was as sweet,
    And every close did meet
    In sentence of as subtle feet,
      As hath the youngest he
That sits in shadow of Apollo's tree.   10

  Oh, but my conscious fears,
    That fly my thoughts between,
    Tell me that she hath seen
    My hundred of gray hairs,

Told seven and forty years,   15
 Read so much waste, as she cannot embrace
 My mountain belly, and my rocky face,
And all these through her eyes, have stopped her ears.

AN ELEGY

Though beauty be the mark of praise,
 And yours of whom I sing be such
 As not the world can praise too much,
Yet is 't your virtue now I raise.

A virtue, like allay, so gone   5
 Throughout your form as, though that move
 And draw and conquer all men's love,
This subjects you to love of one.

Wherein you triumph yet; because
 'Tis of yourself, and that you use   10
 The noblest freedom, not to choose
Against or faith or honor's laws.

But who should less expect from you,
 In whom alone Love lives again?
 By whom he is restored to men,   15
And kept, and bred, and brought up true.

His falling temples you have reared,
 The withered garlands ta'en away;
 His altars kept from the decay
That envy wished, and nature feared;   20

And on them burn so chaste a flame,
 With so much loyalties' expense,
 As Love, t' acquit such excellence,
Is gone himself into your name.

And you are he; the deity   25
 To whom all lovers are designed
 That would their better objects find;
Among which faithful troop am I.

5. *allay*: alloy.

Who, as an off'ring at your shrine,
   Have sung this hymn, and here entreat   30
   One spark of your diviner heat
To light upon a love of mine.

Which, if it kindle not, but scant
   Appear, and that to shortest view,
   Yet give me leave t' adore in you   35
What I, in her, am grieved to want.

John Donne

THE CANONIZATION

For Godsake hold your tongue, and let me love,
   Or chide my palsy, or my gout,
My five gray hairs, or ruin'd fortune flout,
   With wealth your state, your mind with arts improve,
      Take you a course, get you a place,   5
      Observe his honor, or his grace,
Or the King's real, or his stamped face
   Contemplate, what you will, approve,
   So you will let me love.

Alas, alas, who's injur'd by my love?   10
   What merchants' ships have my sighs drown'd?
Who says my tears have overflow'd his ground?
   When did my colds a forward spring remove?
      When did the heats which my veins fill
      Add one more to the plaguy bill?   15
Soldiers find wars, and lawyers find out still
   Litigious men, which quarrels move,
   Though she and I do love.

Call us what you will, we are made such by love;
   Call her one, me another fly,   20

We'are tapers too, and at our own cost die,
   And we in us find the'eagle and the dove.
      The phœnix riddle hath more wit
      By us, we two being one, are it.
So, to one neutral thing both sexes fit,   25
   We die and rise the same, and prove
   Mysterious by this love.

We can die by it, if not live by love,
   And if unfit for tombs and hearse
Our legend be, it will be fit for verse;   30
   And if no piece of chronicle we prove,
      We'll build in sonnets pretty rooms;
      As well a well wrought urn becomes
The greatest ashes, as half-acre tombs,
   And by these hymns, all shall approve   35
   Us *Canoniz'd* for Love:

And thus invoke us; You whom reverend love
   Made one another's hermitage;
You, to whom love was peace, that now is rage;
   Who did the whole world's soul contract, and drove   40
      Into the glasses of your eyes
      (So made such mirrors, and such spies,
That they did all to you epitomize,)
   Countries, towns, courts: Beg from above
   A pattern of your love!   45

THE FLEA

Mark but this flea, and mark in this,
How little that which thou deny'st me is;
It suck'd me first, and now sucks thee,
And in this flea, our two bloods mingled be;
Thou know'st that this cannot be said   5
A sin, nor shame, nor loss of maidenhead,
   Yet this enjoys before it woo,
      And pamper'd swells with one blood made of two,
      And this, alas, is more than we would do.

Oh stay, three lives in one flea spare,   10
Where we almost, yea more than married are.
This flea is you and I, and this
Our marriage bed, and marriage temple is;
Though parents grudge, and you, w'are met,
And cloister'd in these living walls of jet.   15
    Though use make you apt to kill me,
    Let not to that, self murder added be,
    And sacrilege, three sins in killing three.

Cruel and sudden, hast thou since
Purpled thy nail in blood of innocence?   20
Wherein could this flea guilty be,
Except in that drop which it suck'd from thee?
Yet thou triumph'st, and sayst that thou
Find'st not thyself, nor me the weaker now;
    'Tis true, then learn how false fears be;   25
    Just so much honor, when thou yield'st to me,
    Will waste, as this flea's death took life from thee.

A VALEDICTION: FORBIDDING MOURNING

As virtuous men pass mildly away,
    And whisper to their souls, to go,
Whilst some of their sad friends do say,
    The breath goes now, and some say, no:

So let us melt, and make no noise,   5
    No tear-floods, nor sigh-tempests move,
T'were profanation of our joys
    To tell the laity our love.

Moving of th'earth brings harms and fears,
    Men reckon what it did and meant,   10
But trepidation of the spheres,
    Though greater far, is innocent.

11. *trepidation of the spheres:* according to the Ptolemaic astronomy, minor vibrations in the outer spheres of the heavens, producing no harmful consequences on earth.

Dull sublunary lovers' love
    (Whose soul is sense) cannot admit
Absence, because it doth remove   15
    Those things which elemented it.

But we by a love, so much refin'd,
    That ourselves know not what it is,
Inter-assured of the mind,
    Care less eyes, lips, and hands to miss.   20

Our two souls therefore, which are one,
    Though I must go, endure not yet
A breach, but an expansion,
    Like gold to airy thinness beat.

If they be two, they are two so   25
    As stiff twin compasses are two,
Thy soul the fix'd foot, makes no show
    To move, but doth, if th'other do.

And though it in the center sit,
    Yet when the other far doth roam,   30
It leans, and hearkens after it,
    And grows erect, as that comes home.

Such wilt thou be to me, who must
    Like th'other foot, obliquely run;
Thy firmness draws my circle just,   35
    And makes me end, where I begun.

FROM THE *HOLY SONNETS*

7. AT THE ROUND EARTH'S IMAGIN'D CORNERS, BLOW

At the round earth's imagin'd corners, blow
Your trumpets, Angels, and arise, arise
From death, you numberless infinities
Of souls, and to your scatt'red bodies go,
All whom the flood did, and fire shall o'erthrow,   5
All whom war, dearth, age, agues, tyrannies,
Despair, law, chance, hath slain, and you whose eyes,

Shall behold God, and never taste death's woe.
But let them sleep, Lord, and me mourn a space,
For, if above all these, my sins abound,   10
'Tis late to ask abundance of thy grace,
When we are there; here on this lowly ground,
Teach me how to repent; for that's as good
As if thou'hadst seal'd my pardon, with thy blood.

10. DEATH BE NOT PROUD, THOUGH SOME HAVE CALLED THEE

Death be not proud, though some have called thee
Mighty and dreadful, for thou art not so;
For those whom thou think'st thou dost overthrow
Die not, poor death, nor yet canst thou kill me.
From rest and sleep, which but thy pictures be,   5
Much pleasure; then from thee much more must flow,
And soonest our best men with thee do go,
Rest of their bones, and soul's delivery.
Thou art slave to fate, chance, kings, and desperate men,
And dost with poison, war, and sickness dwell,   10
And poppy or charms can make us sleep as well
And better than thy stroke; why swell'st thou then?
One short sleep past, we wake eternally
And death shall be no more; death, thou shalt die.

14. BATTER MY HEART, THREE PERSON'D GOD

Batter my heart, three person'd God; for, you
As yet but knock, breathe, shine, and seek to mend;
That I may rise, and stand, o'erthrow me, and bend
Your force, to break, blow, burn and make me new.
I, like an usurp'd town, to'another due,   5
Labor to'admit you, but Oh, to no end,
Reason your viceroy in me, me should defend,
But is captiv'd, and proves weak or untrue.
Yet dearly I love you, and would be loved fain,
But am betroth'd unto your enemy: 10
Divorce me, untie, or break that knot again,
Take me to you, imprison me, for I
Except you'enthrall me, never shall be free,
Nor ever chaste, except you ravish me.

53

A HYMN TO GOD THE FATHER

[1]

Wilt thou forgive that sin where I begun,
    Which is my sin, though it were done before?
Wilt thou forgive those sins, through which I run,
    And do run still: though still I do deplore?
        When thou hast done, thou hast not done,   5
            For, I have more.

[2]

Wilt thou forgive that sin by which I'have won
    Others to sin, and, made my sin their door?
Wilt thou forgive that sin which I did shun
    A year, or two, but wallowed in, a score?   10
        When thou hast done, thou hast not done,
            For, I have more.

[3]

I have a sin of fear, that when I have spun
    My last thread, I shall perish on the shore;
Swear by thyself, that at my death thy son   15
    Shall shine as he shines now, and heretofore;
        And, having done that, thou hast done,
            I fear no more.

Edward, Lord Herbert of Cherbury

ELEGY OVER A TOMB

Must I then see, alas! eternal night
    Sitting upon those fairest eyes,
And closing all those beams, which once did rise
    So radiant and bright,
That light and heat in them to us did prove   5
    Knowledge and love?

Oh, if you did delight no more to stay
    Upon this low and earthly stage,
But rather chose an endless heritage,
    Tell us at least, we pray, 10
Where all the beauties that those ashes ow'd
    Are now bestow'd?

Doth the sun now his light with yours renew?
    Have waves the curling of your hair?
Did you restore unto the sky and air 15
    The red and white and blue?
Have you vouchsafed to flowers since your death,
    That sweetest breath?

Had not heav'n's lights else in their houses slept,
    Or to some private life retir'd? 20
Must not the sky and air have else conspir'd
    And in their regions wept?
Must not each flower else the earth could breed
    Have been a weed?

But thus enrich'd may we not yield some cause 25
    Why they themselves lament no more,
That must have changed course they held before,
    And broke their proper laws,
Had not your beauties giv'n their second birth
    To heaven and earth? 30

Tell us, for oracles must still ascend
    For those that crave them at your tomb;
Tell us, where are those beauties now become
    And what they now intend;
Tell us, alas! that cannot tell our grief, 35
    Or hope relief.

11. *ow'd:* owned.

Robert Herrick

THE ARGUMENT OF HIS BOOK

I sing of brooks, of blossoms, birds, and bowers,
Of April, May, of June, and July flowers.
I sing of Maypoles, hock carts, wassails, wakes,
Of bridegrooms, brides, and of their bridal cakes.
I write of youth, of love, and have access   5
By these to sing of cleanly wantonness.
I sing of dews, of rains, and, piece by piece,
Of balm, of oil, of spice, and ambergris.
I sing of times trans-shifting, and I write
How roses first came red and lilies white.   10
I write of groves, of twilights, and I sing
The court of Mab and of the fairy king.
I write of hell; I sing (and ever shall)
Of heaven, and hope to have it after all.

TO THE VIRGINS,
TO MAKE MUCH OF TIME

Gather ye rosebuds while ye may,
    Old time is still a-flying;
And this same flower that smiles today
    Tomorrow will be dying.

The glorious lamp of heaven, the sun,   5
    The higher he's a-getting,
The sooner will his race be run,
    And nearer he's to setting.

That age is best which is the first,
    When youth and blood are warmer;   10
But being spent, the worse, and worst
    Times still succeed the former.

Then be not coy, but use your time,
    And, while ye may, go marry;
For, having lost but once your prime,   15
    You may forever tarry.

UPON A CHILD THAT DIED

Here she lies, a pretty bud,
Lately made of flesh and blood,
Who as soon fell fast asleep
As her little eyes did peep.
Give her strewings, but not stir   5
The earth that lightly covers her.

UPON PRUE, HIS MAID

In this little urn is laid
Prudence Baldwin, once my maid,
From whose happy spark here let
Spring the purple violet.

Henry King

THE EXEQUY

Accept, thou shrine of my dead saint,
Instead of dirges, this complaint;
And for sweet flowers to crown thy hearse,
Receive a strew of weeping verse
From thy grieved friend, whom thou might'st see   5
Quite melted into tears for thee.

Dear loss! since thy untimely fate
My task hath been to meditate

On thee, on thee; thou art the book,
The library whereon I look,   10
Though almost blind. For thee, loved clay,
I languish out, not live, the day,
Using no other exercise
But what I practice with mine eyes;
By which wet glasses I find out   15
How lazily time creeps about
To one that mourns: this, only this,
My exercise and business is.
So I compute the weary hours
With sighs dissolvèd into showers.   20

Nor wonder if my time go thus
Backward and most preposterous;
Thou hast benighted me, thy set
This eve of blackness did beget,
Who wast my day, though overcast   25
Before thou hadst thy noontide passed;
And I remember must in tears,
Thou scarce hadst seen so many years
As day tells hours. By thy clear sun
My love and fortune first did run;   30
But thou wilt never more appear
Folded within my hemisphere,
Since both thy light and motion
Like a fled star is fallen and gone;
And 'twixt me and my soul's dear wish   35
An earth now interposèd is,
Which such a strange eclipse doth make
As ne'er was read in almanac.

I could allow thee for a time
To darken me and my sad clime;   40
Were it a month, a year, or ten,
I would thy exile live till then,
And all that space my mirth adjourn,
So thou wouldst promise to return;
And putting off thy ashy shroud,   45
At length disperse this sorrow's cloud.

But woe is me! the longest date
Too narrow is to calculate
These empty hopes; never shall I
Be so much blest as to descry   50
A glimpse of thee, till that day come
Which shall the earth to cinders doom,
And a fierce fever must calcine
The body of this world—like thine,
My little world! That fit of fire   55
Once off, our bodies shall aspire
To our souls' bliss; then we shall rise
And view ourselves with clearer eyes
In that calm region where no night
Can hide us from each other's sight.   60

Meantime, thou hast her, earth: much good
May my harm do thee. Since it stood
With heaven's will I might not call
Her longer mine, I give thee all
My short-lived right and interest   65
In her whom living I loved best;
With a most free and bounteous grief
I give thee what I could not keep.
Be kind to her, and prithee look
Thou write into thy doomsday book   70
Each parcel of this rarity
Which in thy casket shrined doth lie.
See that thou make thy reckoning straight,
And yield her back again by weight;
For thou must audit on thy trust   75
Each grain and atom of this dust,
As thou wilt answer Him that lent,
Not gave thee, my dear monument.

So close the ground, and 'bout her shade
Black curtains draw; my bride is laid.   80

Sleep on, my love, in thy cold bed,
Never to be disquieted!

My last good-night! Thou wilt not wake
Till I thy fate shall overtake;
Till age, or grief, or sickness must   85
Marry my body to that dust
It so much loves; and fill the room
My heart keeps empty in thy tomb.
Stay for me there; I will not fail
To meet thee in that hollow vale.   90
And think not much of my delay;
I am already on the way,
And follow thee with all the speed
Desire can make, or sorrows breed.
Each minute is a short degree,   95
And every hour a step towards thee.
At night when I betake to rest,
Next morn I rise nearer my west
Of life, almost by eight hours' sail,
Than when sleep breathed his drowsy gale.   100

Thus from the sun my bottom steers,
And my day's compass downward bears;
Nor labor I to stem the tide
Through which to thee I swiftly glide.

'Tis true, with shame and grief I yield,   105
Thou like the van first took'st the field,
And gotten hast the victory
In thus adventuring to die
Before me, whose more years might crave
A just precedence in the grave.   110
But hark! my pulse like a soft drum
Beats my approach, tells thee I come;
And slow howe'er my marches be,
I shall at last sit down by thee.

The thought of this bids me go on,   115
And wait my dissolution
With hope and comfort. Dear (forgive
The crime), I am content to live
Divided, with but half a heart,
Till we shall meet and never part.   120

George Herbert

CHURCH–MONUMENTS

While that my soul repairs to her devotion,
Here I intomb my flesh, that it betimes
May take acquaintance of this heap of dust;
To which the blast of death's incessant motion,
Fed with the exhalation of our crimes,   5
Drives all at last. Therefore, I gladly trust

My body to this school, that it may learn
To spell his elements, and find his birth
Written in dusty heraldry and lines;
Which dissolution sure doth best discern,   10
Comparing dust with dust, and earth with earth.
These laugh at jet and marble put for signs,

To sever the good fellowship of dust,
And spoil the meeting. What shall point out them,
When they shall bow, and kneel, and fall down flat   15
To kiss those heaps, which now they have in trust?
Dear flesh, while I do pray, learn here thy stem
And true descent; that when thou shalt grow fat,

And wanton in thy cravings, thou mayst know,
That flesh is but the glass, which holds the dust   20
That measures all our time; which also shall
Be crumbled into dust. Mark here below
How tame these ashes are, how free from lust,
That thou mayst fit thy self against thy fall.

VIRTUE

Sweet day, so cool, so calm, so bright,
The bridal of the earth and sky:
The dew shall weep thy fall tonight;
                    For thou must die.

61

Sweet rose, whose hue angry and brave   5
Bids the rash gazer wipe his eye:
Thy root is ever in its grave,
                    And thou must die.

Sweet spring, full of sweet days and roses,
A box where sweets compacted lie;   10
My music shows ye have your closes,
                    And all must die.

Only a sweet and virtuous soul,
Like season'd timber, never gives;
But though the whole world turn to coal,   15
                    Then chiefly lives.

THE COLLAR

I struck the board, and cried, No more.
                    I will abroad.
          What? shall I ever sigh and pine?
My lines and life are free; free as the road,
          Loose as the wind, as large as store.   5
                    Shall I be still in suit?
          Have I no harvest but a thorn
          To let me blood, and not restore
          What I have lost with cordial fruit?
                    Sure there was wine   10
Before my sighs did dry it: there was corn
          Before my tears did drown it.
          Is the year only lost to me?
                    Have I no bays to crown it?
No flowers, no garlands gay? all blasted?   15
                    All wasted?
          Not so, my heart: but there is fruit,
                    And thou hast hands.
          Recover all thy sigh-blown age
On double pleasures: leave thy cold dispute   20
Of what is fit, and not. Forsake thy cage,
                    Thy rope of sands,

Which petty thoughts have made, and made to thee
  Good cable, to enforce and draw,
     And be thy law,   25
  While thou didst wink and wouldst not see.
    Away; take heed:
    I will abroad.
Call in thy death's head there: tie up thy fears.
    He that forbears   30
  To suit and serve his need,
    Deserves his load.
But as I rav'd and grew more fierce and wild
    At every word,
Methought I heard one calling, *Child!*   35
    And I replied, *My Lord.*

LOVE

Love bade me welcome: yet my soul drew back,
   Guilty of dust and sin.
But quick-ey'd Love, observing me grow slack
   From my first entrance in,
Drew nearer to me, sweetly questioning,   5
   If I lack'd any thing.

A guest, I answer'd, worthy to be here:
   Love said, You shall be he.
I, the unkind, ungrateful? Ah my dear,
   I cannot look on thee.   10
Love took my hand, and smiling did reply,
   Who made the eyes but I?

Truth, Lord, but I have marr'd them: let my shame
   Go where it doth deserve.
And know you not, says Love, who bore the blame?   15
   My dear, then I will serve.
You must sit down, says Love, and taste my meat:
   So I did sit and eat.

Thomas Carew

A SONG

Ask me no more where Jove bestows,
When June is past, the fading rose;
For in your beauties orient deep,
These flowers, as in their causes, sleep.

Ask me no more whither do stray   5
The golden atoms of the day;
For in pure love heaven did prepare
Those powders to enrich your hair.

Ask me no more whither doth haste
The nightingale when May is past;   10
For in your sweet dividing throat
She winters, and keeps warm her note.

Ask me no more where those stars light,
That downwards fall in dead of night;
For in your eyes they sit, and there   15
Fixèd become, as in their sphere.

Ask me no more if east or west
The phoenix builds her spicy nest;
For unto you at last she flies,
And in your fragrant bosom dies.   20

11. *dividing*: harmonious.

SONG

Give me more love, or more disdain;
    The torrid or the frozen zone
Bring equal ease unto my pain;
    The temperate affords me none:
Either extreme, of love or hate,   5
Is sweeter than a calm estate.

64

Give me a storm; if it be love,
　Like Danaë in that golden shower,
I swim in pleasure; if it prove
　Disdain, that torrent will devour　　　　10
My vulture hopes; and he's possessed
Of heaven that's but from hell released.
　Then crown my joys, or cure my pain;
　Give me more love, or more disdain.

Edmund Waller

SONG — *pretty & sweet*

　Go, lovely rose!
Tell her that wastes her time and me
　That now she knows,
When I resemble her to thee,
How sweet and fair she seems to be.　　　　5

　Tell her that's young,
And shuns to have her graces spied,
　That hadst thou sprung
In deserts, where no men abide,
Thou must have uncommended died.　　　　10

　Small is the worth
Of beauty from the light retired;
　Bid her come forth,
Suffer herself to be desired,
And not blush so to be admired.　　　　15

　Then die! that she
The common fate of all things rare
　May read in thee;
How small a part of time they share
That are so wondrous sweet and fair!　　*recurring* 20 (cf.
　　　　　　　　　　　　　　　　　　Herrick)

4. *resemble*: compare.

65

John Milton

HOW SOON HATH TIME, THE SUBTLE THIEF OF YOUTH

How soon hath time, the subtle thief of youth,
Stol'n on his wing my three and twentieth year!
My hasting days fly on with full career,
But my late spring no bud or blossom shew'th.
Perhaps my semblance might deceive the truth,   5
That I to manhood am arriv'd so near,
And inward ripeness doth much less appear,
That some more timely-happy spirits endu'th.
Yet be it less or more, or soon or slow,
It shall be still in strictest measure ev'n,   10
To that same lot, however mean or high,
Toward which Time leads me, and the will of Heav'n;
All is, if I have grace to use it so,
As ever in my great task-Master's eye.

WHEN I CONSIDER HOW MY LIGHT IS SPENT

When I consider how my light is spent,
Ere half my days, in this dark world and wide,
And that one talent which is death to hide,
Lodg'd with me useless, though my soul more bent
To serve therewith my Maker, and present   5
My true account, lest he returning chide,
Doth God exact day-labor, light denied,
I fondly ask; but Patience to prevent
That murmur, soon replies, God doth not need
Either man's work or his own gifts, who best   10
Bear his mild yoke, they serve him best, his state
Is kingly. Thousands at his bidding speed
And post o'er land and ocean without rest:
They also serve who only stand and wait.

METHOUGHT I SAW MY LATE ESPOUSED SAINT

Methought I saw my late espoused saint
Brought to me like Alcestis from the grave,
Whom Jove's great son to her glad husband gave,
Rescu'd from death by force though pale and faint.
Mine as whom wash'd from spot of child-bed taint,   5
Purification in the old law did save,
And such, as yet once more I trust to have
Full sight of her in heaven without restraint,
Came vested all in white, pure as her mind:
Her face was veil'd, yet to my fancied sight,   10
Love, sweetness, goodness, in her person shin'd
So clear, as in no face with more delight.
But O, as to embrace me she inclin'd,
I wak'd, she fled, and day brought back my night.

Sir John Suckling

SONG

Why so pale and wan, fond lover?
  Prithee, why so pale?
Will, when looking well can't move her,
  Looking ill prevail?
  Prithee, why so pale?   5

Why so dull and mute, young sinner?
  Prithee, why so mute?
Will, when speaking well can't win her,
  Saying nothing do't?
  Prithee, why so mute?   10

Quit, quit, for shame; this will not move,
  This cannot take her.
If of herself she will not love,
  Nothing can make her:
  The devil take her!   15

OUT UPON IT!

Out upon it! I have loved
  Three whole days together;
And am like to love three more,
  If it prove fair weather.

Time shall molt away his wings,   5
  Ere he shall discover
In the whole wide world again
  Such a constant lover.

But the spite on 't is, no praise
  Is due at all to me: 10
Love with me had made no stays
  Had it any been but she.

Had it any been but she,
  And that very face,
There had been at least ere this   15
  A dozen dozen in her place.

Anne Bradstreet

TO MY DEAR AND LOVING HUSBAND

If ever two were one, then surely we.
If ever man were loved by wife, then thee;
If ever wife was happy in a man,
Compare with me ye women if you can.

I prize thy love more than whole mines of gold,   5
Or all the riches that the East doth hold.
My love is such that rivers cannot quench,
Nor ought but love from thee give recompense.
Thy love is such I can no way 'repay;
The heavens reward thee manifold, I pray.   10
Then while we live, in love let's so persever,
That when we live no more we may live ever.

Henry Vaughan

MAN

Weighing the steadfastness and state
Of some mean things which here below reside,
Where birds, like watchful clocks, the noiseless date
    And intercourse of times divide,
Where bees at night get home and hive, and flowers,   5
        Early as well as late,
Rise with the sun and set in the same bowers;

    I would (said I) my God would give
The staidness of these things to man! for these
To His divine appointments ever cleave,   10
    And no new business breaks their peace;
The birds nor sow nor reap, yet sup and dine;
        The flowers without clothes live,
Yet Solomon was never dressed so fine.

    Man hath still either toys or care;   15
He hath no root, nor to one place is tied,
But ever restless and irregular
    About this earth doth run and ride.
He knows he hath a home, but scarce knows where;
        He says it is so far   20
That he hath quite forgot how to go there.

He knocks at all doors, strays and roams,
Nay, hath not so much wit as some stones have,
Which in the darkest nights point to their homes,
　　By some hid sense their Maker gave;   25
Man is the shuttle, to whose winding quest
　　　And passage through these looms
God ordered motion, but ordained no rest.

23. *stones*: loadstones; i.e., compasses.

Andrew Marvell

THE GARDEN

　How vainly men themselves amaze
To win the palm, the oak, or bays,
And their incessant labors see
Crowned from some single herb, or tree,
Whose short and narrow-vergèd shade   5
Does prudently their toils upbraid;
While all flowers and all trees do close
To weave the garlands of repose!

　Fair Quiet, have I found thee here,
And Innocence, thy sister dear?   10
Mistaken long, I sought you then
In busy companies of men.
Your sacred plants, if here below,
Only among the plants will grow;
Society is all but rude   15
To this delicious solitude.

　No white nor red was ever seen
So amorous as this lovely green.
Fond lovers, cruel as their flame,
Cut in these trees their mistress' name: 20

Little, alas, they know or heed
How far these beauties hers exceed!
Fair trees, wheresoe'er your barks I wound,
No name shall but your own be found.

When we have run our passion's heat,   25
Love hither makes his best retreat.
The gods, that mortal beauty chase,
Still in a tree did end their race:
Apollo hunted Daphne so,
Only that she might laurel grow;   30
And Pan did after Syrinx speed,
Not as a nymph, but for a reed.

What wondrous life is this I lead!
Ripe apples drop about my head;
The luscious clusters of the vine   35
Upon my mouth do crush their wine;
The nectarine and curious peach
Into my hands themselves do reach;
Stumbling on melons, as I pass,
Insnared with flowers, I fall on grass.   40

Meanwhile the mind, from pleasure less,
Withdraws into its happiness;
The mind, that ocean where each kind
Does straight its own resemblance find;
Yet it creates, transcending these,   45
Far other worlds and other seas,
Annihilating all that's made
To a green thought in a green shade.

Here at the fountain's sliding foot,
Or at some fruit tree's mossy root,   50
Casting the body's vest aside,
My soul into the boughs does glide:
There, like a bird, it sits and sings,
Then whets and combs its silver wings,
And, till prepared for longer flight,   55
Waves in its plumes the various light.

Such was that happy garden-state,
While man there walked without a mate:
After a place so pure and sweet,
What other help could yet be meet!   60
But 'twas beyond a mortal's share
To wander solitary there:
Two paradises 'twere in one
To live in paradise alone.

How well the skillful gardener drew   65
Of flowers and herbs this dial new,
Where, from above, the milder sun
Does through a fragrant zodiac run;
And as it works, th' industrious bee
Computes its time as well as we!   70
How could such sweet and wholesome hours
Be reckoned but with herbs and flowers?

TO HIS COY MISTRESS

Had we but world enough, and time,
This coyness, lady, were no crime.
We would sit down, and think which way
To walk, and pass our long love's day.
Thou by the Indian Ganges' side   5
Shouldst rubies find; I by the tide
Of Humber would complain. I would
Love you ten years before the flood,
And you should, if you please, refuse
Till the conversion of the Jews.   10
My vegetable love should grow
Vaster than empires and more slow;
An hundred years should go to praise
Thine eyes, and on thy forehead gaze;
Two hundred to adore each breast,   15
But thirty thousand to the rest;
An age at least to every part,
And the last age should show your heart.

7. *Humber*: tidal river flowing past Marvell's home city of Hull.

For, lady, you deserve this state,
Nor would I love at lower rate.   20
    But at my back I always hear
Time's wingèd chariot hurrying near;
And yonder all before us lie
Deserts of vast eternity.
Thy beauty shall no more be found,   25
Nor, in thy marble vault, shall sound
My echoing song; then worms shall try
That long-preserved virginity,
And your quaint honor turn to dust,
And into ashes all my lust: 30
The grave's a fine and private place,
But none, I think, do there embrace.
    Now therefore, while the youthful hue
Sits on thy skin like morning dew,
And while thy willing soul transpires   35
At every pore with instant fires,
Now let us sport us while we may,
And now, like amorous birds of prey,
Rather at once our time devour
Than languish in his slow-chapped power.   40
Let us roll all our strength and all
Our sweetness up into one ball
And tear our pleasures with rough strife
Through the iron gates of life:
Thus, though we cannot make our sun   45
Stand still, yet we will make him run.

THE DEFINITION OF LOVE

My love is of a birth as rare
As 'tis, for object, strange and high;
It was begotten by despair
Upon impossibility.
Magnanimous despair alone   5
Could show me so divine a thing,

73

Where feeble hope could ne'er have flown
But vainly flapped its tinsel wing.

And yet I quickly might arrive
Where my extended soul is fixed;   10
But fate does iron wedges drive,
And always crowds itself betwixt.

For fate with jealous eye does see
Two perfect loves, nor lets them close;
Their union would her ruin be,   15
And her tyrannic power depose.

And therefore her decrees of steel
Us as the distant poles have placed
(Though love's whole world on us doth wheel),
Not by themselves to be embraced,   20

Unless the giddy heaven fall,
And earth some new convulsion tear,
And, us to join, the world should all
Be cramped into a planisphere.

As lines, so loves oblique may well   25
Themselves in every angle greet,
But ours, so truly parallel,
Though infinite, can never meet.

Therefore the love which us doth bind,
But fate so enviously debars,   30
Is the conjunction of the mind,
And opposition of the stars.

John Dryden

MACFLECKNOE

OR A SATIRE UPON THE TRUE-BLUE PROTESTANT POET, T. S.*

All human things are subject to decay,
And when fate summons, monarchs must obey.
This Flecknoe found, who, like Augustus, young
Was called to empire, and had governed long;
In prose and verse, was owned, without dispute,   5
Through all the realms of nonsense, absolute.
This aged prince, now flourishing in peace,
And blest with issue of a large increase,
Worn out with business, did at length debate
To settle the succession of the state;   10
And, pondering which of all his sons was fit
To reign, and wage immortal war with wit,
Cried: " 'Tis resolved; for nature pleads that he
Should only rule, who most resembles me.
Sh—— alone my perfect image bears,   15
Mature in dullness from his tender years:
Sh—— alone, of all my sons, is he
Who stands confirmed in full stupidity.
The rest to some faint meaning make pretense,
But Sh—— never deviates into sense.   20
Some beams of wit on other souls may fall,
Strike through, and make a lucid interval;
But Sh——'s genuine night admits no ray,
His rising fogs prevail upon the day.
Besides, his goodly fabric fills the eye,   25
And seems designed for thoughtless majesty:
Thoughtless as monarch oaks that shade the plain,
And, spread in solemn state, supinely reign.

---

* T. S.: Thomas Shadwell, a corpulent playwright who considered himself
the artistic heir of Ben Jonson.
3. Flecknoe: Richard Flecknoe, a notoriously bad Irish poet and playwright.

Heywood and Shirley were but types of thee,
Thou last great prophet of tautology.   30
Even I, a dunce of more renown than they,
Was sent before but to prepare thy way;
And, coarsely clad in Norwich drugget, came
To teach the nations in thy greater name.
My warbling lute, the lute I whilom strung,   35
When to King John of Portugal I sung,
Was but the prelude to that glorious day,
When thou on silver Thames didst cut thy way,
With well-timed oars before the royal barge,
Swelled with the pride of thy celestial charge;   40
And big with hymn, commander of a host,
The like was ne'er in Epsom blankets tossed.
Methinks I see the new Arion sail,
The lute still trembling underneath thy nail.
At thy well-sharpened thumb from shore to shore   45
The treble squeaks for fear, the basses roar;
Echoes from Pissing Alley Sh—— call,
And Sh—— they resound from Aston Hall.
About thy boat the little fishes throng,
As at the morning toast that floats along.   50
Sometimes, as prince of thy harmonious band,
Thou wield'st thy papers in thy threshing hand.
St. André's feet ne'er kept more equal time,
Not ev'n the feet of thy own *Psyche's* rhyme;
Though they in number as in sense excel: 55
So just, so like tautology, they fell
That, pale with envy, Singleton forswore
The lute and sword, which he in triumph bore,
And vowed he ne'er would act Villerius more."
Here stopped the good old sire, and wept for joy   60
In silent raptures of the hopeful boy.
All arguments, but most his plays, persuade,
That for anointed dullness he was made.

33. *Norwich drugget:* rough woolen cloth.
53. *St. André:* Shadwell's French choreographer.
57. *Singleton:* an opera singer.

Close to the walls which fair Augusta bind
(The fair Augusta much to fears inclined),   65
An ancient fabric raised to inform the sight,
There stood of yore, and Barbican it hight:
A watchtower once; but now, so fate ordains,
Of all the pile an empty name remains.
From its old ruins brothel houses rise,   70
Scenes of lewd loves, and of polluted joys,
Where their vast courts the mother-strumpets keep,
And, undisturbed by watch, in silence sleep.
Near these a Nursery erects its head,
Where queens are formed, and future heroes bred;   75
Where unfledged actors learn to laugh and cry,
Where infant punks their tender voices try,
And little Maximins the gods defy.
Great Fletcher never treads in buskins here,
Nor greater Jonson dares in socks appear;   80
But gentle Simkin just reception finds
Amidst this monument of vanished minds:
Pure clinches the suburbian Muse affords,
And Panton waging harmless war with words.
Here Flecknoe, as a place to fame well known,   85
Ambitiously design'd his Sh——'s throne;
For ancient Dekker prophesied long since,
That in this pile would reign a mighty prince,
Born for a scourge of wit, and flail of sense;
To whom true dullness should some *Psyches* owe,   90
But worlds of *Misers* from his pen should flow;
Humorists and *Hypocrites* it should produce,
Whole Raymond families, and tribes of Bruce.
Now Empress Fame had published the renown
Of Sh——'s coronation through the town.   95
Roused by report of Fame, the nations meet,
From near Bunhill, and distant Watling Street.

64. *Augusta:* London.
74. *Nursery:* a training school for actors.
78. *Maximin:* the emperor in Dryden's play *Tyrannic Love.*
81. *Simkin:* a type character in farces.
90–93. Four of Shadwell's plays, and the names of two of his characters.

No Persian carpets spread the imperial way,
But scattered limbs of mangled poets lay;
From dusty shops neglected authors come,   100
Martyrs of pies, and relics of the bum.
Much Heywood, Shirley, Ogilby there lay,
But loads of Sh—— almost choked the way.
Bilked stationers for yeomen stood prepared,
And Herringman was captain of the guard.   105
The hoary prince in majesty appeared,
High on a throne of his own labors reared.
At his right hand our young Ascanius sate,
Rome's other hope, and pillar of the state.
His brows thick fogs, instead of glories, grace,   110
And lambent dullness played around his face.
As Hannibal did to the altars come,
Sworn by his sire a mortal foe to Rome,
So Sh—— swore, nor should his vow be vain,
That he till death true dullness would maintain;   115
And, in his father's right, and realm's defense,
Ne'er to have peace with wit, nor truce with sense.
The king himself the sacred unction made,
As king by office, and as priest by trade.
In his sinister hand, instead of ball,   120
He placed a mighty mug of potent ale;
Love's Kingdom to his right he did convey,
At once his scepter, and his rule of sway;
Whose righteous lore the prince had practiced young,
And from whose loins recorded *Psyche* sprung.   125
His temples, last, with poppies were o'erspread,
That nodding seemed to consecrate his head.
Just at that point of time, if fame not lie,
On his left hand twelve reverend owls did fly.
So Romulus, 'tis sung, by Tiber's brook,   130
Presage of sway from twice six vultures took.
The admiring throng loud acclamations make,
And omens of his future empire take.
The sire then shook the honors of his head,

101. *Martyrs . . . bum*: unsold books were torn apart and used for wrapping
or as toilet paper.

And from his brows damps of oblivion shed 135
Full on the filial dullness: long he stood,
Repelling from his breast the raging god;
At length burst out in this prophetic mood:
   "Heavens bless my son, from Ireland let him reign
To far Barbadoes on the western main; 140
Of his dominion may no end be known,
And greater than his father's be his throne;
Beyond *Love's Kingdom* let him stretch his pen!"
He paused, and all the people cried, "Amen."
Then thus continued he: "My son, advance 145
Still in new impudence, new ignorance.
Success let others teach, learn thou from me
Pangs without birth, and fruitless industry.
Let *Virtuosos* in five years be writ;
Yet not one thought accuse thy toil of wit. 150
Let gentle George in triumph tread the stage,
Make Dorimant betray, and Loveit rage;
Let Cully, Cockwood, Fopling, charm the pit,
And in their folly show the writer's wit.
Yet still thy fools shall stand in thy defense, 155
And justify their author's want of sense.
Let 'em be all by thy own model made
Of dullness, and desire no foreign aid;
That they to future ages may be known,
Not copies drawn, but issue of thy own. 160
Nay, let thy men of wit too be the same,
All full of thee, and differing but in name.
But let no alien S——dl——y interpose,
To lard with wit thy hungry *Epsom* prose.
And when false flowers of rhetoric thou wouldst cull, 165
Trust nature, do not labor to be dull;
But write thy best, and top; and, in each line,
Sir Formal's oratory will be thine:
Sir Formal, though unsought, attends thy quill,
And does thy northern dedications fill. 170

151. *George:* Sir George Etherege, a leading Restoration playwright; Dryden names several of his characters in the next lines.
168. *Sir Formal:* one of Shadwell's long-winded characters.

Nor let false friends seduce thy mind to fame,
By arrogating Jonson's hostile name.
Let father Flecknoe fire thy mind with praise,
And uncle Ogilby thy envy raise.
Thou art my blood, where Jonson has no part: 175
What share have we in nature, or in art?
Where did his wit on learning fix a brand,
And rail at arts he did not understand?
Where made he love in Prince Nicander's vein,
Or swept the dust in *Psyche's* humble strain?   180
Where sold he bargains, 'whip-stitch, kiss my arse,'
Promised a play and dwindled to a farce?
When did his Muse from Fletcher scenes purloin,
As thou whole Eth'rege dost transfuse to thine?
But so transfused, as oil on water's flow,   185
His always floats above, thine sinks below.
This is thy province, this thy wondrous way,
New humors to invent for each new play:
This is that boasted bias of thy mind,
By which one way, to dullness, 'tis inclined;   190
Which makes thy writings lean on one side still,
And, in all changes, that way bends thy will.
Nor let thy mountain-belly make pretense
Of likeness; thine's a tympany of sense.
A tun of man in thy large bulk is writ,   195
But sure thou'rt but a kilderkin of wit.
Like mine, thy gentle numbers feebly creep;
Thy tragic Muse gives smiles, thy comic sleep.
With whate'er gall thou sett'st thyself to write,
Thy inoffensive satires never bite.   200
In thy felonious heart though venom lies,
It does but touch thy Irish pen, and dies.
Thy genius calls thee not to purchase fame
In keen iambics, but mild anagram.
Leave writing plays, and choose for thy command   205
Some peaceful province in acrostic land.
There thou may'st wings display and altars raise,
And torture one poor word ten thousand ways.

181. *sold he bargains:* answered simple questions crudely.

Or, if thou wouldst thy different talent suit,
Set thy own songs, and sing them to thy lute." 210
    He said: but his last words were scarcely heard
For Bruce and Longville had a trap prepared,
And down they sent the yet declaiming bard.
Sinking he left his drugget robe behind,
Borne upwards by a subterranean wind. 215
The mantle fell to the young prophet's part,
With double portion of his father's art.

TO THE MEMORY OF MR. OLDHAM*

Farewell, too little, and too lately known,
Whom I began to think and call my own:
For sure our souls were near allied, and thine
Cast in the same poetic mold with mine.
One common note on either lyre did strike, 5
And knaves and fools we both abhorred alike.
To the same goal did both our studies drive;
The last set out the soonest did arrive.
Thus Nisus fell upon the slippery place,
While his young friend performed and won the race. 10
O early ripe! to thy abundant store
What could advancing age have added more?
It might (what nature never gives the young)
Have taught the numbers of thy native tongue.
But satire needs not those, and wit will shine 15
Through the harsh cadence of a rugged line:
A noble error, and but seldom made,
When poets are by too much force betrayed.
Thy generous fruits, though gathered ere their prime,
Still showed a quickness; and maturing time 20
But mellows what we write to the dull sweets of rhyme.
Once more, hail and farewell; farewell, thou young,
But ah too short, Marcellus of our tongue;
Thy brows with ivy, and with laurels bound;
But fate and gloomy night encompass thee around. 25

* *Mr. Oldham:* John Oldham, a poet who died at the age of 27.

Edward Taylor

HUSWIFERY

Make me, O Lord, thy spinning wheel complete.
　Thy holy Word my distaff make for me.
Make mine affections thy swift flyers neat
　And make my soul thy holy spool to be.
　My conversation make to be thy reel　　　　　5
　And reel the yarn thereon spun of thy wheel.

Make me thy loom then, knit therein this twine,
　And make thy holy spirit, Lord, wind quills.
Then weave the web thyself. The yarn is fine.
　Thine ordinances make my fulling mills.　　　10
　Then dye the same in heavenly colors choice,
　All pinked with varnished flowers of paradise.

Then clothe therewith mine understanding, will,
　Affections, judgment, conscience, memory,
My words, and actions, that their shine may fill　15
　My ways with glory and thee glorify.
　Then mine apparel shall display before ye
　That I am clothed in holy robes for glory.

MEDITATION ONE

What love is this of thine, that cannot be
　In thine infinity, O Lord, confined,
Unless it in thy very person see,
　Infinity and finity conjoined?
　What hath thy godhead, as not satisfied,　　　5
　Married our manhood, making it its bride?

Oh, matchless love! Filling heaven to the brim!
　O'er running it: all running o'er beside
This world! Nay, overflowing hell; wherein
　For thine elect, there rose a mighty tide!　　　10

That there our veins might through thy person bleed,
To quench those flames, that else would on us feed.

Oh! that thy love might overflow my heart!
　To fire the same with love: for love I would.
But oh! my straightened breast! my lifeless spark!　　15
　My fireless flame! what chilly love, and cold?
　In measure small! in manner chilly! see.
　Lord, blow the coal: thy love enflame in me.

Jonathan Swift

THE PROGRESS OF BEAUTY

　When first Diana leaves her bed
Vapors and steams her looks disgrace,
A frouzy dirty colored red
Sits on her cloudy wrinkled face.

　But by degrees when mounted high　　　　　5
Her artificial face appears
Down from her window in the sky,
Her spots are gone, her visage clears.

　'Twixt earthly females and the moon
All parallels exactly run;　　　　　　　　10
If Celia should appear too soon
Alas, the nymph would be undone.

　To see her from her pillow rise
All reeking in a cloudy steam,
Cracked lips, foul teeth, and gummy eyes,　　15
Poor Strephon, how would he blaspheme!

　The soot or powder which was wont
To make her hair look black as jet,
Falls from her tresses on her front
A mingled mass of dirt and sweat.　　　　　20

Three colors, black, and red, and white,
So graceful in their proper place,
Remove them to a diff'rent light
They form a frightful hideous face;

For instance: when the lily slips 25
Into the precincts of the rose,
And takes possession of the lips,
Leaving the purple to the nose.

So Celia went entire to bed,
All her complexions safe and sound, 30
But when she rose, the black and red,
Though still in sight, had changed their ground.

The black, which would not be confined,
A more inferior station seeks,
Leaving the fiery red behind, 35
And mingles in her muddy cheeks.

The paint by perspiration cracks,
And falls in rivulets of sweat,
On either side you see the tracks,
While at her chin the confluents met. 40

A skillful housewife thus her thumb
With spittle while she spins, anoints,
And thus the brown meanders come
In trickling streams betwixt her joints.

But Celia can with ease reduce 45
By help of pencil, paint and brush
Each color to its place and use,
And teach her cheeks again to blush.

She knows her early self no more,
But filled with admiration, stands, 50
As other painters oft adore
The workmanship of their own hands.

Thus after four important hours
Celia's the wonder of her sex;

Say, which among the heavenly powers   55
Could cause such wonderful effects?

Venus, indulgent to her kind,
Gave women all their hearts could wish
When first she taught them where to find
White lead, and Lusitanian dish.   60

Love with white lead cements his wings,
White lead was sent us to repair
Two brightest, brittlest earthly things,
A lady's face, and china ware.

She ventures now to lift the sash,   65
The window is her proper sphere;
Ah lovely nymph, be not too rash,
Nor let the beaux approach too near.

Take pattern by your sister star,
Delude at once and bless our sight;   70
When you are seen, be seen from far,
And chiefly choose to shine by night.

In the Pell-Mell when passing by,
Keep up the glasses of your chair;
Then each transported fop will cry,   75
"G——d d——m me, Jack, she's wondrous fair."

But art no longer can prevail
When the materials all are gone;
The best mechanic hand must fail
Where nothing's left to work upon.   80

Matter, as wise logicians say,
Cannot without a form subsist,
And form, say I, as well as they,
Must fail if matter brings no grist.

And this is fair Diana's case,   85
For all astrologers maintain
Each night a bit drops off her face
When mortals say she's in her wane.

While Partridge wisely shows the cause
Efficient of the moon's decay,   90
That Cancer with his pois'nous claws
Attacks her in the Milky Way;

But Gadbury in art profound
From her pale cheeks pretends to show
That swain Endymion is not sound,   95
Or else, that Mercury's her foe.

But, let the cause be what it will,
In half a month she looks so thin
That Flamstead can with all his skill
See but her forehead and her chin.   100

Yet as she wastes, she grows discreet,
Till midnight never shows her head;
So rotting Celia strolls the street
When sober folks are all a-bed.

For sure if this be Luna's fate,   105
Poor Celia, but of mortal race,
In vain expects a longer date
To the materials of her face.

When mercury her tresses mows
To think of oil and soot is vain;   110
No painting can restore a nose,
Nor will her teeth return again.

Two balls of glass may serve for eyes,
White lead can plaster up a cleft,
But these, alas, are poor supplies   115
If neither cheeks, nor lips, be left.

Ye powers who over love preside,
Since mortal beauties drop so soon,
If you would have us well supplied,
Send us new nymphs with each new moon.   120

89. *Partridge*: a writer on astrology.
93. *Gadbury*: another astrologer.
99. *Flamstead*: the royal astronomer.
109. *mercury*: a cure for venereal disease.

Alexander Pope

THE RAPE OF THE LOCK

TO MRS. ARABELLA FERMOR

[Canto 1]

What dire offense from amorous causes springs,
What mighty contests rise from trivial things,
I sing—This verse to Caryll, Muse! is due:
This, even Belinda may vouchsafe to view:
Slight is the subject, but not so the praise,   5
If she inspire, and he approve my lays.
  Say what strange motive, Goddess! could compel
A well-bred lord to assault a gentle belle?
Oh, say what stranger cause, yet unexplored,
Could make a gentle belle reject a lord?   10
In tasks so bold can little men engage,
And in soft bosoms dwells such mighty rage?
  Sol through white curtains shot a timorous ray,
And oped those eyes that must eclipse the day.
Now lapdogs give themselves the rousing shake,   15
And sleepless lovers just at twelve awake:
Thrice rung the bell, the slipper knocked the ground,
And the pressed watch returned a silver sound.
Belinda still her downy pillow pressed,
Her guardian sylph prolonged the balmy rest: 20
'Twas he had summoned to her silent bed
The morning dream that hovered o'er her head.
A youth more glittering than a birthnight beau
(That even in slumber caused her cheek to glow)
Seemed to her ear his winning lips to lay,   25
And thus in whispers said, or seemed to say:
  "Fairest of mortals, thou distinguished care
Of thousand bright inhabitants of air!
If e'er one vision touched thy infant thought,
Of all the nurse and all the priest have taught,   30

Of airy elves by moonlight shadows seen,
The silver token, and the circled green,
Or virgins visited by angel powers,
With golden crowns and wreaths of heavenly flowers,
Hear and believe! thy own importance know,   35
Nor bound thy narrow views to things below.
Some secret truths, from learned pride concealed,
To maids alone and children are revealed:
What though no credit doubting wits may give?
The fair and innocent shall still believe.   40
Know, then, unnumbered spirits round thee fly,
The light militia of the lower sky:
These, though unseen, are ever on the wing,
Hang o'er the box, and hover round the ring.
Think what an equipage thou hast in air,   45
And view with scorn two pages and a chair.
As now your own, our beings were of old,
And once enclosed in woman's beauteous mold;
Thence, by a soft transition, we repair
From earthly vehicles to these of air.   50
Think not, when woman's transient breath is fled,
That all her vanities at once are dead:
Succeeding vanities she still regards,
And though she plays no more, o'erlooks the cards.
Her joy in gilded chariots, when alive,   55
And love of ombre, after death survive.
For when the fair in all their pride expire,
To their first elements their souls retire:
The sprites of fiery termagants in flame
Mount up, and take a salamander's name.   60
Soft yielding minds to water glide away,
And sip, with nymphs, their elemental tea.
The graver prude sinks downward to a gnome,
In search of mischief still on earth to roam.
The light coquettes in sylphs aloft repair,   65
And sport and flutter in the fields of air.
   "Know further yet; whoever fair and chaste
Rejects mankind, is by some sylph embraced:
For spirits, freed from mortal laws, with ease

Assume what sexes and what shapes they please.   70
What guards the purity of melting maids,
In courtly balls, and midnight masquerades,
Safe from the treacherous friend, the daring spark,
The glance by day, the whisper in the dark,
When kind occasion prompts their warm desires,   75
When music softens, and when dancing fires?
'Tis but their sylph, the wise celestials know,
Though honor is the word with men below.
    "Some nymphs there are, too conscious of their face,
For life predestined to the gnomes' embrace.   80
These swell their prospects and exalt their pride,
When offers are disdained, and love denied:
Then gay ideas crowd the vacant brain,
While peers, and dukes, and all their sweeping train,
And garters, stars, and coronets appear,   85
And in soft sounds, 'your Grace' salutes their ear.
'Tis these that early taint the female soul,
Instruct the eyes of young coquettes to roll,
Teach infant cheeks a bidden blush to know,
And little hearts to flutter at a beau.   90
    "Oft, when the world imagine women stray,
The sylphs through mystic mazes guide their way,
Through all the giddy circle they pursue,
And old impertinence expel by new.
What tender maid but must a victim fall   95
To one man's treat, but for another's ball?
When Florio speaks what virgin could withstand,
If gentle Damon did not squeeze her hand?
With varying vanities, from every part,
They shift the moving toyshop of their heart;   100
Where wigs with wigs, with sword-knots sword-knots strive,
Beaux banish beaux, and coaches coaches drive.
This erring mortals levity may call;
Oh, blind to truth! the sylphs contrive it all.
    "Of these am I, who thy protection claim,   105
A watchful sprite, and Ariel is my name.
Late, as I ranged the crystal wilds of air,
In the clear mirror of thy ruling star

I saw, alas! some dread event impend,
Ere to the main this morning sun descend,   110
But heaven reveals not what, or how, or where:
Warned by the sylph, O pious maid, beware!
This to disclose is all thy guardian can:
Beware of all, but most beware of man!"
      He said; when Shock, who thought she slept too long,   115
Leaped up, and waked his mistress with his tongue.
'Twas then, Belinda, if report say true,
Thy eyes first opened on a billet-doux;
Wounds, charms, and ardors were no sooner read,
But all the vision vanished from thy head.   120
      And now, unveiled, the toilet stands displayed,
Each silver vase in mystic order laid.
First, robed in white, the nymph intent adores,
With head uncovered, the cosmetic powers.
A heavenly image in the glass appears;   125
To that she bends, to that her eyes she rears.
The inferior priestess, at her altar's side,
Trembling begins the sacred rites of Pride.
Unnumbered treasures ope at once, and here
The various offerings of the world appear;   130
From each she nicely culls with curious toil,
And decks the goddess with the glittering spoil.
This casket India's glowing gems unlocks,
And all Arabia breathes from yonder box.
The tortoise here and elephant unite,   135
Transformed to combs, the speckled and the white.
Here files of pins extend their shining rows,
Puffs, powders, patches, Bibles, billet-doux.
Now awful Beauty puts on all its arms;
The fair each moment rises in her charms,   140
Repairs her smiles, awakens every grace,
And calls forth all the wonders of her face;
Sees by degrees a purer blush arise,
And keener lightnings quicken in her eyes.
The busy sylphs surround their darling care,   145
These set the head, and those divide the hair,

Some fold the sleeve, whilst others plait the gown;
And Betty's praised for labors not her own.

[Canto 2]

Not with more glories, in the ethereal plain,
The sun first rises o'er the purpled main,
Than, issuing forth, the rival of his beams
Launched on the bosom of the silver Thames.
Fair nymphs and well-dressed youths around her shone,   5
But every eye was fixed on her alone.
On her white breast a sparkling cross she wore,
Which Jews might kiss, and infidels adore.
Her lively looks a sprightly mind disclose,
Quick as her eyes, and as unfixed as those: 10
Favors to none, to all she smiles extends;
Oft she rejects, but never once offends.
Bright as the sun, her eyes the gazers strike,
And, like the sun, they shine on all alike.
Yet graceful ease, and sweetness void of pride,   15
Might hide her faults, if belles had faults to hide:
If to her share some female errors fall,
Look on her face, and you'll forget 'em all.
    This nymph, to the destruction of mankind,
Nourished two locks which graceful hung behind   20
In equal curls, and well conspired to deck
With shining ringlets the smooth ivory neck.
Love in these labyrinths his slaves detains,
And mighty hearts are held in slender chains.
With hairy springes we the birds betray,   25
Slight lines of hair surprise the finny prey,
Fair tresses man's imperial race ensnare,
And beauty draws us with a single hair.
    The adventurous Baron the bright locks admired,
He saw, he wished, and to the prize aspired.   30
Resolved to win, he meditates the way,
By force to ravish, or by fraud betray;
For when success a lover's toil attends,
Few ask if fraud or force attained his ends.

For this, ere Phoebus rose, he had implored   35
Propitious heaven, and every power adored,
But chiefly love—to love an altar built,
Of twelve vast French romances, neatly gilt.
There lay three garters, half a pair of gloves,
And all the trophies of his former loves.   40
With tender billet-doux he lights the pyre,
And breathes three amorous sighs to raise the fire.
Then prostrate falls, and begs with ardent eyes
Soon to obtain, and long possess the prize:
The powers gave ear, and granted half his prayer, 45
The rest the winds dispersed in empty air.
    But now secure the painted vessel glides,
The sunbeams trembling on the floating tides,
While melting music steals upon the sky,
And softened sounds along the waters die.   50
Smooth flow the waves, the zephyrs gently play,
Belinda smiled, and all the world was gay.
All but the sylph—with careful thoughts oppressed,
The impending woe sat heavy on his breast.
He summons straight his denizens of air;   55
The lucid squadrons round the sails repair:
Soft o'er the shrouds aërial whispers breathe
That seemed but zephyrs to the train beneath.
Some to the sun their insect-wings unfold,
Waft on the breeze, or sink in clouds of gold.   60
Transparent forms too fine for mortal sight,
Their fluid bodies half dissolved in light,
Loose to the wind their airy garments flew,
Thin glittering textures of the filmy dew,
Dipped in the richest tincture of the skies,   65
Where light disports in ever-mingling dyes,
While every beam new transient colors flings,
Colors that change whene'er they wave their wings.
Amid the circle, on the gilded mast,
Superior by the head was Ariel placed;   70
His purple pinions opening to the sun,
He raised his azure wand, and thus begun:

"Ye sylphs and sylphids, to your chief give ear!
Fays, fairies, genii, elves, and daemons, hear!
Ye know the spheres and various tasks assigned   75
By laws eternal to the aërial kind.
Some in the fields of purest ether play,
And bask and whiten in the blaze of day.
Some guide the course of wandering orbs on high,
Or roll the planets through the boundless sky.   80
Some less refined, beneath the moon's pale light
Pursue the stars that shoot athwart the night,
Or suck the mists in grosser air below,
Or dip their pinions in the painted bow,
Or brew fierce tempests on the wintry main,   85
Or o'er the glebe distill the kindly rain.
Others on earth o'er human race preside,
Watch all their ways, and all their actions guide:
Of these the chief the care of nations own,
And guard with arms divine the British throne.   90
     "Our humbler province is to tend the fair,
Not a less pleasing, though less glorious care:
To save the powder from too rude a gale,
Nor let the imprisoned essences exhale;
To draw fresh colors from the vernal flowers;   95
To steal from rainbows ere they drop in showers
A brighter wash; to curl their waving hairs,
Assist their blushes, and inspire their airs;
Nay oft, in dreams invention we bestow,
To change a flounce, or add a furbelow.   100
     "This day black omens threat the brightest fair,
That e'er deserved a watchful spirit's care;
Some dire disaster, or by force or slight,
But what, or where, the Fates have wrapped in night:
Whether the nymph shall break Diana's law,   105
Or some frail china jar receive a flaw,
Or stain her honor or her new brocade,
Forget her prayers, or miss a masquerade,
Or lose her heart, or necklace, at a ball;
Or whether heaven has doomed that Shock must fall.   110

Haste, then, ye spirits! to your charge repair:
The fluttering fan be Zephyretta's care;
The drops to thee, Brillante, we consign;
And, Momentilla, let the watch be thine;
Do thou, Crispissa, tend her favorite lock;   115
Ariel himself shall be the guard of Shock.
   "To fifty chosen sylphs, of special note,
We trust the important charge, the petticoat;
Oft have we known that sevenfold fence to fail,
Though stiff with hoops, and armed with ribs of whale.   120
Form a strong line about the silver bound,
And guard the wide circumference around.
   "Whatever spirit, careless of his charge,
His post neglects, or leaves the fair at large,
Shall feel sharp vengeance soon o'ertake his sins,   125
Be stopped in vials, or transfixed with pins,
Or plunged in lakes of bitter washes lie,
Or wedged whole ages in a bodkin's eye;
Gums and pomatums shall his flight restrain,
While clogged he beats his silken wings in vain,   130
Or alum styptics with contracting power
Shrink his thin essence like a riveled flower:
Or, as Ixion fixed, the wretch shall feel
The giddy motion of the whirling mill,
In fumes of burning chocolate shall glow,   135
And tremble at the sea that froths below!"
   He spoke; the spirits from the sails descend;
Some, orb in orb, around the nymph extend;
Some thread the mazy ringlets of her hair;
Some hang upon the pendants of her ear: 140
With beating hearts the dire event they wait,
Anxious, and trembling for the birth of Fate.

[Canto 3]

   Close by those meads, forever crowned with flowers,
Where Thames with pride surveys his rising towers,
There stands a structure of majestic frame,
Which from the neighboring Hampton takes its name.
Here Britain's statesmen oft the fall foredoom   5

Of foreign tyrants and of nymphs at home;
Here thou, great Anna! whom three realms obey,
Dost sometimes counsel take—and sometimes tea.

Hither the heroes and the nymphs resort,
To taste awhile the pleasures of a court; 10
In various talk the instructive hours they passed,
Who gave the ball, or paid the visit last;
One speaks the glory of the British queen,
And one describes a charming Indian screen;
A third interprets motions, looks, and eyes; 15
At every word a reputation dies.
Snuff, or the fan, supply each pause of chat,
With singing, laughing, ogling, and all that.

Meanwhile, declining from the noon of day,
The sun obliquely shoots his burning ray; 20
The hungry judges soon the sentence sign,
And wretches hang that jurymen may dine;
The merchant from the Exchange returns in peace,
And the long labors of the toilet cease.

Belinda now, whom thirst of fame invites, 25
Burns to encounter two adventurous knights,
At ombre singly to decide their doom,
And swells her breast with conquests yet to come.
Straight the three bands prepare in arms to join,
Each band the number of the sacred nine. 30
Soon as she spreads her hand, the aërial guard
Descend, and sit on each important card:
First Ariel perched upon a matadore,
Then each according to the rank they bore;
For sylphs, yet mindful of their ancient race, 35
Are, as when women, wondrous fond of place.

Behold, four kings in majesty revered,
With hoary whiskers and a forky beard;
And four fair queens whose hands sustain a flower,
The expressive emblem of their softer power; 40
Four knaves in garbs succinct, a trusty band,
Caps on their heads, and halberts in their hand;
And parti-colored troops, a shining train,
Draw forth to combat on the velvet plain.

The skillful nymph reviews her force with care;   45
"Let spades be trumps!" she said, and trumps they were.
    Now move to war her sable matadores,
In show like leaders of the swarthy Moors.
Spadillio first, unconquerable lord!
Led off two captive trumps, and swept the board.   50
As many more Manillio forced to yield,
And marched a victor from the verdant field.
Him Basto followed, but his fate more hard
Gained but one trump and one plebeian card.
With his broad saber next, a chief in years,   55
The hoary Majesty of Spades appears,
Puts forth one manly leg, to sight revealed,
The rest his many-colored robe concealed.
The rebel knave, who dares his prince engage,
Proves the just victim of his royal rage.   60
Even mighty Pam, that kings and queens o'erthrew
And mowed down armies in the fights of loo,
Sad chance of war! now destitute of aid,
Falls undistinguished by the victor spade.
    Thus far both armies to Belinda yield;   65
Now to the Baron fate inclines the field.
His warlike amazon her host invades,
The imperial consort of the crown of spades.
The club's black tyrant first her victim died,
Spite of his haughty mien and barbarous pride.   70
What boots the regal circle on his head,
His giant limbs, in state unwieldy spread?
That long behind he trails his pompous robe,
And of all monarchs only grasps the globe?
    The Baron now his diamonds pours apace;   75
The embroidered king who shows but half his face,
And his refulgent queen, with powers combined
Of broken troops an easy conquest find.
Clubs, diamonds, hearts, in wild disorder seen,
With throngs promiscuous strew the level green.   80
Thus when dispersed a routed army runs,
Of Asia's troops, and Afric's sable sons,
With like confusion different nations fly,

Of various habit, and of various dye,
The pierced battalions disunited fall   85
In heaps on heaps; one fate o'erwhelms them all.
   The knave of diamonds tries his wily arts,
And wins (oh, shameful chance!) the queen of hearts.
At this, the blood the virgin's cheek forsook,
A livid paleness spreads o'er all her look;   90
She sees, and trembles at the approaching ill,
Just in the jaws of ruin, and Codille,
And now (as oft in some distempered state)
On one nice trick depends the general fate.
An ace of hearts steps forth: the king unseen   95
Lurked in her hand, and mourned his captive queen.
He springs to vengeance with an eager pace,
And falls like thunder on the prostrate ace.
The nymph exulting fills with shouts the sky,
The walls, the woods, and long canals reply.   100
   O thoughtless mortals! ever blind to fate,
Too soon dejected, and too soon elate:
Sudden these honors shall be snatched away,
And cursed forever this victorious day.
   For lo! the board with cups and spoons is crowned,   105
The berries crackle, and the mill turns round;
On shining altars of Japan they raise
The silver lamp; the fiery spirits blaze:
From silver spouts the grateful liquors glide,
While China's earth receives the smoking tide.   110
At once they gratify their scent and taste,
And frequent cups prolong the rich repast.
Straight hover round the fair her airy band;
Some, as she sipped, the fuming liquor fanned,
Some o'er her lap their careful plumes displayed,   115
Trembling, and conscious of the rich brocade.
Coffee (which makes the politician wise,
And see through all things with his half-shut eyes)
Sent up in vapors to the Baron's brain
New stratagems, the radiant lock to gain.   120
Ah, cease, rash youth! desist ere 'tis too late,
Fear the just gods, and think of Scylla's fate!

Changed to a bird, and sent to flit in air,
She dearly pays for Nisus' injured hair!
   But when to mischief mortals bend their will,   125
How soon they find fit instruments of ill!
Just then Clarissa drew with tempting grace
A two-edged weapon from her shining case:
So ladies in romance assist their knight,
Present the spear, and arm him for the fight.   130
He takes the gift with reverence, and extends
The little engine on his fingers' ends;
This just behind Belinda's neck he spread,
As o'er the fragrant steams she bends her head.
Swift to the lock a thousand sprites repair,   135
A thousand wings, by turns, blow back the hair,
And thrice they twitched the diamond in her ear,
Thrice she looked back, and thrice the foe drew near.
Just in that instant, anxious Ariel sought
The close recesses of the virgin's thought;   140
As on the nosegay in her breast reclined,
He watched the ideas rising in her mind,
Sudden he viewed, in spite of all her art,
An earthly lover lurking at her heart.
Amazed, confused, he found his power expired,   145
Resigned to fate, and with a sigh retired.
   The peer now spreads the glittering forfex wide,
To enclose the lock; now joins it, to divide.
Even then, before the fatal engine closed,
A wretched sylph too fondly interposed;   150
Fate urged the shears, and cut the sylph in twain
(But airy substance soon unites again):
The meeting points the sacred hair dissever
From the fair head, forever, and forever!
   Then flashed the living lightning from her eyes,   155
And screams of horror rend the affrighted skies.
Not louder shrieks to pitying heaven are cast,
When husbands, or when lapdogs breathe their last;
Or when rich china vessels fallen from high,
In glittering dust and painted fragments lie!   160
"Let wreaths of triumph now my temples twine,"

The victor cried, "the glorious prize is mine!
While fish in streams, or birds delight in air,
Or in a coach and six the British fair,
As long as *Atalantis* shall be read,   165
Or the small pillow grace a lady's bed,
While visits shall be paid on solemn days,
When numerous wax-lights in bright order blaze,
While nymphs take treats, or assignations give,
So long my honor, name, and praise shall live!   170
What time would spare, from steel receive its date,
And monuments, like men, submit to fate!
Steel could the labor of the gods destroy,
And strike to dust the imperial towers of Troy;
Steel could the works of mortal pride confound,   175
And hew triumphal arches to the ground.
What wonder then, fair nymph! thy hairs should feel,
The conquering force of unresisted steel?"

[Canto 4]

But anxious cares the pensive nymph oppressed,
And secret passions labored in her breast.
Not youthful kings in battle seized alive,
Not scornful virgins who their charms survive,
Not ardent lovers robbed of all their bliss,   5
Not ancient ladies when refused a kiss,
Not tyrants fierce that unrepenting die,
Not Cynthia when her manteau's pinned awry,
E'er felt such rage, resentment, and despair,
As thou, sad virgin! for thy ravished hair.   10
    For, that sad moment, when the sylphs withdrew
And Ariel weeping from Belinda flew,
Umbriel, a dusky, melancholy sprite
As ever sullied the fair face of light,
Down to the central earth, his proper scene,   15
Repaired to search the gloomy Cave of Spleen.
    Swift on his sooty pinions flits the gnome,
And in a vapor reached the dismal dome.
No cheerful breeze this sullen region knows,
The dreaded east is all the wind that blows.   20

99

Here in a grotto, sheltered close from air,
And screened in shades from day's detested glare,
She sighs forever on her pensive bed,
Pain at her side, and Megrim at her head.
   Two handmaids wait the throne: alike in place,   25
But differing far in figure and in face.
Here stood Ill-Nature like an ancient maid,
Her wrinkled form in black and white arrayed;
With store of prayers for mornings, nights, and noons,
Her hand is filled; her bosom with lampoons.   30
   There Affectation, with a sickly mien,
Shows in her cheek the roses of eighteen,
Practiced to lisp, and hang the head aside,
Faints into airs, and languishes with pride,
On the rich quilt sinks with becoming woe,   35
Wrapped in a gown, for sickness and for show.
The fair ones feel such maladies as these,
When each new nightdress gives a new disease.
   A constant vapor o'er the palace flies,
Strange phantoms rising as the mists arise;   40
Dreadful as hermit's dreams in haunted shades,
Or bright as visions of expiring maids.
Now glaring fiends, and snakes on rolling spires,
Pale specters, gaping tombs, and purple fires;
Now lakes of liquid gold, Elysian scenes,   45
And crystal domes, and angels in machines.
   Unnumbered throngs on every side are seen
Of bodies changed to various forms by Spleen.
Here living teapots stand, one arm held out,
One bent; the handle this, and that the spout: 50
A pipkin there, like Homer's tripod, walks;
Here sighs a jar, and there a goose pie talks;
Men prove with child, as powerful fancy works,
And maids, turned bottles, call aloud for corks.
   Safe passed the gnome through this fantastic band,   55
A branch of healing spleenwort in his hand.
Then thus addressed the Power: "Hail, wayward Queen!
Who rule the sex to fifty from fifteen:
Parent of vapors and of female wit,

Who give the hysteric or poetic fit,   60
On various tempers act by various ways,
Make some take physic, others scribble plays;
Who cause the proud their visits to delay,
And send the godly in a pet to pray.
A nymph there is that all your power disdains,   65
And thousands more in equal mirth maintains.
But oh! if e'er thy gnome could spoil a grace,
Or raise a pimple on a beauteous face,
Like citron-waters matrons' cheeks inflame,
Or change complexions at a losing game;   70
If e'er with airy horns I planted heads,
Or rumpled petticoats, or tumbled beds,
Or caused suspicion when no soul was rude,
Or discomposed the headdress of a prude,
Or e'er to costive lapdog gave disease,   75
Which not the tears of brightest eyes could ease,
Hear me, and touch Belinda with chagrin:
That single act gives half the world the spleen."
    The Goddess with a discontented air
Seems to reject him though she grants his prayer.   80
A wondrous bag with both her hands she binds,
Like that where once Ulysses held the winds;
There she collects the force of female lungs,
Sighs, sobs, and passions, and the war of tongues.
A vial next she fills with fainting fears,   85
Soft sorrows, melting griefs, and flowing tears.
The gnome rejoicing bears her gifts away,
Spreads his black wings, and slowly mounts to day.
    Sunk in Thalestris' arms the nymph he found,
Her eyes dejected and her hair unbound.   90
Full o'er their heads the swelling bag he rent,
And all the Furies issued at the vent.
Belinda burns with more than mortal ire,
And fierce Thalestris fans the rising fire.
"O wretched maid!" she spread her hands, and cried   95
(While Hampton's echoes, "Wretched maid!" replied),
"Was it for this you took such constant care
The bodkin, comb, and essence to prepare?

For this your locks in paper durance bound,
For this with torturing irons wreathed around? 100
For this with fillets strained your tender head,
And bravely bore the double loads of lead?
Gods! shall the ravisher display your hair,
While the fops envy, and the ladies stare!
Honor forbid! at whose unrivaled shrine 105
Ease, pleasure, virtue, all, our sex resign.
Methinks already I your tears survey,
Already hear the horrid things they say,
Already see you a degraded toast,
And all your honor in a whisper lost! 110
How shall I, then, your helpless fame defend?
'Twill then be infamy to seem your friend!
And shall this prize, the inestimable prize,
Exposed through crystal to the gazing eyes,
And heightened by the diamond's circling rays, 115
On that rapacious hand forever blaze?
Sooner shall grass in Hyde Park Circus grow,
And wits take lodgings in the sound of Bow;
Sooner let earth, air, sea, to chaos fall,
Men, monkeys, lapdogs, parrots, perish all!" 120
    She said; then raging to Sir Plume repairs,
And bids her beau demand the precious hairs
(Sir Plume of amber snuffbox justly vain,
And the nice conduct of a clouded cane).
With earnest eyes, and round unthinking face, 125
He first the snuffbox opened, then the case,
And thus broke out—"My Lord, why, what the devil!
Z——ds! damn the lock! 'fore Gad, you must be civil!
Plague on't! 'tis past a jest—nay prithee, pox!
Give her the hair"—he spoke, and rapped his box. 130
    "It grieves me much," replied the Peer again,
"Who speaks so well should ever speak in vain.
But by this lock, this sacred lock I swear
(Which never more shall join its parted hair;
Which never more its honors shall renew, 135
Clipped from the lovely head where late it grew),
That while my nostrils draw the vital air,

This hand, which won it, shall forever wear."
He spoke, and speaking, in proud triumph spread
The long-contended honors of her head.   140
    But Umbriel, hateful gnome, forbears not so;
He breaks the vial whence the sorrows flow.
Then see! the nymph in beauteous grief appears,
Her eyes half languishing, half drowned in tears;
On her heaved bosom hung her drooping head,   145
Which with a sigh she raised, and thus she said:
    "Forever cursed be this detested day,
Which snatched my best, my favorite curl away!
Happy! ah, ten times happy had I been,
If Hampton Court these eyes had never seen!   150
Yet am not I the first mistaken maid,
By love of courts to numerous ills betrayed.
Oh, had I rather unadmired remained
In some lone isle, or distant northern land;
Where the gilt chariot never marks the way,   155
Where none learn ombre, none e'er taste bohea!
There kept my charms concealed from mortal eye,
Like roses that in deserts bloom and die.
What moved my mind with youthful lords to roam?
Oh, had I stayed, and said my prayers at home!   160
'Twas this the morning omens seemed to tell,
Thrice from my trembling hand the patch box fell;
The tottering china shook without a wind,
Nay, Poll sat mute, and Shock was most unkind!
A sylph too warned me of the threats of fate,   165
In mystic visions, now believed too late!
See the poor remnants of these slighted hairs!
My hands shall rend what e'en thy rapine spares.
These in two sable ringlets taught to break,
Once gave new beauties to the snowy neck;   170
The sister lock now sits uncouth, alone,
And in its fellow's fate foresees its own;
Uncurled it hangs, the fatal shears demands,
And tempts once more thy sacrilegious hands.
Oh, hadst thou, cruel! been content to seize   175
Hairs less in sight, or any hairs but these!"

[Canto 5]

She said: the pitying audience melt in tears.
But Fate and Jove had stopped the Baron's ears.
In vain Thalestris with reproach assails,
For who can move when fair Belinda fails?
Not half so fixed the Trojan could remain,   5
While Anna begged and Dido raged in vain.
Then grave Clarissa graceful waved her fan;
Silence ensued, and thus the nymph began:
    "Say why are beauties praised and honored most,
The wise man's passion, and the vain man's toast?   10
Why decked with all that land and sea afford,
Why angels called, and angel-like adored?
Why round our coaches crowd the white-gloved beaux,
Why bows the side box from its inmost rows?
How vain are all these glories, all our pains,   15
Unless good sense preserve what beauty gains;
That men may say when we the front box grace,
'Behold the first in virtue as in face!'
Oh! if to dance all night, and dress all day,
Charmed the smallpox, or chased old age away,   20
Who would not scorn what housewife's cares produce,
Or who would learn one earthly thing of use?
To patch, nay ogle, might become a saint,
Nor could it sure be such a sin to paint.
But since, alas! frail beauty must decay,   25
Curled or uncurled, since locks will turn to gray;
Since painted, or not painted, all shall fade,
And she who scorns a man must die a maid;
What then remains but well our power to use,
And keep good humor still whate'er we lose?   30
And trust me, dear, good humor can prevail
When airs, and flights, and screams, and scolding fail.
Beauties in vain their pretty eyes may roll;
Charms strike the sight, but merit wins the soul."
    So spoke the dame, but no applause ensued;   35
Belinda frowned, Thalestris called her prude.
"To arms, to arms!" the fierce virago cries,

And swift as lightning to the combat flies.
All side in parties, and begin the attack;
Fans clap, silks rustle, and tough whalebones crack;　　　40
Heroes' and heroines' shouts confusedly rise,
And bass and treble voices strike the skies.
No common weapons in their hands are found,
Like Gods they fight, nor dread a mortal wound.
　　So when bold Homer makes the Gods engage,　　　45
And heavenly breasts with human passions rage;
'Gainst Pallas, Mars; Latona, Hermes arms;
And all Olympus rings with loud alarms:
Jove's thunder roars, heaven trembles all around,
Blue Neptune storms, the bellowing deeps resound:　　　50
Earth shakes her nodding towers, the ground gives way,
And the pale ghosts start at the flash of day!
　　Triumphant Umbriel on a sconce's height
Clapped his glad wings, and sat to view the fight:
Propped on the bodkin spears, the sprites survey　　　55
The growing combat, or assist the fray.
　　While through the press enraged Thalestris flies,
And scatters death around from both her eyes,
A beau and witling perished in the throng,
One died in metaphor, and one in song.　　　60
"O cruel nymph! a living death I bear,"
Cried Dapperwit, and sunk beside his chair.
A mournful glance Sir Fopling upwards cast,
"Those eyes are made so killing"—was his last.
Thus on Maeander's flowery margin lies　　　65
The expiring swan, and as he sings he dies.
　　When bold Sir Plume had drawn Clarissa down,
Chloe stepped in, and killed him with a frown;
She smiled to see the doughty hero slain,
But, at her smile, the beau revived again.　　　70
　　Now Jove suspends his golden scales in air,
Weighs the men's wits against the lady's hair;
The doubtful beam long nods from side to side;
At length the wits mount up, the hairs subside.
　　See, fierce Belinda on the Baron flies,　　　75
With more than usual lightning in her eyes;

Nor feared the chief the unequal fight to try,
Who sought no more than on his foe to die.
   But this bold lord with manly strength endued,
She with one finger and a thumb subdued: 80
Just where the breath of life his nostrils drew,
A charge of snuff the wily virgin threw;
The gnomes direct, to every atom just,
The pungent grains of titillating dust.
Sudden, with starting tears each eye o'erflows,   85
And the high dome re-echoes to his nose.
   "Now meet thy fate," incensed Belinda cried,
And drew a deadly bodkin from her side.
(The same, his ancient personage to deck,
Her great-great-grandsire wore about his neck,   90
In three seal rings; which after, melted down,
Formed a vast buckle for his widow's gown:
Her infant grandame's whistle next it grew,
The bells she jingled, and the whistle blew;
Then in a bodkin graced her mother's hairs,   95
Which long she wore, and now Belinda wears.)
   "Boast not my fall," he cried, "insulting foe!
Thou by some other shalt be laid as low.
Nor think to die dejects my lofty mind:
All that I dread is leaving you behind!   100
Rather than so, ah, let me still survive,
And burn in Cupid's flames—but burn alive."
   "Restore the lock!" she cries; and all around
"Restore the lock!" the vaulted roofs rebound.
Not fierce Othello in so loud a strain   105
Roared for the handkerchief that caused his pain.
But see how oft ambitious aims are crossed,
And chiefs contend till all the prize is lost!
The lock, obtained with guilt, and kept with pain,
In every place is sought, but sought in vain: 110
With such a prize no mortal must be blessed,
So Heaven decrees! with Heaven who can contest?
   Some thought it mounted to the lunar sphere,
Since all things lost on earth are treasured there.
There heroes' wits are kept in ponderous vases,   115

And beaux' in snuffboxes and tweezer cases.
There broken vows and deathbed alms are found,
And lovers' hearts with ends of riband bound,
The courtier's promises, and sick man's prayers,
The smiles of harlots, and the tears of heirs, 120
Cages for gnats, and chains to yoke a flea,
Dried butterflies, and tomes of casuistry.
  But trust the Muse—she saw it upward rise,
Though marked by none but quick, poetic eyes
(So Rome's great founder to the heavens withdrew, 125
To Proculus alone confessed in view);
A sudden star, it shot through liquid air,
And drew behind a radiant trail of hair.
Not Berenice's locks first rose so bright,
The heavens bespangling with disheveled light. 130
The sylphs behold it kindling as it flies
And pleased pursue its progress through the skies.
  This the beau monde shall from the Mall survey,
And hail with music its propitious ray.
This the blest lover shall for Venus take, 135
And send up vows from Rosamonda's Lake.
This Partridge soon shall view in cloudless skies,
When next he looks through Galileo's eyes;
And hence the egregious wizard shall foredoom
The fate of Louis, and the fall of Rome. 140
  Then cease, bright nymph! to mourn thy ravished hair,
Which adds new glory to the shining sphere!
Not all the tresses that fair head can boast,
Shall draw such envy as the lock you lost.
For, after all the murders of your eye, 145
When, after millions slain, yourself shall die:
When those fair suns shall set, as set they must,
And all those tresses shall be laid in dust,
This lock the Muse shall consecrate to fame,
And 'midst the stars inscribe Belinda's name. 150

William Collins

A SONG FROM SHAKESPEARE'S CYMBELINE

Sung by Guiderus and Arviragus
over Fidele, supposed to be dead

To fair Fidele's grassy tomb
  Soft maids and village hinds shall bring
Each opening sweet, of earliest bloom,
  And rifle all the breathing spring.

No wailing ghost shall dare appear   5
  To vex with shrieks this quiet grove:
But shepherd lads assemble here,
  And melting virgins own their love.

No withered witch shall here be seen,
  No goblins lead their nightly crew: 10
The female fays shall haunt the green,
  And dress thy grave with pearly dew!

The red-breast oft at evening hours
  Shall kindly lend his little aid:
With hoary moss, and gathered flowers,   15
  To deck the ground where thou art laid.

When howling winds, and beating rain,
  In tempests shake the sylvan cell:
Or midst the chace on every plain,
  The tender thought on thee shall dwell.   20

Each lonely scene shall thee restore,
  For thee the tear be duly shed:
Beloved till life can charm no more,
  And mourned, till pity's self be dead.

William Cowper

THE POPLAR FIELD

The poplars are felled; farewell to the shade
And the whispering sound of the cool colonnade;
The winds play no longer and sing in the leaves,
Nor Ouse on his bosom their image receives.

Twelve years have elapsed since I first took a view   5
Of my favourite field, and the bank where they grew;
And now in the grass behold they are laid,
And the tree is my seat that once lent me a shade.

The blackbird has fled to another retreat
Where the hazels afford him a screen from the heat,   10
And the scene where his melody charmed me before
Resounds with his sweet-flowing ditty no more.

My fugitive years are all hasting away,
And I must ere long lie as lowly as they
With a turf on my breast, and a stone at my head,   15
Ere another such grove shall arise in its stead.

'Tis a sight to engage me, if anything can,
To muse on the perishing pleasures of man;
Though his life be a dream, his enjoyments, I see,
Have a being less durable even than he.   20

4. *Ouse:* Great Ouse River, central and eastern England.

Philip Freneau

THE INDIAN BURYING GROUND*

In spite of all the learned have said,
    I still my old opinion keep;
The posture, that we give the dead,
    Points out the soul's eternal sleep.

Not so the ancients of these lands—   5
    The Indian, when from life released,
Again is seated with his friends,
    And shares again the joyous feast.

His imaged birds, and painted bowl,
    And venison, for a journey dressed,   10
Bespeak the nature of the soul,
    Activity, that knows no rest.

His bow, for action ready bent,
    And arrows, with a head of stone,
Can only mean that life is spent,   15
    And not the old ideas gone.

Thou, stranger, that shalt come this way,
    No fraud upon the dead commit—
Observe the swelling turf, and say
    They do not lie, but here they sit.   20

Here still a lofty rock remains,
    On which the curious eye may trace
(Now wasted, half, by wearing rains)
    The fancies of a ruder race.

Here still an aged elm aspires,   25
    Beneath whose far-projecting shade

"The North American Indians bury their dead in a sitting posture; deco-
rating the corpse with wampum, the images of birds, quadrupeds, &c:
And (if that of a warrior) with bows, arrows, tomahawks, and other military weapons." (Freneau's note.)

(And which the shepherd still admires)
 The children of the forest played!

There oft a restless Indian queen
 (Pale Shebah, with her braided hair)   30
And many a barbarous form is seen
 To chide the man that lingers there.

By midnight moons, o'er moistening dews;
 In habit for the chase arrayed,
The hunter still the deer pursues,   35
 The hunter and the deer, a shade!

And long shall timorous fancy see
 The painted chief, and pointed spear,
And reason's self shall bow the knee
 To shadows and delusions here.   40

ON THE UNIVERSALITY AND OTHER ATTRIBUTES OF THE GOD OF NATURE

All that we see, about, abroad,
What is it all, but nature's God?
In meaner works discovered here
No less than in the starry sphere.

In seas, on earth, this God is seen;   5
All that exist, upon him lean;
He lives in all, and never strayed
A moment from the works he made:

His system fixed on general laws
Bespeaks a wise creating cause;   10
Impartially he rules mankind
And all that on this globe we find.

Unchanged in all that seems to change,
Unbounded space is his great range;
To one vast purpose always true,   15
No time, with him, is old or new.

In all the attributes divine
Unlimited perfectings shine;
In these enwrapt, in these complete,
All virtues in that center meet.   20

This power doth all powers transcend,
To all intelligence a friend,
Exists, the greatest and the best
Throughout all the worlds, to make them blest.

All that he did he first approved,   25
He all things into being loved;
O'er all he made he still presides,
For them in life, or death provides.

William Blake

FROM SONGS OF INNOCENCE

THE LAMB

Little lamb, who made thee?
Dost thou know who made thee?
Gave thee life, and bid thee feed
By the stream and o'er the mead;
Gave thee clothing of delight,   5
Softest clothing, woolly, bright;
Gave thee such a tender voice,
Making all the vales rejoice?
  Little lamb, who made thee?
  Dost thou know who made thee?   10

  Little lamb, I'll tell thee,
  Little lamb, I'll tell thee:
He is callèd by thy name,
For he calls himself a Lamb.

He is meek, and he is mild;   15
He became a little child.
I a child, and thou a lamb,
We are callèd by his name.
    Little lamb, God bless thee!
    Little lamb, God bless thee!   20

THE LITTLE BLACK BOY

My mother bore me in the southern wild,
And I am black, but O! my soul is white;
White as an angel is the English child,
But I am black, as if bereaved of light.

My mother taught me underneath a tree,   5
And sitting down before the heat of day,
She took me on her lap and kissèd me,
And pointing to the east, began to say:

"Look on the rising sun: there God does live,
And gives his light, and gives his heat away;   10
And flowers and trees and beasts and men receive
Comfort in morning, joy in the noonday.

"And we are put on earth a little space,
That we may learn to bear the beams of love;
And these black bodies and this sunburnt face   15
Is but a cloud, and like a shady grove.

"For when our souls have learned the heat to bear,
The cloud will vanish; we shall hear his voice,
Saying: 'Come out from the grove, my love and care,
And round my golden tent like lambs rejoice.'"   20

Thus did my mother say, and kissèd me;
And thus I say to little English boy.
When I from black and he from white cloud free,
And round the tent of God like lambs we joy,

I'll shade him from the heat, till he can bear   25
To lean in joy upon our father's knee;
And then I'll stand and stroke his silver hair,
And be like him, and he will then love me.

FROM *SONGS OF EXPERIENCE*

THE CLOD AND THE PEBBLE

"Love seeketh not itself to please,
Nor for itself hath any care,
But for another gives its ease,
And builds a heaven in hell's despair."

So sang a little clod of clay   5
Trodden with the cattle's feet,
But a pebble of the brook
Warbled out these meters meet:

"Love seeketh only self to please,
To bind another to its delight,   10
Joys in another's loss of ease,
And builds a hell in heaven's despite."

THE CHIMNEY SWEEPER

A little black thing among the snow,
Crying " 'weep! 'weep!" in notes of woe!
"Where are thy father and mother? say?"
"They are both gone up to the church to pray.

"Because I was happy upon the heath,   5
And smiled among the winter's snow,
They clothèd me in the clothes of death,
And taught me to sing the notes of woe.

"And because I am happy and dance and sing,
They think they have done me no injury,   10
And are gone to praise God and his priest and king,
Who make up a heaven of our misery."

THE SICK ROSE

O rose, thou art sick!
The invisible worm
That flies in the night,
In the howling storm,

Has found out thy bed   5
Of crimson joy:
And his dark secret love
Does thy life destroy.

THE TIGER

Tiger! Tiger! burning bright
In the forests of the night,
What immortal hand or eye
Could frame thy fearful symmetry?

In what distant deeps or skies   5
Burnt the fire of thine eyes?
On what wings dare he aspire?
What the hand dare seize the fire?

And what shoulder, and what art,
Could twist the sinews of thy heart?   10
And when thy heart began to beat,
What dread hand? and what dread feet?

What the hammer? what the chain?
In what furnace was thy brain?
What the anvil? what dread grasp   15
Dare its deadly terrors clasp?

When the stars threw down their spears,
And watered heaven with their tears,
Did he smile his work to see?
Did he who made the Lamb make thee?   20

Tiger! Tiger! burning bright
In the forests of the night,
What immortal hand or eye
Dare frame thy fearful symmetry?

AH SUNFLOWER

Ah, sunflower, weary of time,
Who countest the steps of the sun,
Seeking after that sweet golden clime
Where the traveler's journey is done:

Where the youth pined away with desire, 5
And the pale virgin shrouded in snow
Arise from their graves, and aspire
Where my sunflower wishes to go.

LONDON

I wander through each chartered street,
Near where the chartered Thames does flow,
And mark in every face I meet
Marks of weakness, marks of woe.

In every cry of every man, 5
In every infant's cry of fear,
In every voice, in every ban,
The mind-forged manacles I hear.

How the chimney-sweeper's cry
Every blackening church appalls; 10
And the hapless soldier's sigh
Runs in blood down palace walls.

But most through midnight streets I hear
How the youthful harlot's curse
Blasts the new born infant's tear, 15
And blights with plagues the marriage hearse.

Robert Burns

AE FOND KISS

Ae fond kiss, and then we sever!
Ae fareweel, and then forever!
Deep in heart-wrung tears I'll pledge thee,
Warring sighs and groans I'll wage thee.
Who shall say that fortune grieves him 5
While the star of hope she leaves him?
Me, nae cheerfu' twinkle lights me,
Dark despair around benights me.

I'll ne'er blame my partial fancy,
Naething could resist my Nancy;   10
But to see her was to love her,
Love but her, and love forever.
Had we never loved sae kindly,
Had we never loved sae blindly,
Never met—or never parted,   15
We had ne'er been broken-hearted.

Fare thee weel, thou first and fairest!
Fare thee weel, thou best and dearest!
Thine be ilka joy and treasure,
Peace, enjoyment, love, and pleasure!   20
Ae fond kiss, and then we sever;
Ae fareweel, alas, forever!
Deep in heart-wrung tears I'll pledge thee,
Warring sighs and groans I'll wage thee.

19. *ilka*: every.

YE FLOWERY BANKS

Ye flowery banks o' bonnie Doon,
 How can ye blume sae fair?
How can ye chant, ye little birds,
 And I sae fu' o' care?

Thou'll break my heart, thou bonnie bird,   5
 That sings upon the bough;
Thou minds me o' the happy days,
 When my fause luve was true.

Thou'll break my heart, thou bonnie bird,
 That sings beside thy mate;   10
For sae I sat, and sae I sang,
 And wist na o' my fate.

Aft hae I roved by bonnie Doon,
 To see the woodbine twine,
And ilka bird sang o' its luve,   15
 And sae did I o' mine.

15. *ilka*: each.

Wi' lightsome heart I pu'd a rose
  Frae aff its thorny tree;
But my fause luver staw my rose,
  And left the thorn wi' me.   20

Wi' lightsome heart I pu'd a rose
  Upon a morn in June;
And sae I flourished on the morn,
  And sae was pu'd ere noon.

A RED, RED ROSE

O my luve's like a red, red rose,
  That's newly sprung in June;
O my luve's like the melodie
  That's sweetly played in tune.

As fair art thou, my bonnie lass,   5
  So deep in luve am I;
And I will luve thee still, my dear,
  Till a' the seas gang dry.

Till a' the seas gang dry, my dear,
  And the rocks melt wi' the sun: 10
O I will love thee still, my dear,
  While the sands o' life shall run.

And fare thee weel, my only luve,
  And fare thee weel awhile!
And I will come again, my luve,   15
  Though it were ten thousand mile.

William Wordsworth

LINES

COMPOSED A FEW MILES ABOVE TINTERN ABBEY
ON REVISITING THE BANKS OF THE WYE
DURING A TOUR. JULY 13, 1798

Five years have passed; five summers, with the length
Of five long winters! and again I hear
These waters, rolling from their mountain-springs
With a soft inland murmur. Once again
Do I behold these steep and lofty cliffs,   5
That on a wild secluded scene impress
Thoughts of more deep seclusion; and connect
The landscape with the quiet of the sky.
The day is come when I again repose
Here, under this dark sycamore, and view   10
These plots of cottage ground, these orchard tufts,
Which at this season, with their unripe fruits,
Are clad in one green hue, and lose themselves
'Mid groves and copses. Once again I see
These hedgerows, hardly hedgerows, little lines   15
Of sportive wood run wild; these pastoral farms,
Green to the very door; and wreaths of smoke
Sent up, in silence, from among the trees!
With some uncertain notice, as might seem
Of vagrant dwellers in the houseless woods,   20
Or of some hermit's cave, where by his fire
The hermit sits alone.
                    These beauteous forms,
Through a long absence, have not been to me
As is a landscape to a blind man's eye;
But oft, in lonely rooms, and 'mid the din   25
Of towns and cities, I have owed to them,
In hours of weariness, sensations sweet,
Felt in the blood, and felt along the heart;

And passing even into my purer mind,
With tranquil restoration—feelings too   30
Of unremembered pleasure; such, perhaps,
As have no slight or trivial influence
On that best portion of a good man's life,
His little, nameless, unremembered, acts
Of kindness and of love. Nor less, I trust,   35
To them I may have owed another gift,
Of aspect more sublime; that blessed mood,
In which the burthen of the mystery,
In which the heavy and the weary weight
Of all this unintelligible world,   40
Is lightened—that serene and blessed mood,
In which the affections gently lead us on—
Until, the breath of this corporeal frame
And even the motion of our human blood
Almost suspended, we are laid asleep   45
In body, and become a living soul;
While with an eye made quiet by the power
Of harmony, and the deep power of joy,
We see into the life of things.
                                    If this
Be but a vain belief, yet, oh! how oft—   50
In darkness and amid the many shapes
Of joyless daylight; when the fretful stir
Unprofitable, and the fever of the world,
Have hung upon the beatings of my heart—
How oft, in spirit, have I turned to thee,   55
O sylvan Wye! thou wanderer through the woods,
How often has my spirit turned to thee!

   And now, with gleams of half-extinguished thought,
With many recognitions dim and faint,
And somewhat of a sad perplexity,   60
The picture of the mind revives again;
While here I stand, not only with the sense
Of present pleasure, but with pleasing thoughts
That in this moment there is life and food
For future years. And so I dare to hope,   65

Though changed, no doubt, from what I was when first
I came among these hills; when like a roe
I bounded o'er the mountains, by the sides
Of the deep rivers, and the lonely streams,
Wherever nature led—more like a man   70
Flying from something that he dreads than one
Who sought the thing he loved. For nature then
(The coarser pleasures of my boyish days,
And their glad animal movements all gone by)
To me was all in all.—I cannot paint   75
What then I was. The sounding cataract
Haunted me like a passion; the tall rock,
The mountain, and the deep and gloomy wood,
Their colors and their forms, were then to me
An appetite; a feeling and a love,   80
That had no need of a remoter charm,
By thought supplied, nor any interest
Unborrowed from the eye.—That time is past,
And all its aching joys are now no more,
And all its dizzy raptures. Not for this   85
Faint I, nor mourn nor murmur; other gifts
Have followed; for such loss, I would believe,
Abundant recompense. For I have learned
To look on nature, not as in the hour
Of thoughtless youth; but hearing oftentimes   90
The still, sad music of humanity,
Nor harsh nor grating, though of ample power
To chasten and subdue. And I have felt
A presence that disturbs me with the joy
Of elevated thoughts; a sense sublime   95
Of something far more deeply interfused,
Whose dwelling is the light of setting suns,
And the round ocean and the living air,
And the blue sky, and in the mind of man:
A motion and a spirit, that impels   100
All thinking things, all objects of all thought,
And rolls through all things. Therefore am I still
A lover of the meadows and the woods,
And mountains; and of all that we behold

From this green earth; of all the mighty world 105
Of eye, and ear—both what they half create,
And what perceive; well pleased to recognize
In nature and the language of the sense
The anchor of my purest thoughts, the nurse,
The guide, the guardian of my heart, and soul 110
Of all my moral being.
                  Nor perchance,
If I were not thus taught, should I the more
Suffer my genial spirits to decay:
For thou art with me here upon the banks
Of this fair river; thou my dearest friend, 115
My dear, dear friend; and in thy voice I catch
The language of my former heart, and read
My former pleasures in the shooting lights
Of thy wild eyes. Oh! yet a little while
May I behold in thee what I was once, 120
My dear, dear sister! and this prayer I make,
Knowing that nature never did betray
The heart that loved her; 'tis her privilege,
Through all the years of this our life, to lead
From joy to joy: for she can so inform 125
The mind that is within us, so impress
With quietness and beauty, and so feed
With lofty thoughts, that neither evil tongues,
Rash judgments, nor the sneers of selfish men,
Nor greetings where no kindness is, nor all 130
The dreary intercourse of daily life,
Shall e'er prevail against us, or disturb
Our cheerful faith, that all which we behold
Is full of blessings. Therefore let the moon
Shine on thee in thy solitary walk; 135
And let the misty mountain winds be free
To blow against thee: and, in after years,
When these wild ecstasies shall be matured
Into a sober pleasure; when thy mind
Shall be a mansion for all lovely forms, 140
Thy memory be as a dwelling place
For all sweet sounds and harmonies; oh! then,

If solitude, or fear, or pain, or grief
Should be thy portion, with what healing thoughts
Of tender joy wilt thou remember me,   145
And these my exhortations! Nor, perchance—
If I should be where I no more can hear
Thy voice, nor catch from thy wild eyes these gleams
Of past existence—wilt thou then forget
That on the banks of this delightful stream   150
We stood together; and that I, so long
A worshiper of nature, hither came
Unwearied in that service; rather say
With warmer love—oh! with far deeper zeal
Of holier love. Nor wilt thou then forget,   155
That after many wanderings, many years
Of absence, these steep woods and lofty cliffs,
And this green pastoral landscape, were to me
More dear, both for themselves and for thy sake!

A SLUMBER DID MY SPIRIT SEAL

A slumber did my spirit seal;
    I had no human fears:
She seemed a thing that could not feel
    The touch of earthly years.

No motion has she now, no force;   5
    She neither hears nor sees;
Rolled round in earth's diurnal course,
    With rocks, and stones, and trees.

ODE

INTIMATIONS OF IMMORTALITY FROM RECOLLECTIONS
OF EARLY CHILDHOOD

The Child is father of the Man:
And I could wish my days to be
Bound each to each by natural piety.

[1]

There was a time when meadow, grove, and stream,
The earth, and every common sight,
    To me did seem
    Appareled in celestial light,
The glory and the freshness of a dream.   5
It is not now as it hath been of yore—
    Turn whereso'er I may,
      By night or day,
The things which I have seen I now can see no more.

[2]

    The rainbow comes and goes,   10
    And lovely is the rose,
    The moon doth with delight
Look round her when the heavens are bare,
    Waters on a starry night
    Are beautiful and fair;   15
  The sunshine is a glorious birth;
  But yet I know, where'er I go,
That there hath passed away a glory from the earth.

[3]

Now, while the birds thus sing a joyous song,
  And while the young lambs bound   20
    As to the tabor's sound,
To me alone there came a thought of grief:
A timely utterance gave that thought relief,
    And I again am strong:
The cataracts blow their trumpets from the steep;   25
No more shall grief of mine the season wrong;

I hear the echoes through the mountains throng,
The winds come to me from the fields of sleep,
    And all the earth is gay;
        Land and sea   30
    Give themselves up to jollity,
      And with the heart of May
    Doth every beast keep holiday—
      Thou child of joy,
Shout round me, let me hear thy shouts, thou happy   35
    Shepherd-boy!

[4]

Ye blessed creatures, I have heard the call
    Ye to each other make; I see
The heavens laugh with you in your jubilee;
    My heart is at your festival,   40
    My head hath its coronal,
The fullness of your bliss, I feel—I feel it all.
      Oh, evil day! if I were sullen
      While earth herself is adorning,
        This sweet May morning,   45
      And the children are culling
        On every side,
      In a thousand valleys far and wide,
      Fresh flowers; while the sun shines warm,
And the babe leaps up on his mother's arm—   50
      I hear, I hear, with joy I hear!
    —But there's a tree, of many, one,
A single field which I have looked upon,
Both of them speak of something that is gone:
      The pansy at my feet   55
      Doth the same tale repeat:
Whither is fled the visionary gleam?
Where is it now, the glory and the dream?

[5]

Our birth is but a sleep and a forgetting:
The soul that rises with us, our life's star,   60
    Hath had elsewhere its setting,

And cometh from afar:
Not in entire forgetfulness,
And not in utter nakedness,
But trailing clouds of glory do we come   65
    From God, who is our home:
Heaven lies about us in our infancy!
Shades of the prison-house begin to close
    Upon the growing boy
        But he   70
Beholds the light, and whence it flows,
    He sees it in his joy;
The youth, who daily farther from the east
    Must travel, still is nature's priest,
    And by the vision splendid   75
    Is on his way attended;
At length the man perceives it die away,
And fade into the light of common day.

[6]

Earth fills her lap with pleasures of her own;
Yearnings she hath in her own natural kind,   80
And, even with something of a mother's mind,
    And no unworthy aim,
    The homely nurse doth all she can
To make her foster child, her inmate man,
    Forget the glories he hath known,   85
And that imperial palace whence he came.

[7]

Behold the child among his newborn blisses,
A six-years' darling of a pygmy size!
See, where 'mid work of his own hand he lies,
Fretted by sallies of his mother's kisses,   90
With light upon him from his father's eyes!
See, at his feet, some little plan or chart,
Some fragment from his dream of human life,
Shaped by himself with newly-learned art;

A wedding or a festival, 95
A mourning or a funeral;
    And this hath now his heart,
    And unto this he frames his song;
        Then will he fit his tongue
To dialogues of business, love, or strife; 100
        But it will not be long
        Ere this be thrown aside,
        And with new joy and pride
The little actor cons another part;
Filling from time to time his "humorous stage" 105
With all the persons, down to palsied age,
That life brings with her in her equipage;
        As if his whole vocation
        Were endless imitation.

[8]

Thou, whose exterior semblance doth belie 110
        Thy soul's immensity;
Thou best philosopher, who yet dost keep
Thy heritage, thou eye among the blind,
That, deaf and silent, read'st the eternal deep,
Haunted forever by the eternal mind— 115
        Mighty prophet! Seer blest!
        On whom those truths do rest,
Which we are toiling all our lives to find,
In darkness lost, the darkness of the grave;
Thou, over whom thy immortality 120
Broods like the day, a master o'er a slave,
A presence which is not to be put by;
Thou little child, yet glorious in the might
Of heaven-born freedom on thy being's height,
Why with such earnest pains dost thou provoke 125
The years to bring the inevitable yoke,
Thus blindly with thy blessedness at strife?
Full soon thy soul shall have her earthly freight,
And custom lie upon thee with a weight,
Heavy as frost, and deep almost as life! 130

[9]

O joy! that in our embers
Is something that doth live,
That nature yet remembers
What was so fugitive!
The thought of our past years in me doth breed   135
Perpetual benediction: not indeed
For that which is most worthy to be blest;
Delight and liberty, the simple creed
Of childhood, whether busy or at rest,
With new-fledged hope still fluttering in his breast—   140
    Not for these I raise
    The song of thanks and praise;
    But for those obstinate questionings
    Of sense and outward things,
    Fallings from us, vanishings;   145
    Blank misgivings of a creature
Moving about in worlds not realized,
High instincts before which our mortal nature
Did tremble like a guilty thing surprised;
    But for those first affections,   150
    Those shadowy recollections,
    Which, be they what they may,
Are yet the fountain light of all our day,
Are yet a master light of all our seeing;
    Uphold us, cherish, and have power to make   155
Our noisy years seem moments in the being
Of the eternal silence: truths that wake,
    To perish never;
Which neither listlessness, nor mad endeavor,
    Nor man nor boy,   160
Nor all that is at enmity with joy,
Can utterly abolish or destroy!
    Hence in a season of calm weather
    Though inland far we be,
Our souls have sight of that immortal sea   165
    Which brought us hither,
    Can in a moment travel thither,

And see the children sport upon the shore,
And hear the mighty waters rolling evermore.

[10]

Then sing, ye birds, sing, sing a joyous song!   170
  And let the young lambs bound
  As to the tabor's sound!
We in thought will join your throng,
  Ye that pipe and ye that play,
  Ye that through your hearts today   175
  Feel the gladness of the May!
What though the radiance which was once so bright
Be now forever taken from my sight,
  Though nothing can bring back the hour
Of splendor in the grass, of glory in the flower;   180
  We will grieve not, rather find
  Strength in what remains behind;
  In the primal sympathy
  Which having been must ever be;
  In the soothing thoughts that spring   185
  Out of human suffering;
  In the faith that looks through death,
In years that bring the philosophic mind.

[11]

And O, ye fountains, meadows, hills, and groves,
Forebode not any severing of our loves!   190
Yet in my heart of hearts I feel your might;
I only have relinquished one delight
To live beneath your more habitual sway.
I love the brooks which down their channels fret,
Even more than when I tripped lightly as they;   195
The innocent brightness of a newborn day
  Is lovely yet;
The clouds that gather round the setting sun
Do take a sober coloring from an eye
That hath kept watch o'er man's mortality;   200
Another race hath been, and other palms are won.

Thanks to the human heart by which we live,
Thanks to its tenderness, its joys, and fears,
To me the meanest flower that blows can give
Thoughts that do often lie too deep for tears.   205

THE SOLITARY REAPER

Behold her, single in the field,
Yon solitary highland lass!
Reaping and singing by herself;
Stop here, or gently pass!
Alone she cuts and binds the grain,   5
And sings a melancholy strain;
O listen! for the vale profound
Is overflowing with the sound.

No nightingale did ever chaunt
More welcome notes to weary bands   10
Of travelers in some shady haunt,
Among Arabian sands;
A voice so thrilling ne'er was heard
In springtime from the cuckoo bird,
Breaking the silence of the seas   15
Among the farthest Hebrides.

Will no one tell me what she sings?—
Perhaps the plaintive numbers flow
For old, unhappy, far-off things,
And battles long ago;   20
Or is it some more humble lay,
Familiar matter of today?
Some natural sorrow, loss, or pain,
That has been, and may be again?

Whate'er the theme, the maiden sang   25
As if her song could have no ending;
I saw her singing at her work,
And o'er the sickle bending—
I listened, motionless and still;
And, as I mounted up the hill,   30

The music in my heart I bore,
Long after it was heard no more.

COMPOSED UPON WESTMINSTER BRIDGE, SEPTEMBER 3, 1802

Earth has not anything to show more fair:
Dull would he be of soul who could pass by
A sight so touching in its majesty;
This city now doth, like a garment, wear
The beauty of the morning; silent, bare,   5
Ships, towers, domes, theaters, and temples lie
Open unto the fields, and to the sky;
All bright and glittering in the smokeless air.
Never did sun more beautifully steep
In his first splendor, valley, rock, or hill;   10
Ne'er saw I, never felt, a calm so deep!
The river glideth at his own sweet will:
Dear God! the very houses seem asleep;
And all that mighty heart is lying still!

IT IS A BEAUTEOUS EVENING

It is a beauteous evening, calm and free,
The holy time is quiet as a nun
Breathless with adoration; the broad sun
Is sinking down in its tranquility;
The gentleness of heaven broods o'er the sea: 5
Listen! the mighty being is awake,
And doth with his eternal motion make
A sound like thunder—everlastingly.
Dear child! dear girl! that walkest with me here,
If thou appear untouched by solemn thought,   10
Thy nature is not therefore less divine:
Thou liest in Abraham's bosom all the year,
And worship'st at the temple's inner shrine,
God being with thee when we know it not.

Samuel Taylor Coleridge

KUBLA KHAN

OR A VISION IN A DREAM. A FRAGMENT

In Xanadu did Kubla Khan
A stately pleasure dome decree:
Where Alph, the sacred river, ran
Through caverns measureless to man
    Down to a sunless sea.   5
So twice five miles of fertile ground
With walls and towers were girdled round:
And there were gardens bright with sinuous rills,
Where blossomed many an incense-bearing tree;
And here were forests ancient as the hills,   10
Enfolding sunny spots of greenery.

But oh! that deep romantic chasm which slanted
Down the green hill athwart a cedarn cover!
A savage place! as holy and enchanted
As e'er beneath a waning moon was haunted   15
By woman wailing for her demon lover!
And from this chasm, with ceaseless turmoil seething,
As if this earth in fast thick pants were breathing,
A mighty fountain momently was forced:
Amid whose swift half-intermitted burst   20
Huge fragments vaulted like rebounding hail,
Or chaffy grain beneath the thresher's flail:
And 'mid these dancing rocks at once and ever
It flung up momently the sacred river.
Five miles meandering with a mazy motion   25
Through wood and dale the sacred river ran,
Then reached the caverns measureless to man,
And sank in tumult to a lifeless ocean:
And 'mid this tumult Kubla heard from far
Ancestral voices prophesying war!   30
    The shadow of the dome of pleasure

Floated midway on the waves;
Where was heard the mingled measure
From the fountain and the caves.
It was a miracle of rare device,   35
A sunny pleasure dome with caves of ice!

A damsel with a dulcimer
In a vision once I saw:
It was an Abyssinian maid,
And on her dulcimer she played,   40
Singing of Mount Abora.
Could I revive within me
Her symphony and song,
To such a deep delight 'twould win me,
That with music loud and long,   45
I would build that dome in air,
That sunny dome! those caves of ice!
And all who heard should see them there,
And all should cry, Beware! Beware!
His flashing eyes, his floating hair!   50
Weave a circle round him thrice,
And close your eyes with holy dread,
For he on honeydew hath fed,
And drunk the milk of Paradise.

DEJECTION: AN ODE

Late, late yestreen I saw the new Moon,
With the old Moon in her arms;
And I fear, I fear, my master dear!
We shall have a deadly storm.
        Ballad of Sir Patrick Spence

[I]

Well! If the bard was weather-wise, who made
    The grand old ballad of Sir Patrick Spence,
    This night, so tranquil now, will not go hence
Unroused by winds, that ply a busier trade
Than those which mold yon cloud in lazy flakes,   5
Or the dull sobbing draft, that moans and rakes

Upon the strings of this Aeolian lute,
    Which better far were mute.
  For lo! the new moon winter-bright!
And overspread with phantom light,   10
  (With swimming phantom light o'erspread
  But rimmed and circled by a silver thread)
I see the old moon in her lap, foretelling
  The coming-on of rain and squally blast.
And oh! that even now the gust were swelling,   15
  And the slant night shower driving loud and fast!
Those sounds which oft have raised me, whilst they awed,
    And sent my soul abroad,
Might now perhaps their wonted impulse give,
Might startle this dull pain, and make it move and live!   20

[2]

A grief without a pang, void, dark, and drear,
  A stifled, drowsy, unimpassioned grief,
  Which finds no natural outlet, no relief,
    In word, or sigh, or tear—
O lady! in this wan and heartless mood,   25
To other thoughts by yonder throstle wooed,
  All this long eve, so balmy and serene,
Have I been gazing on the western sky,
  And its peculiar tint of yellow green:
And still I gaze—and with how blank an eye!   30
And those thin clouds above, in flakes and bars,
That give away their motion to the stars;
Those stars, that glide behind them or between,
Now sparkling, now bedimmed, but always seen:
Yon crescent moon, as fixed as if it grew   35
In its own cloudless, starless lake of blue;
I see them all so excellently fair,
I see, not feel, how beautiful they are!

[3]

  My genial spirits fail;
  And what can these avail   40

To lift the smothering weight from off my breast?
    It were a vain endeavor,
    Though I should gaze forever
On that green light that lingers in the west:
I may not hope from outward forms to win   45
The passion and the life, whose fountains are within.

[4]

O lady! we receive but what we give,
And in our life alone does nature live:
Ours is her wedding garment, ours her shroud!
    And would we aught behold, of higher worth,   50
Than that inanimate cold world allowed
To the poor loveless ever-anxious crowd,
    Ah! from the soul itself must issue forth
A light, a glory, a fair luminous cloud
        Enveloping the earth—   55
And from the soul itself must there be sent
    A sweet and potent voice, of its own birth,
Of all sweet sounds the life and element!

[5]

O pure of heart! thou need'st not ask of me
What this strong music in the soul may be!   60
What, and wherein it doth exist,
This light, this glory, this fair luminous mist,
This beautiful and beauty-making power.
    Joy, virtuous lady! Joy that ne'er was given,
Save to the pure, and in their purest hour,   65
Life, and life's effluence, cloud at once and shower,
Joy, lady! is the spirit and the power,
Which wedding nature to us gives in dower
    A new earth and new heaven,
Undreamt of by the sensual and the proud—   70
Joy is the sweet voice, joy the luminous cloud—
        We in ourselves rejoice!
And thence flows all that charms or ear or sight,
    All melodies the echoes of that voice,
All colors a suffusion from that light.   75

[6]

There was a time when, though my path was rough,
    This joy within me dallied with distress,
And all misfortunes were but as the stuff
    Whence fancy made me dreams of happiness:
For hope grew round me, like the twining vine,   80
And fruits, and foliage, not my own, seemed mine.
But now afflictions bow me down to earth:
Nor care I that they rob me of my mirth;
        But oh! each visitation
Suspends what nature gave me at my birth,   85
    My shaping spirit of imagination.
For not to think of what I needs must feel,
    But to be still and patient, all I can;
And haply by abstruse research to steal
    From my own nature all the natural man—   90
    This was my sole resource, my only plan:
Till that which suits a part infects the whole,
And now is almost grown the habit of my soul.

[7]

Hence, viper thoughts, that coil around my mind,
        Reality's dark dream!   95
I turn from you, and listen to the wind,
    Which long has raved unnoticed. What a scream
Of agony by torture lengthened out
That lute sent forth! Thou wind, that rav'st without,
    Bare crag, or mountain tairn, or blasted tree,   100
Or pine grove whither woodman never clomb,
Or lonely house, long held the witches' home,
    Methinks were fitter instruments for thee,
Mad lutanist! who in this month of showers,
Of dark-brown gardens, and of peeping flowers,   105
Mak'st devils' yule, with worse than wintry song,
The blossoms, buds, and timorous leaves among.
    Thou actor, perfect in all tragic sounds!
Thou mighty poet, e'en to frenzy bold!
        What tell'st thou now about?   110

'Tis of the rushing of an host in rout,
With groans, of trampled men, with smarting wounds—
At once they groan with pain, and shudder with the cold!
But hush! there is a pause of deepest silence!
And all that noise, as of a rushing crowd,   115
With groans, and tremulous shudderings—all is over—
It tells another tale, with sounds less deep and loud!
A tale of less affright,
And tempered with delight,
As Otway's self had framed the tender lay—   120
'Tis of a little child
Upon a lonesome wild,
Not far from home, but she hath lost her way:
And now moans low in bitter grief and fear,
And now screams loud, and hopes to make her mother hear. 125

[8]

'Tis midnight, but small thoughts have I of sleep:
Full seldom may my friend such vigils keep!
Visit her, gentle sleep! with wings of healing,
And may this storm be but a mountain birth,
May all the stars hang bright above her dwelling,   130
Silent as though they watched the sleeping earth!
With light heart may she rise,
Gay fancy, cheerful eyes,
Joy lift her spirit, joy attune her voice;
To her may all things live, from pole to pole,   135
Their life the eddying of her living soul!
O simple spirit, guided from above,
Dear lady! friend devoutest of my choice,
Thus mayest thou ever, evermore rejoice.

George Gordon, Lord Byron

WHEN WE TWO PARTED

When we two parted
  In silence and tears,
Half broken-hearted
  To sever for years,
Pale grew thy cheek and cold,   5
  Colder thy kiss;
Truly that hour foretold
  Sorrow to this.

The dew of the morning
  Sunk chill on my brow—   10
It felt like the warning
  Of what I feel now.
Thy vows are all broken,
  And light is thy fame;
I hear thy name spoken,   15
  And share in its shame.

They name thee before me,
  A knell to mine ear;
A shudder comes o'er me—
  Why wert thou so dear?   20
They know not I knew thee,
  Who knew thee too well—
Long, long shall I rue thee,
  Too deeply to tell.

In secret we met—   25
  In silence I grieve,
That thy heart could forget,
  Thy spirit deceive.
If I should meet thee
  After long years,   30
How should I greet thee?—
  With silence and tears.

STANZAS FOR MUSIC

THERE BE NONE OF BEAUTY'S DAUGHTERS

[1]

There be none of Beauty's daughters
  With a magic like thee;
And like music on the waters
  Is thy sweet voice to me:
When, as if its sound were causing   5
The charmèd ocean's pausing,
The waves lie still and gleaming,
And the lulled winds seem dreaming;

[2]

And the midnight moon is weaving
  Her bright chain o'er the deep;   10
Whose breast is gently heaving,
  As an infant's asleep:
So the spirit bows before thee,
To listen and adore thee;
With a full but soft emotion,   15
Like the swell of summer's ocean.

THEY SAY THAT HOPE IS HAPPINESS

[1]

They say that hope is happiness;
  But genuine love must prize the past,
And memory wakes the thoughts that bless:
  They rose the first—they set the last;

[2]

And all that memory loves the most   5
  Was once our only hope to be,
And all that hope adored and lost
  Hath melted into memory.

[3]

Alas! it is delusion all;
    The future cheats us from afar,   10
Nor can we be what we recall,
    Nor dare we think on what we are.

Percy Bysshe Shelley

OZYMANDIAS*

I met a traveler from an antique land
Who said: Two vast and trunkless legs of stone
Stand in the desert . . . Near them, on the sand,
Half sunk, a shattered visage lies, whose frown,
And wrinkled lip, and sneer of cold command,   5
Tell that its sculptor well those passions read
Which yet survive, stamped on these lifeless things,
The hand that mocked them, and the heart that fed:
And on the pedestal these words appear:
"My name is Ozymandias, king of kings: 10
Look on my works, ye Mighty, and despair!"
Nothing beside remains. Round the decay
Of that colossal wreck, boundless and bare
The lone and level sands stretch far away.

* *Ozymandias:* Pharaoh Ramses II of Egypt, 13th century B.C.

ODE TO THE WEST WIND

[1]

O wild West Wind, thou breath of autumn's being,
Thou, from whose unseen presence the leaves dead
Are driven, like ghosts from an enchanter fleeing,

Yellow, and black, and pale, and hectic red,
Pestilence-stricken multitudes: O thou,   5
Who chariotest to their dark wintry bed

The wingèd seeds, where they lie cold and low,
Each like a corpse within its grave, until
Thine azure sister of the spring shall blow

Her clarion o'er the dreaming earth, and fill   10
(Driving sweet buds like flocks to feed in air)
With living hues and odors plain and hill:

Wild Spirit, which art moving everywhere;
Destroyer and preserver; hear, oh, hear!

[2]

Thou on whose stream, mid the steep sky's commotion,   15
Loose clouds like earth's decaying leaves are shed,
Shook from the tangled bough of heaven and ocean,

Angels of rain and lightning: there are spread
On the blue surface of thine aery surge,
Like the bright hair uplifted from the head   20

Of some fierce Maenad, even from the dim verge
Of the horizon to the zenith's height,
The locks of the approaching storm. Thou dirge

Of the dying year, to which this closing night
Will be the dome of a vast sepulcher,   25
Vaulted with all thy congregated might

Of vapors, from whose solid atmosphere
Black rain, and fire, and hail will burst: oh, hear!

[3]

Thou who didst waken from his summer dreams
The blue Mediterranean, where he lay,   30
Lulled by the coil of his crystalline streams,

Beside a pumice isle in Baiae's bay,
And saw in sleep old palaces and towers
Quivering within the wave's intenser day,

All overgrown with azure moss and flowers   35
So sweet, the sense faints picturing them! Thou
For whose path the Atlantic's level powers

Cleave themselves into chasms, while far below
The sea-blooms and the oozy woods which wear
The sapless foliage of the ocean, know   40

Thy voice, and suddenly grow gray with fear,
And tremble and despoil themselves: or, hear!

[4]

If I were a dead leaf thou mightest bear;
If I were a swift cloud to fly with thee;
A wave to pant beneath thy power, and share   45

The impulse of thy strength, only less free
Than thou, O uncontrollable! If even
I were as in my boyhood, and could be

The comrade of thy wanderings over heaven,
As then, when to outstrip thy skyey speed   50
Scarce seemed a vision; I would ne'er have striven

As thus with thee in prayer in my sore need.
Oh, lift me as a wave, a leaf, a cloud!
I fall upon the thorns of life! I bleed!

A heavy weight of hours has chained and bowed   55
One too like thee: tameless, and swift, and proud.

[5]

Make me thy lyre, even as the forest is:
What if my leaves are falling like its own!
The tumult of thy mighty harmonies

Will take from both a deep, autumnal tone,   60
Sweet though in sadness. Be thou, Spirit fierce,
My spirit! Be thou me, impetuous one!

Drive my dead thoughts over the universe
Like withered leaves to quicken a new birth!
And, by the incantation of this verse,   65

Scatter, as from an unextinguished hearth
Ashes and sparks, my words among mankind!
Be through my lips to unawakened earth

The trumpet of a prophecy! O Wind,
If winter comes, can spring be far behind?   70

MUSIC, WHEN SOFT VOICES DIE

Music, when soft voices die,
Vibrates in the memory—
Odors, when sweet violets sicken,
Live within the sense they quicken.
Rose leaves, when the rose is dead,   5
Are heaped for the belovèd's bed;
And so thy thoughts, when thou art gone,
Love itself shall slumber on.

LINES: WHEN THE LAMP IS SHATTERED

[1]

When the lamp is shattered
The light in the dust lies dead—
When the cloud is scattered
The rainbow's glory is shed.
When the lute is broken,   5
Sweet tones are remembered not;
When the lips have spoken,
Loved accents are soon forgot.

[2]

As music and splendor
Survive not the lamp and the lute,   10
The heart's echoes render
No song when the spirit is mute—
No song but sad dirges,
Like the wind through a ruined cell,
Or the mournful surges   15
That ring the dead seaman's knell.

143

[3]

When hearts have once mingled
Love first leaves the well-built nest;
   The weak one is singled
To endure what it once possessed.   20
   O Love! who bewailest
The frailty of all things here,
   Why choose you the frailest
For your cradle, your home, and your bier?

[4]

   Its passions will rock thee   25
As the storms rock the ravens on high;
   Bright reason will mock thee,
Like the sun from a wintry sky.
   From thy nest every rafter
Will rot, and thine eagle home   30
   Leave the naked to laughter,
When leaves fall and cold winds come.

William Cullen Bryant

TO A WATERFOWL

Whither, 'midst falling dew,
While glow the heavens with the last steps of day,
Far, through their rosy depths, dost thou pursue
   Thy solitary way?

Vainly the fowler's eye   5
Might mark thy distant flight, to do thee wrong,
As, darkly seen against the crimson sky,
   Thy figure floats along.

Seek'st thou the plashy brink
Of weedy lake, or marge of river wide,   10
Or where the rocking billows rise and sink
    On the chafed ocean side?

There is a Power, whose care
Teaches thy way along that pathless coast—
The desert and illimitable air,   15
    Lone wandering, but not lost.

All day thy wings have fann'd,
At that far height, the cold thin atmosphere;
Yet stoop not, weary, to the welcome land,
    Though the dark night is near.   20

And soon that toil shall end,
Soon shalt thou find a summer home, and rest,
And scream among thy fellows; reeds shall bend,
    Soon, o'er thy sheltered nest.

Thou'rt gone, the abyss of heaven   25
Hath swallowed up thy form, yet, on my heart
Deeply hath sunk the lesson thou hast given,
    And shall not soon depart.

He, who, from zone to zone,
Guides through the boundless sky thy certain flight,   30
In the long way that I must trace alone,
    Will lead my steps aright.

THE DEATH OF LINCOLN

Oh, slow to smite and swift to spare,
    Gentle and merciful and just!
Who, in the fear of God, didst bear
    The sword of power, a nation's trust!

In sorrow by thy bier we stand,   5
    Amid the awe that hushes all,
And speak the anguish of a land
    That shook with horror at thy fall.

Thy task is done; the bond are free:
   We bear thee to an honored grave,   10
Whose proudest monument shall be
   The broken fetters of the slave.

Pure was thy life; its bloody close
   Hath placed thee with the sons of light,
Among the noble host of those   15
   Who perished in the cause of right.

John Keats

ON FIRST LOOKING INTO CHAPMAN'S HOMER

Much have I traveled in the realms of gold,
   And many goodly states and kingdoms seen;
   Round many western islands have I been
Which bards in fealty to Appollo hold.
Oft of one wide expanse had I been told   5
   That deep-browed Homer ruled as his demesne;
   Yet did I never breathe its pure serene
Till I heard Chapman speak out loud and bold:
Then felt I like some watcher of the skies
   When a new planet swims into his ken;   10
Or like stout Cortez when with eagle eyes
   He stared at the Pacific—and all his men
Looked at each other with a wild surmise—
   Silent, upon a peak in Darien.

BRIGHT STAR

Bright star, would I were steadfast as thou art—
   Not in lone splendor hung aloft the night
And watching, with eternal lids apart,
   Like nature's patient, sleepless Eremite,

The moving waters at their priestlike task 5
   Of pure ablution round earth's human shores,
Or gazing on the new soft fallen mask
   Of snow upon the mountains and the moors—
No—yet still steadfast, still unchangeable,
   Pillowed upon my fair love's ripening breast, 10
To feel forever its soft fall and swell,
   Awake forever in a sweet unrest,
Still, still to hear her tender-taken breath,
And so live ever—or else swoon to death.

LA BELLE DAME SANS MERCI

O what can ail thee, knight at arms,
   Alone and palely loitering?
The sedge has withered from the lake
   And no birds sing!

O what can ail thee, knight at arms, 5
   So haggard, and so woebegone?
The squirrel's granary is full
   And the harvest's done.

I see a lily on thy brow
   With anguish moist and fever dew, 10
And on thy cheeks a fading rose
   Fast withereth too.

I met a lady in the meads,
   Full beautiful, a faery's child,
Her hair was long, her foot was light 15
   And her eyes were wild.

I made a garland for her head,
   And bracelets too, and fragrant zone;
She looked at me as she did love
   And made sweet moan. 20

I set her on my pacing steed
   And nothing else saw all day long,
For sidelong would she bend and sing
   A faery's song.

She found me roots of relish sweet,   25
   And honey wild, and manna dew,
And sure in language strange she said
   "I love thee true."

She took me to her elfin grot
   And there she wept and sighed full sore,   30
And there I shut her wild wild eyes
   With kisses four.

And there she lulled me asleep,
   And there I dreamed, ah woe betide!
The latest dream I ever dreamt   35
   On the cold hill side.

I saw pale kings, and princes too,
   Pale warriors, death-pale were they all;
They cried, "La belle dame sans merci
   Thee hath in thrall!"   40

I saw their starved lips in the gloam
   With horrid warning gaped wide,
And I awoke, and found me here
   On the cold hill's side.

And this is why I sojourn here,   45
   Alone and palely loitering;
Though the sedge is withered from the lake
   And no birds sing.

ODE ON A GRECIAN URN

[I]

Thou still unravished bride of quietness,
   Thou foster child of silence and slow time,
Sylvan historian, who canst thus express
   A flowery tale more sweetly than our rhyme:
What leaf-fringed legend haunts about thy shape
   Of deities or mortals, or of both,
     In Tempe or the dales of Arcady?

148

What men or gods are these? What maidens loath?
What mad pursuit? What struggle to escape?
    What pipes and timbrels? What wild ecstasy?   10

[2]

Heard melodies are sweet, but those unheard
  Are sweeter; therefore, ye soft pipes, play on;
Not to the sensual ear, but, more endeared,
  Pipe to the spirit ditties of no tone:
Fair youth, beneath the trees, thou canst not leave   15
  Thy song, nor ever can those trees be bare;
    Bold lover, never, never canst thou kiss,
Though winning near the goal—yet, do not grieve;
    She cannot fade, though thou hast not thy bliss,
Forever wilt thou love, and she be fair!   20

[3]

Ah, happy, happy boughs! that cannot shed
  Your leaves, nor ever bid the spring adieu;
And, happy melodist, unwearied,
  Forever piping songs forever new;
More happy love! more happy, happy love!   25
  Forever warm and still to be enjoyed,
    Forever panting, and forever young;
All breathing human passion far above,
  That leaves a heart high-sorrowful and cloyed,
    A burning forehead, and a parching tongue.   30

[4]

Who are these coming to the sacrifice?
  To what green altar, O mysterious priest,
Lead'st thou that heifer lowing at the skies,
  And all her silken flanks with garlands dressed?
What little town by river or sea shore,   35
  Or mountain-built with peaceful citadel,
    Is emptied of this folk, this pious morn?
And, little town, thy streets forevermore
  Will silent be; and not a soul to tell
    Why thou art desolate, can e'er return.   40

[5]

O Attic shape! Fair attitude! with brede
　　Of marble men and maidens overwrought,
With forest branches and the trodden weed;
　　Thou, silent form, dost tease us out of thought
As doth eternity: Cold pastoral!　　　　　　　　　　45
　　When old age shall this generation waste,
　　　　Thou shalt remain, in midst of other woe
　　Than ours, a friend to man, to whom thou say'st,
　　"Beauty is truth, truth beauty,"—that is all
　　　　Ye know on earth, and all ye need to know.　　50

ODE TO A NIGHTINGALE

[1]

My heart aches, and a drowsy numbness pains
　　My sense, as though of hemlock I had drunk,
Or emptied some dull opiate to the drains
　　One minute past, and Lethe-wards had sunk:
'Tis not through envy of thy happy lot,　　　　　　　5
　　But being too happy in thine happiness—
　　　　That thou, light-wingèd Dryad of the trees,
　　　　　　In some melodious plot
　　Of beechen green, and shadows numberless,
　　　　Singest of summer in full-throated ease.　　10

[2]

O, for a draught of vintage! that hath been
　　Cooled a long age in the deep-delvèd earth,
Tasting of Flora and the country green,
　　Dance, and Provençal song, and sunburnt mirth!
O for a beaker full of the warm South,　　　　　　15
　　Full of the true, the blushful Hippocrene,
　　　　With beaded bubbles winking at the brim,
　　　　　　And purple-stainèd mouth;
　　That I might drink, and leave the world unseen,
　　　　And with thee fade away into the forest dim:　　20

[3]

Fade far away, dissolve, and quite forget
    What thou among the leaves hast never known,
The weariness, the fever, and the fret
    Here, where men sit and hear each other groan;
Where palsy shakes a few, sad, last gray hairs,   25
    Where youth grows pale, and specter-thin, and dies;
        Where but to think is to be full of sorrow
            And leaden-eyed despairs,
    Where Beauty cannot keep her lustrous eyes,
        Or new Love pine at them beyond tomorrow.   30

[4]

Away! away! for I will fly to thee,
    Not charioted by Bacchus and his pards,
But on the viewless wings of Poesy,
    Though the dull brain perplexes and retards:
Already with thee! tender is the night,   35
    And haply the Queen-Moon is on her throne,
        Clustered around by all her starry Fays;
            But here there is no light,
    Save what from heaven is with the breezes blown
        Through verdurous glooms and winding mossy ways.   40

[5]

I cannot see what flowers are at my feet,
    Nor what soft incense hangs upon the boughs,
But, in embalmèd darkness, guess each sweet
    Wherewith the seasonable month endows
The grass, the thicket, and the fruit tree wild;   45
    White hawthorn, and the pastoral eglantine;
        Fast fading violets covered up in leaves;
            And mid-May's eldest child,
    The coming musk-rose, full of dewy wine,
        The murmurous haunt of flies on summer eves.   50

[6]

Darkling I listen; and, for many a time
  I have been half in love with easeful Death,
Called him soft names in many a musèd rhyme,
  To take into the air my quiet breath;
Now more than ever seems it rich to die, 55
  To cease upon the midnight with no pain,
    While thou art pouring forth thy soul abroad
      In such an ecstasy!
  Still wouldst thou sing, and I have ears in vain—
    To thy high requiem become a sod. 60

[7]

Thou wast not born for death, immortal Bird!
  No hungry generations tread thee down;
The voice I hear this passing night was heard
  In ancient days by emperor and clown:
Perhaps the selfsame song that found a path 65
  Through the sad heart of Ruth, when, sick for home,
    She stood in tears amid the alien corn;
      The same that ofttimes hath
  Charmed magic casements, opening on the foam
    Of perilous seas, in faery lands forlorn. 70

[8]

Forlorn! the very word is like a bell
  To toll me back from thee to my sole self!
Adieu! the fancy cannot cheat so well
  As she is famed to do, deceiving elf.
Adieu! adieu! thy plaintive anthem fades 75
  Past the near meadows, over the still stream,
    Up the hill side; and now 'tis buried deep
      In the next valley-glades:
  Was it a vision, or a waking dream?
    Fled is that music:—Do I wake or sleep? 80

ODE ON MELANCHOLY

[1]

No, no, go not to Lethe, neither twist
   Wolfsbane, tight-rooted, for its poisonous wine;
Nor suffer thy pale forehead to be kissed
   By nightshade, ruby grape of Proserpine;
Make not your rosary of yew-berries,   5
   Nor let the beetle, nor the death-moth be
      Your mournful Psyche, nor the downy owl
A partner in your sorrow's mysteries;
   For shade to shade will come too drowsily,
      And drown the wakeful anguish of the soul.   10

[2]

But when the melancholy fit shall fall
   Sudden from heaven like a weeping cloud,
That fosters the droop-headed flowers all,
   And hides the green hill in an April shroud;
Then glut thy sorrow on a morning rose,   15
   Or on the rainbow of the salt sand-wave,
      Or on the wealth of globèd peonies;
Or if thy mistress some rich anger shows,
   Imprison her soft hand, and let her rave,
      And feed deep, deep upon her peerless eyes.   20

[3]

She dwells with Beauty—Beauty that must die;
   And Joy, whose hand is ever at his lips
Bidding adieu; and aching Pleasure nigh,
   Turning to Poison while the bee-mouth sips:
Aye, in the very temple of Delight   25
   Veiled Melancholy has her sov'reign shrine,
      Though seen of none save him whose strenuous tongue
Can burst Joy's grape against his palate fine;
His soul shall taste the sadness of her might,
      And be among her cloudy trophies hung.   30

TO AUTUMN

[1]

visual

Season of mists and mellow fruitfulness,
  Close bosom-friend of the maturing sun;
Conspiring with him how to load and bless
  With fruit the vines that round the thatch-eaves run;

Action

To bend with apples the mossed cottage-trees,   5
  And fill all fruit with ripeness to the core;
    To swell the gourd, and plump the hazel shells
With a sweet kernel; to set budding more,
  And still more, later flowers for the bees,
  Until they think warm days will never cease,   10
    For summer has o'er-brimmed their clammy cells.

[2]

Who hath not seen thee oft amid thy store?
  Sometimes whoever seeks abroad may find
Thee sitting careless on a granary floor,
  Thy hair soft-lifted by the winnowing wind;   15
Or on a half-reaped furrow sound asleep,
  Drowsed with the fume of poppies, while thy hook
    Spares the next swath and all its twined flowers:
And sometimes like a gleaner thou dost keep
  Steady thy laden head across a brook;   20
  Or by a cider-press, with patient look,
    Thou watchest the last oozings hours by hours.

[3]

Where are the songs of spring? Aye, where are they?
  Think not of them, thou hast thy music too—
While barred clouds bloom the soft-dying day,   25
  And touch the stubble-plains with rosy hue;
Then in a wailful choir the small gnats mourn
  Among the river sallows, borne aloft
    Or sinking as the light wind lives or dies;
And full-grown lambs loud bleat from hilly bourn;   30
  Hedge crickets sing; and now with treble soft
  The redbreast whistles from a garden croft;
    And gathering swallows twitter in the skies.

Ralph Waldo Emerson

FATE

Deep in the man sits fast his fate
To mold his fortunes, mean or great:
Unknown to Cromwell as to me
Was Cromwell's measure or degree;
Unknown to him as to his horse,   5
If he than his groom be better or worse.
He works, plots, fights, in rude affairs,
With squires, lords, kings, his craft compares,
Till late he learned, through doubt and fear,
Broad England harbored not his peer: 10
Obeying time, the last to own
The genius from its cloudy throne.
For the prevision is allied
Unto the thing so signified;
Or say, the foresight that awaits   15
Is the same genius that creates.

COMPENSATION

[1]

The wings of time are black and white,
Pied with morning and with night.
Mountain tall and ocean deep
Trembling balance duly keep.
In changing moon and tidal wave   5
Glows the feud of want and have.
Gauge of more and less through space,
Electric star or pencil plays,
The lonely earth amid the balls
That hurry through the eternal halls,   10
A makeweight flying to the void,
Supplemental asteroid,

Or compensatory spark,
Shoots across the neutral dark.

[2]

Man's the elm, and wealth the vine;   15
Stanch and strong the tendrils twine:
Though the frail ringlets thee deceive,
None from its stock that vine can reave.
Fear not, then, thou child infirm,
There's no god dare wrong a worm;   20
Laurel crowns cleave to deserts,
And power to him who power exerts.
Hast not thy share? On winged feet,
Lo! it rushes thee to meet;
And all that nature made thy own,   25
Floating in air or pent in stone,
Will rive the hills, and swim the sea,
And, like thy shadow, follow thee.

ODE TO BEAUTY

Who gave thee, O Beauty,
The keys of this breast,—
Too credulous lover
Of blest and unblest?
Say, when in lapsed ages   5
Thee knew I of old?
Or what was the service
For which I was sold?
When first my eyes saw thee,
I found me thy thrall,   10
By magical drawings,
Sweet tyrant of all!
I drank at thy fountain
False waters of thirst;
Thou intimate stranger,   15
Thou latest and first!

Thy dangerous glances
Make women of men;
New-born, we are melting
Into nature again.   20

Lavish, lavish promiser,
Nigh persuading gods to err!
Guest of million painted forms,
Which in turn thy glory warms!
The frailest leaf, the mossy bark,   25
The acorn's cup, the raindrop's arc,
The swinging spider's silver line,
The ruby of the drop of wine,
The shining pebble of the pond,
Thou inscribest with a bond,   30
In thy momentary play,
Would bankrupt nature to repay.
Ah, what avails it
To hide or shun
Whom the Infinite One   35
Hath granted his throne?
The heaven high over
Is the deep's lover;
The sun and sea,
Informed by thee,   40
Before me run
And draw me on,
Yet fly me still,
As Fate refuses
To me the heart Fate for me chooses.   45
Is it that my opulent soul
Was mingled from the generous whole;
Sea-valleys and the deep of skies
Furnished several supplies;
And the sands whereof I'm made   50
Draw me to them, self-betrayed?
I turn the proud portfolio
Which holds the grand designs
Of Salvator, of Guercino,

And Piranesi's lines.   55
I hear the lofty paeans
Of the masters of the shell,
Who heard the starry music
And recount the numbers well;
Olympian bards who sung   60
Divine ideas below,
Which always find us young
And always keep us so.
Oft, in streets or humblest places,
I detect far-wandered graces,   65
Which, from Eden wide astray,
In lowly homes have lost their way.

Thee gliding through the sea of form,
Like the lightning through the storm,
Somewhat not to be possessed,   70
Somewhat not to be caressed,
No feet so fleet could ever find,
No perfect form could ever bind.
Thou eternal fugitive,
Hovering over all that live,   75
Quick and skillful to inspire
Sweet, extravagant desire,
Starry space and lily-bell
Filling with thy roseate smell,
Wilt not give the lips to taste   80
Of the nectar which thou hast.

All that's good and great with thee
Works in close conspiracy;
Thou hast bribed the dark and lonely
To report thy features only,   85
And the cold and purple morning
Itself with thoughts of thee adorning;
The leafy dell, the city mart,
Equal trophies of thine art;
E'en the flowing azure air   90
Thou hast touched for my despair;

And, if I languish into dreams,
Again I meet the ardent beams.
Queen of things! I dare not die
In Being's deeps past ear and eye;   95
Lest there I find the same deceiver
And be the sport of Fate forever.
Dread Power, but dear! if God thou be,
Unmake me quite, or give thyself to me!

DAYS

Daughters of Time, the hypocritic Days,
Muffled and dumb like barefoot dervishes,
And marching single in an endless file,
Bring diadems and fagots in their hands.
To each they offer gifts after his will,   5
Bread, kingdoms, stars, and sky that holds them all.
I, in my pleached garden, watched the pomp,
Forgot my morning wishes, hastily
Took a few herbs and apples, and the Day
Turned and departed silent. I, too late,   10
Under her solemn fillet saw the scorn.

Henry Wadsworth Longfellow

THE JEWISH CEMETERY AT NEWPORT

How strange it seems! These Hebrews in their graves,
   Close by the street of this fair seaport town,
Silent beside the never-silent waves,
   At rest in all this moving up and down!

The trees are white with dust, that o'er their sleep   5
   Wave their broad curtains in the southwind's breath,
While underneath these leafy tents they keep
   The long, mysterious exodus of death.

And these sepulchral stones, so old and brown,
  That pave with level flags their burial-place,   10
Seem like the tablets of the law, thrown down
  And broken by Moses at the mountain's base.

The very names recorded here are strange,
  Of foreign accent, and of different climes;
Alvares and Rivera interchange   15
  With Abraham and Jacob of old times.

"Blessed be God! for he created death!"
  The mourners said, "and death is rest and peace;"
Then added, in the certainty of faith,
  "And giveth life that nevermore shall cease."   20

Closed are the portals of their synagogue,
  No psalms of David now the silence break,
No rabbi reads the ancient Decalogue
  In the grand dialect the prophets spake.

Gone are the living, but the dead remain,   25
  And not neglected; for a hand unseen,
Scattering its bounty, like a summer rain,
  Still keeps their graves and their remembrance green.

How came they here? What burst of Christian hate,
  What persecution, merciless and blind,   30
Drove o'er the sea—that desert desolate—
  These Ishmaels and Hagars of mankind?

They lived in narrow streets and lanes obscure,
  Ghetto and Judenstrass, in mirk and mire;
Taught in the school of patience to endure   35
  The life of anguish and the death of fire.

All their lives long, with the unleavened bread
  And bitter herbs of exile and its fears,
The wasting famine of the heart they fed,
  And slaked its thirst with marah of their tears.   40

40. *marah:* undrinkable bitter water (from the spring of Marah, Exodus 15:23).

Anathema maranatha! was the cry
   That rang from town to town, from street to street;
At every gate the accursed Mordecai
   Was mocked and jeered, and spurned by Christian feet.

Pride and humiliation hand in hand   45
   Walked with them through the world where'er they went;
Trampled and beaten were they as the sand,
   And yet unshaken as the continent.

For in the background figures vague and vast
   Of patriarchs and of prophets rose sublime,   50
And all the great traditions of the past
   They saw reflected in the coming time.

And thus forever with reverted look
   The mystic volume of the world they read,
Spelling it backward, like a Hebrew book,   55
   Till life became a legend of the dead.

But ah! what once has been shall be no more!
   The groaning earth in travail and in pain
Brings forth its races, but does not restore,
   And the dead nations never rise again.   60

41. *Anathema maranatha:* marked for destruction at the coming of the Lord (see I Corinthians 16:22).

Edgar Allan Poe

THE CITY IN THE SEA

   Lo! Death has reared himself a throne
   In a strange city lying alone
   Far down within the dim west,
   Where the good and the bad and the worst and the best
   Have gone to their eternal rest.   5
   There shrines and palaces and towers

(Time-eaten towers that tremble not!)
Resemble nothing that is ours.
Around, by lifting winds forgot,
Resignedly beneath the sky   10
The melancholy waters lie.

No rays from the holy heaven come down
On the long night-time of that town;
But light from out the lurid sea
Streams up the turrets silently—   15
Gleams up the pinnacles far and free—
Up domes—up spires—up kingly halls—
Up fanes—up Babylon-like walls—
Up shadowy long-forgotten bowers
Of sculptured ivy and stone flowers—   20
Up many and many a marvelous shrine
Whose wreathèd friezes intertwine
The viol, the violet, and the vine.

Resignedly beneath the sky
The melancholy waters lie.   25
So blend the turrets and shadows there
That all seem pendulous in air,
While from a proud tower in the town
Death looks gigantically down.

There open fanes and gaping graves   30
Yawn level with the luminous waves;
But not the riches there that lie
In each idol's diamond eye—
Not the gaily-jeweled dead
Tempt the waters from their bed;   35
For no ripples curl, alas!
Along that wilderness of glass—
No swellings tell that winds may be
Upon some far-off happier sea—
No heavings hint that winds have been   40
On seas less hideously serene.

But lo, a stir is in the air!
The wave—there is a movement there!

As if the towers had thrust aside,
In slightly sinking, the dull tide— 45
As if their tops had feebly given
A void within the filmy heaven.
The waves have now a redder glow—
The hours are breathing faint and low—
And when, amid no earthly moans, 50
Down, down that town shall settle hence,
Hell, rising from a thousand thrones,
Shall do it reverence.

Alfred, Lord Tennyson

THE LOTOS-EATERS

"Courage!" he said, and pointed toward the land,
"This mounting wave will roll us shoreward soon."
In the afternoon they came unto a land
In which it seemèd always afternoon.
All round the coast the languid air did swoon, 5
Breathing like one that hath a weary dream.
Full-faced above the valley stood the moon;
And, like a downward smoke, the slender stream
Along the cliff to fall and pause and fall did seem.

A land of streams! some, like a downward smoke, 10
Slow-dropping veils of thinnest lawn, did go;
And some through wavering lights and shadows broke,
Rolling a slumbrous sheet of foam below.
They saw the gleaming river seaward flow
From the inner land; far off, three mountaintops 15
Three silent pinnacles of aged snow,
Stood sunset-flushed; and, dewed with showery drops,
Up-clomb the shadowy pine above the woven copse.

The charmèd sunset lingered low adown
In the red West; through mountain clefts the dale   20
Was seen far inland, and the yellow down
Bordered with palm, and many a winding vale
And meadow, set with slender galingale;
A land where all things always seemed the same!
And round about the keel with faces pale,   25
Dark faces pale against that rosy flame,
The mild-eyed melancholy lotos-eaters came.

Branches they bore of that enchanted stem,
Laden with flower and fruit, whereof they gave
To each, but whoso did receive of them   30
And taste, to him the gushing of the wave
Far far away did seem to mourn and rave
On alien shores; and if his fellow spake,
His voice was thin, as voices from the grave;
And deep-asleep he seemed, yet all awake,   35
And music in his ears his beating heart did make.

They sat them down upon the yellow sand,
Between the sun and moon upon the shore;
And sweet it was to dream of fatherland,
Of child, and wife, and slave; but evermore   40
Most weary seemed the sea, weary the oar,
Weary the wandering fields of barren foam.
Then some one said, "We will return no more";
And all at once they sang, "Our island home
Is far beyond the wave; we will no longer roam."   45

CHORIC SONG

[1]

There is sweet music here that softer falls
Than petals from blown roses on the grass,
Or night-dews on still waters between walls
Of shadowy granite, in a gleaming pass;
Music that gentlier on the spirit lies,   50
Than tired eyelids upon tired eyes;
Music that brings sweet sleep down from the blissful skies.

Here are cool mosses deep,
And through the moss the ivies creep,
And in the stream the long-leaved flowers weep,   55
And from the craggy ledge the poppy hangs in sleep.

[2]

Why are we weighed upon with heaviness,
And utterly consumed with sharp distress,
While all things else have rest from weariness?
All things have rest: why should we toil alone,   60
We only toil, who are the first of things,
And make perpetual moan,
Still from one sorrow to another thrown;
Nor ever fold our wings,
And cease from wanderings,   65
Nor steep our brows in slumber's holy balm;
Nor harken what the inner spirit sings,
"There is no joy but calm!"—
Why should we only toil, the roof and crown of things?

[3]

Lo! in the middle of the wood,   70
The folded leaf is wooed from out the bud
With winds upon the branch, and there
Grows green and broad, and takes no care,
Sun-steeped at noon, and in the moon
Nightly dew-fed; and turning yellow   75
Falls, and floats adown the air.
Lo! sweetened with the summer light,
The full-juiced apple, waxing over-mellow,
Drops in a silent autumn night.
All its allotted length of days   80
The flower ripens in its place,
Ripens and fades, and falls, and hath no toil,
Fast-rooted in the fruitful soil.

[4]

Hateful is the dark blue sky,
Vaulted o'er the dark blue sea.   85

Death is the end of life; ah, why
Should life all labor be?
Let us alone. Time driveth onward fast,
And in a little while our lips are dumb.
Let us alone. What is it that will last? 90
All things are taken from us, and become
Portions and parcels of the dreadful past.
Let us alone. What pleasure can we have
To war with evil? Is there any peace
In ever climbing up the climbing wave? 95
All things have rest, and ripen toward the grave
In silence—ripen, fall, and cease:
Give us long rest or death, dark death, or dreamful ease.

[5]

How sweet it were, hearing the downward stream,
With half-shut eyes ever to seem 100
Falling asleep in a half-dream!
To dream and dream, like yonder amber light,
Which will not leave the myrrh-bush on the height;
To hear each other's whispered speech;
Eating the lotos day by day, 105
To watch the crisping ripples on the beach,
And tender curving lines of creamy spray;
To lend our hearts and spirits wholly
To the influence of mild-minded melancholy;
To muse and brood and live again in memory, 110
With those old faces of our infancy
Heaped over with a mound of grass,
Two handfuls of white dust, shut in an urn of brass!

[6]

Dear is the memory of our wedded lives,
And dear the last embraces of our wives 115
And their warm tears; but all hath suffered change;
For surely now our household hearths are cold,
Our sons inherit us, our looks are strange,
And we should come like ghosts to trouble joy.
Or else the island princes overbold 120

Have eat our substance, and the minstrel sings
Before them of the ten years' war in Troy,
And our great deeds, as half-forgotten things.
Is there confusion in the little isle?
Let what is broken so remain.   125
The Gods are hard to reconcile;
'Tis hard to settle order once again.
There *is* confusion worse than death,
Trouble on trouble, pain on pain,
Long labor unto aged breath,   130
Sore tasks to hearts worn out by many wars
And eyes grown dim with gazing on the pilot-stars.

[7]

But, propped on beds of amaranth and moly,
How sweet—while warm airs lull us, blowing lowly—
With half-dropped eyelid still,   135
Beneath a heaven dark and holy,
To watch the long bright river drawing slowly
His waters from the purple hill—
To hear the dewy echoes calling
From cave to cave through the thick-twined vine—   140
To watch the emerald-colored water falling
Through many a woven acanthus wreath divine!
Only to hear and see the far-off sparkling brine,
Only to hear were sweet, stretched out beneath the pine.

[8]

The lotos blooms below the barren peak,   145
The lotos blows by every winding creek;
All day the wind breathes low with mellower tone;
Through every hollow cave and alley lone
Round and round the spicy downs the yellow lotos dust is blown.
We have had enough of action, and of motion we,   150
Rolled to starboard, rolled to larboard, when the surge was seeth-
    ing free,
Where the wallowing monster spouted his foam-fountains in the
    sea.

Let us swear an oath, and keep it with an equal mind,
In the hollow lotos land to live and lie reclined
On the hills like Gods together, careless of mankind.   155
For they lie beside their nectar, and the bolts are hurled
Far below them in the valleys, and the clouds are lightly curled
Round their golden houses, girdled with the gleaming world;
Where they smile in secret, looking over wasted lands,
Blight and famine, plague and earthquake, roaring deeps and
    fiery sands,   160
Clanging fights, and flaming towns, and sinking ships, and pray-
    ing hands.
But they smile, they find a music centered in a doleful song
Steaming up, a lamentation and an ancient tale of wrong,
Like a tale of little meaning though the words are strong;
Chanted from an ill-used race of men that cleave the soil,   165
Sow the seed, and reap the harvest with enduring toil,
Storing yearly little dues of wheat, and wine and oil;
Till they perish and they suffer—some, 'tis whispered—down in
    hell
Suffer endless anguish, others in Elysian valleys dwell,
Resting weary limbs at last on beds of asphodel.   170
Surely, surely, slumber is more sweet than toil, the shore
Than labor in the deep mid-ocean, wind and wave and oar;
O, rest ye, brother mariners, we will not wander more.

ULYSSES

   It little profits that an idle king,
By this still hearth, among these barren crags,
Matched with an aged wife, I mete and dole
Unequal laws unto a savage race,
That hoard, and sleep, and feed, and know not me.   5
I cannot rest from travel; I will drink
Life to the lees. All times I have enjoyed
Greatly, have suffered greatly, both with those
That loved me, and alone; on shore, and when
Through scudding drifts the rainy Hyades   10
Vexed the dim sea. I am become a name;

For always roaming with a hungry heart
Much have I seen and known—cities of men
And manners, climates, councils, governments,
Myself not least, but honored of them all—   15
And drunk delight of battle with my peers,
Far on the ringing plains of windy Troy.
I am a part of all that I have met;
Yet all experience is an arch wherethrough
Gleams that untraveled world whose margin fades   20
Forever and forever when I move.
How dull it is to pause, to make an end,
To rust unburnished, not to shine in use!
As though to breathe were life! Life piled on life
Were all too little, and of one to me   25
Little remains; but every hour is saved
From that eternal silence, something more,
A bringer of new things; and vile it were
For some three suns to store and hoard myself,
And this gray spirit yearning in desire   30
To follow knowledge like a sinking star,
Beyond the utmost bound of human thought.
    This is my son, mine own Telemachus,
To whom I leave the scepter and the isle—
Well-loved of me, discerning to fulfill   35
This labor, by slow prudence to make mild
A rugged people, and through soft degrees
Subdue them to the useful and the good.
Most blameless is he, centered in the sphere
Of common duties, decent not to fail   40
In offices of tenderness, and pay
Meet adoration to my household gods,
When I am gone. He works his work, I mine.
    There lies the port; the vessel puffs her sail;
There gloom the dark, broad seas. My mariners,   45
Souls that have toiled, and wrought, and thought with me—
That ever with a frolic welcome took
The thunder and the sunshine, and opposed
Free hearts, free foreheads—you and I are old;
Old age hath yet his honor and his toil.   50

Death closes all; but something ere the end,
Some work of noble note, may yet be done,
Not unbecoming men that strove with Gods.
The lights begin to twinkle from the rocks;
The long day wanes; the slow moon climbs; the deep   55
Moans round with many voices. Come, my friends,
'Tis not too late to seek a newer world.
Push off, and sitting well in order smite
The sounding furrows; for my purpose holds
To sail beyond the sunset, and the baths   60
Of all the western stars, until I die.
It may be that the gulfs will wash us down;
It may be we shall touch the Happy Isles,
And see the great Achilles, whom we knew.
Though much is taken, much abides; and though   65
We are not now that strength which in old days
Moved earth and heaven, that which we are, we are—
One equal temper of heroic hearts,
Made weak by time and fate, but strong in will
To strive, to seek, to find, and not to yield.   70

TITHONUS

The woods decay, the woods decay and fall,
The vapors weep their burthen to the ground,
Man comes and tills the field and lies beneath,
And after many a summer dies the swan.
Me only cruel immortality   5
Consumes; I wither slowly in thine arms,
Here at the quiet limit of the world,
A white-haired shadow roaming like a dream
The ever-silent spaces of the East,
Far-folded mists, and gleaming halls of morn.   10
Alas! for this gray shadow, once a man—
So glorious in his beauty and thy choice,
Who madest him thy chosen, that he seemed
To his great heart none other than a God!
I asked thee, "Give me immortality."   15

Then didst thou grant mine asking with a smile,
Like wealthy men who care not how they give.
But thy strong hours indignant worked their wills,
And beat me down and marred and wasted me,
And though they could not end me, left me maimed   20
To dwell in presence of immortal youth,
Immortal age beside immortal youth,
And all I was in ashes. Can thy love,
Thy beauty, make amends, though even now,
Close over us, the silver star, thy guide,   25
Shines in those tremulous eyes that fill with tears
To hear me? Let me go; take back thy gift.
Why should a man desire in any way
To vary from the kindly race of men,
Or pass beyond the goal of ordinance   30
Where all should pause, as is most meet for all?
    A soft air fans the cloud apart; there comes
A glimpse of that dark world where I was born.
Once more the old mysterious glimmer steals
From thy pure brows, and from thy shoulders pure,   35
And bosom beating with a heart renewed.
Thy cheek begins to redden through the gloom,
Thy sweet eyes brighten slowly close to mine,
Ere yet they blind the stars, and the wild team
Which love thee, yearning for thy yoke, arise,   40
And shake the darkness from their loosened manes,
And beat the twilight into flakes of fire.
    Lo! ever thus thou growest beautiful
In silence, then before thine answer given
Departest, and thy tears are on my cheek.   45
    Why wilt thou ever scare me with thy tears,
And make me tremble lest a saying learnt,
In days far-off, on that dark earth, be true?
"The Gods themselves cannot recall their gifts."
    Ay me! ay me! with what another heart   50
In days far-off, and with what other eyes
I used to watch—if I be he that watched—
The lucid outline forming round thee; saw
The dim curls kindle into sunny rings;

Changed with thy mystic change, and felt my blood   55
Glow with the glow that slowly crimsoned all
Thy presence and thy portals, while I lay,
Mouth, forehead, eyelids, growing dewy-warm
With kisses balmier than half-opening buds
Of April, and could hear the lips that kissed   60
Whispering I knew not what of wild and sweet,
Like that strange song I heard Apollo sing,
While Ilion like a mist rose into towers.

  Yet hold me not forever in thine East;
How can my nature longer mix with thine?   65
Coldly thy rosy shadows bathe me, cold
Are all thy lights, and cold my wrinkled feet
Upon thy glimmering thresholds, when the steam
Floats up from those dim fields about the homes
Of happy men that have the power to die,   70
And grassy barrows of the happier dead.
Release me, and restore me to the ground.
Thou seest all things, thou wilt see my grave;
Thou wilt renew thy beauty morn by morn,
I earth in earth forget these empty courts,   75
And thee returning on thy silver wheels.

TEARS, IDLE TEARS

  Tears, idle tears, I know not what they mean,
Tears from the depth of some divine despair
Rise in the heart, and gather to the eyes,
In looking on the happy autumn-fields,
And thinking of the days that are no more.   5

  Fresh as the first beam glittering on a sail,
That brings our friends up from the underworld,
Sad as the last which reddens over one
That sinks with all we love below the verge;
So sad, so fresh, the days that are no more.   10

  Ah, sad and strange as in dark summer dawns
The earliest pipe of half-awaken'd birds

To dying ears, when unto dying eyes
The casement slowly grows a glimmering square;
So sad, so strange, the days that are no more.   15

Dear as remember'd kisses after death,
And sweet as those by hopeless fancy feign'd
On lips that are for others; deep as love,
Deep as first love, and wild with all regret;
O Death in Life, the days that are no more!   20

CALM IS THE MORN WITHOUT A SOUND

Calm is the morn without a sound,
    Calm as to suit a calmer grief,
    And only thro' the faded leaf
The chestnut pattering to the ground;

Calm and deep peace on this high wold,   5
    And on these dews that drench the furze,
    And all the silvery gossamers
That twinkle into green and gold;

Calm and still light on yon great plain
    That sweeps with all its autumn bowers,   10
    And crowded farms and lessening towers,
To mingle with the bounding main;

Calm and deep peace in this wide air,
    These leaves that redden to the fall,
    And in my heart, if calm at all,   15
If any calm, a calm despair;

Calm on the seas, and silver sleep,
    And waves that sway themselves in rest,
    And dead calm in that noble breast
Which heaves but with the heaving deep.   20

O LIVING WILL THAT SHALT ENDURE

O living will that shalt endure
  When all that seems shall suffer shock,
  Rise in the spiritual rock,
Flow thro' our deeds and make them pure,

That we may lift from out of dust   5
  A voice as unto him that hears,
  A cry above the conquer'd years
To one that with us works, and trust,

With faith that comes of self-control,
  The truths that never can be proved   10
  Until we close with all we loved,
And all we flow from, soul in soul.

Robert Browning

SOLILOQUY OF THE SPANISH CLOISTER

[1]

Gr-r-r—there go, my heart's abhorrence!
  Water your damned flowerpots, do!
If hate killed men, Brother Lawrence,
  God's blood, would not mine kill you!
What? your myrtle bush wants trimming?   5
  Oh, that rose has prior claims—
Needs its leaden vase filled brimming?
  Hell dry you up with its flames!

[2]

At the meal we sit together:
  Salve tibi! I must hear   10
Wise talk of the kind of weather,
  Sort of season, time of year:

10. *Salve tibi:* hail to thee.

Not a plenteous cork crop: scarcely
    Dare we hope oak-galls, I doubt:
What's the Latin name for "parsley"?   15
    What's the Greek name for Swine's Snout?

[3]

Whew! We'll have our platter burnished,
    Laid with care on our own shelf!
With a fire-new spoon we're furnished,
    And a goblet for ourself,   20
Rinsed like something sacrificial
    Ere 'tis fit to touch our chaps—
Marked with L. for our initial!
    (He-he! There his lily snaps!)

[4]

Saint, forsooth! While brown Dolores   25
    Squats outside the Convent bank
With Sanchicha, telling stories,
    Steeping tresses in the tank,
Blue-black, lustrous, thick like horsehairs,
    —Can't I see his dead eye glow,   30
Bright as 'twere a Barbary corsair's?
    (That is, if he'd let it show!)

[5]

When he finishes refection,
    Knife and fork he never lays
Cross-wise, to my recollection,   35
    As do I, in Jesu's praise.
I the Trinity illustrate,
    Drinking watered orange pulp—
In three sips the Arian frustrate;
    While he drains his at one gulp.   40

[6]

Oh, those melons? If he's able
    We're to have a feast! so nice!
One goes to the Abbot's table,
    All of us get each a slice.

How go on your flowers? None double? 45
      Not one fruit-sort can you spy?
Strange!—And I, too, at such trouble,
      Keep them close-nipped on the sly!

[7]

There's a great text in Galatians,
      Once you trip on it, entails 50
Twenty-nine distinct damnations,
      One sure, if another fails:
If I trip him just a-dying,
      Sure of heaven as sure can be,
Spin him round and send him flying
      Off to hell, a Manichee? 55

[8]

Or, my scrofulous French novel
      On gray paper with blunt type!
Simply glance at it, you grovel
      Hand and foot in Belial's gripe: 60
If I double down its pages
      At the woeful sixteenth print,
When he gathers his greengages,
      Ope a sieve and slip it in't?

[9]

Or, there's Satan!—one might venture 65
      Pledge one's soul to him, yet leave
Such a flaw in the indenture
      As he'd miss till, past retrieve,
Blasted lay that rose-acacia
      We're so proud of! *Hy, Zy, Hine* . . . 70
'St, there's Vespers! *Plena gratiá*
      Ave, Virgo! Gr-r-r—you swine!

71–72. *Plena . . . Virgo:* Hail Virgin, full of grace.

MY LAST DUCHESS

FERRARA

Drama

That's my last Duchess painted on the wall,
Looking as if she were alive. I call
That piece a wonder, now: Frà Pandolf's hands
Worked busily a day, and there she stands.
Will't please you sit and look at her? I said   5
"Frà Pandolf" by design, for never read
Strangers like you that pictured countenance,
The depth and passion of its earnest glance,
But to myself they turned (since none puts by
The curtain I have drawn for you, but I)   10
And seemed as they would ask me, if they durst,
How such a glance came there; so, not the first
Are you to turn and ask thus. Sir, 'twas not
Her husband's presence only, called that spot
Of joy into the Duchess' cheek: perhaps   15
Frà Pandolf chanced to say "Her mantle laps
Over my lady's wrist too much," or "Paint
Must never hope to reproduce the faint
Half-flush that dies along her throat": such stuff
Was courtesy, she thought, and cause enough   20
For calling up that spot of joy. She had
A heart—how shall I say?—too soon made glad,
Too easily impressed; she liked whate'er
She looked on, and her looks went everywhere.
Sir, 'twas all one! My favor at her breast,   25
The dropping of the daylight in the West,
The bough of cherries some officious fool
Broke in the orchard for her, the white mule
She rode with round the terrace—all and each
Would draw from her alike the approving speech,   30
Or blush, at least. She thanked men—good! but thanked
Somehow—I know not how—as if she ranked
My gift of a nine-hundred-years-old name
With anybody's gift. Who'd stoop to blame
This sort of trifling? Even had you skill   35
In speech—(which I have not)—to make your will

177

Quite clear to such an one, and say, "Just this
Or that in you disgusts me; here you miss,
Or there exceed the mark"—and if she let
Herself be lessoned so, nor plainly set   40
Her wits to yours, forsooth, and made excuse
—E'en then would be some stooping; and I choose
Never to stoop. Oh sir, she smiled, no doubt,
Whene'er I passed her; but who passed without
Much the same smile? This grew; I gave commands;   45
Then all smiles stopped together. There she stands
As if alive. Will't please you rise? We'll meet
The company below, then. I repeat,
The Count your master's known munificence
Is ample warrant that no just pretense   50
Of mine for dowry will be disallowed;
Though his fair daughter's self, as I avowed
At starting, is my object. Nay, we'll go
Together down, sir. Notice Neptune, though,
Taming a sea horse, thought a rarity,   55
Which Claus of Innsbruck cast in bronze for me!

THE BISHOP ORDERS HIS TOMB AT
SAINT PRAXED'S CHURCH

ROME, 15—

Vanity, saith the preacher, vanity!
Draw round my bed: is Anselm keeping back?
Nephews—sons mine . . . ah God, I know not! Well—
She, men would have to be your mother once,
Old Gandolf envied me, so fair she was!   5
What's done is done, and she is dead beside,
Dead long ago, and I am Bishop since,
And as she died so must we die ourselves,
And thence ye may perceive the world's a dream.
Life, how and what is it? As here I lie   10
In this state chamber, dying by degrees,
Hours and long hours in the dead night, I ask
"Do I live, am I dead?" Peace, peace seems all.

Saint Praxed's ever was the church for peace;
And so, about this tomb of mine. I fought   15
With tooth and nail to save my niche, ye know:
—Old Gandolf cozened me, despite my care;
Shrewd was that snatch from out the corner south
He graced his carrion with, God curse the same!
Yet still my niche is not so cramped but thence   20
One sees the pulpit o' the epistle side,
And somewhat of the choir, those silent seats,
And up into the aery dome where live
The angels, and a sunbeam's sure to lurk:
And I shall fill my slab of basalt there,   25
And 'neath my tabernacle take my rest,
With those nine columns round me, two and two,
The odd one at my feet where Anselm stands:
Peach-blossom marble all, the rare, the ripe
As fresh-poured red wine of a mighty pulse.   30
—Old Gandolf with his paltry onion-stone,
Put me where I may look at him! True peach,
Rosy and flawless: how I earned the prize!
Draw close: that conflagration of my church
—What then? So much was saved if aught were missed!   35
My sons, ye would not be my death? Go dig
The white-grape vineyard where the oil-press stood,
Drop water gently till the surface sink,
And if ye find . . . Ah God, I know not, I! . . .
Bedded in store of rotten fig leaves soft,   40
And corded up in a tight olive-frail,
Some lump, ah God, of *lapis lazuli*,
Big as a Jew's head cut off at the nape,
Blue as a vein o'er the Madonna's breast . . .
Sons, all have I bequeathed you, villas, all,   45
That brave Frascati villa with its bath,
So, let the blue lump poise between my knees,
Like God the Father's globe on both his hands
Ye worship in the Jesu Church so gay,
For Gandolf shall not choose but see and burst!   50
Swift as a weaver's shuttle fleet our years:
Man goeth to the grave, and where is he?

Did I say basalt for my slab, sons? Black—
'Twas ever antique-black I meant! How else
Shall ye contrast my frieze to come beneath?   55
The bas-relief in bronze ye promised me,
Those Pans and Nymphs ye wot of, and perchance
Some tripod, thyrsus, with a vase or so,
The Saviour at his sermon on the mount,
Saint Praxed in a glory, and one Pan   60
Ready to twitch the Nymph's last garment off,
And Moses with the tables . . . but I know
Ye mark me not! What do they whisper thee,
Child of my bowels, Anselm? Ah, ye hope
To revel down my villas while I gasp   65
Bricked o'er with beggar's moldy travertine
Which Gandolf from his tomb-top chuckles at!
Nay, boys, ye love me—all of jasper, then!
'Tis jasper ye stand pledged to, lest I grieve
My bath must needs be left behind, alas!   70
One block, pure green as a pistachio nut,
There's plenty jasper somewhere in the world—
And have I not Saint Praxed's ear to pray
Horses for ye, and brown Greek manuscripts,
And mistresses with great smooth marbly limbs?   75
—That's if ye carve my epitaph aright,
Choice Latin, picked phrase, Tully's every word,
No gaudy ware like Gandolf's second line—
Tully, my masters? Ulpian serves his need!
And then how I shall lie through centuries,   80
And hear the blessed mutter of the mass,
And see God made and eaten all day long,
And feel the steady candle flame, and taste
Good strong thick stupefying incense-smoke!
For as I lie here, hours of the dead night,   85
Dying in state and by such slow degrees,
I fold my arms as if they clasped a crook,
And stretch my feet forth straight as stone can point,
And let the bedclothes, for a mortcloth, drop
Into great laps and folds of sculptor's-work: 90
And as yon tapers dwindle, and strange thoughts

Grow, with a certain humming in my ears,
About the life before I lived this life,
And this life too, popes, cardinals, and priests,
Saint Praxed at his sermon on the mount, 95
Your tall pale mother with her talking eyes,
And new-found agate urns as fresh as day,
And marble's language, Latin pure, discreet
—Aha, ELUCESCEBAT quoth our friend?
No Tully, said I, Ulpian at the best! 100
Evil and brief hath been my pilgrimage.
All *lapis,* all, sons! Else I give the Pope
My villas! Will ye ever eat my heart?
Ever your eyes were as a lizard's quick,
They glitter like your mother's for my soul, 105
Or ye would heighten my impoverished frieze,
Piece out its starved design, and fill my vase
With grapes, and add a vizor and a term,
And to the tripod ye would tie a lynx
That in his struggle throws the thyrsus down, 110
To comfort me on my entablature
Whereon I am to lie till I must ask
"Do I live, am I dead?" There, leave me, there!
For ye have stabbed me with ingratitude
To death—ye wish it—God, ye wish it! Stone— 115
Gritstone, a-crumble! Clammy squares which sweat
As if the corpse they keep were oozing through—
And no more *lapis* to delight the world!
Well go! I bless ye. Fewer tapers there,
But in a row: and, going, turn your backs 120
—Aye, like departing altar-ministrants,
And leave me in my church, the church for peace,
That I may watch at leisure if he leers—
Old Gandolf, at me, from his onion-stone,
As still he envied me, so fair she was! 125

99. *ELUCESCEBAT:* Late Latin for *elucebat,* "he was illustrious."

Emily Brontë

REMEMBRANCE

Cold in the earth—and the deep snow piled above thee,
Far, far removed, cold in the dreary grave!
Have I forgot, my only love, to love thee,
Severed at last by time's all-severing wave?

Now, when alone, do my thoughts no longer hover   5
Over the mountains, on that northern shore,
Resting their wings where heath and fern leaves cover
Thy noble heart forever, ever more?

Cold in the earth—and fifteen wild Decembers,
From those brown hills, have melted into spring;   10
Faithful, indeed, is the spirit that remembers
After such years of change and suffering!

Sweet love of youth, forgive, if I forget thee,
While the world's tide is bearing me along;
Other desires and other hopes beset me,   15
Hopes which obscure, but cannot do thee wrong!

No later light has lightened up my heaven,
No second morn has ever shone for me;
All my life's bliss from thy dear life was given,
All my life's bliss is in the grave with thee.   20

But, when the days of golden dreams had perished,
And even despair was powerless to destroy,
Then did I learn how existence could be cherished,
Strengthened, and fed without the aid of joy.

Then did I check the tears of useless passion—   25
Weaned my young soul from yearning after thine;
Sternly denied its burning wish to hasten
Down to that tomb already more than mine.

And, even yet, I dare not let it languish,
Dare not indulge in memory's rapturous pain;   30
Once drinking deep of that divinest anguish,
How could I seek the empty world again?

NO COWARD SOUL IS MINE

No coward soul is mine,
No trembler in the world's storm-troubled sphere;
I see heaven's glories shine,
And faith shines equal, arming me from fear.

O God within my breast,   5
Almighty, ever-present Deity!
Life—that in me has rest,
As I—undying life—have power in thee!

Vain are the thousand creeds
That move men's hearts—unutterably vain;   10
Worthless as withered weeds,
Or idlest froth amid the boundless main,

To waken doubt in one
Holding so fast by thine infinity;
So surely anchored on   15
The steadfast rock of immortality.

With wide-embracing love
Thy spirit animates eternal years,
Pervades and broods above,
Changes, sustains, dissolves, creates, and rears.   20

Though earth and man were gone,
And suns and universes ceased to be,
And thou were left alone,
Every existence would exist in thee.

There is not room for death,   25
Nor atom that his might could render void;
Thou—thou art being and breath,
And what thou art may never be destroyed.

Walt Whitman

OUT OF THE CRADLE ENDLESSLY ROCKING

Out of the cradle endlessly rocking,
Out of the mocking-bird's throat, the musical shuttle,
Out of the Ninth-month midnight,
Over the sterile sands and the fields beyond, where the child
    leaving his bed wander'd alone, bareheaded, barefoot,
Down from the shower'd halo,   5
Up from the mystic play of shadows twining and twisting as if
    they were alive,
Out from the patches of briers and blackberries,
From the memories of the bird that chanted to me,
From your memories sad brother, from the fitful risings and
    fallings I heard,
From under that yellow half-moon late-risen and swollen as if
    with tears,   10
From those beginning notes of yearning and love there in the
    mist,
From the thousand responses of my heart never to cease,
From the myriad thence-arous'd words,
From the word stronger and more delicious than any,
From such as now they start the scene revisiting,   15
As a flock, twittering, rising, or overhead passing,
Borne hither, ere all eludes me, hurriedly,
A man, yet by these tears a little boy again,
Throwing myself on the sand, confronting the waves,
I, chanter of pains and joys, uniter of here and hereafter,   20
Taking all hints to use them, but swiftly leaping beyond them,
A reminiscence sing.

Once Paumanok,
When the lilac-scent was in the air and Fifth-month grass was
    growing,

23. *Paumanok*: American Indian name for Long Island.

Up this seashore in some briers,   25
Two feather'd guests from Alabama, two together,
And their nest, and four light-green eggs spotted with brown,
And every day the he-bird to and fro near at hand,
And every day the she-bird crouch'd on her nest, silent, with
      bright eyes,
And every day I, a curious boy, never too close, never disturbing
      them,   30
Cautiously peering, absorbing, translating.

Shine! shine! shine!
Pour down your warmth, great sun!
While we bask, we two together.
Two together!   35
Winds blow south, or winds blow north,
Day come white, or night come black.
Home, or rivers and mountains from home,
Singing all time, minding no time,
While we two keep together.   40

Till of a sudden,
Maybe kill'd, unknown to her mate,
One forenoon the she-bird crouch'd not on the nest,
Nor return'd that afternoon, nor the next,
Nor ever appear'd again.   45

And thenceforward all summer in the sound of the sea,
And at night under the full of the moon in calmer weather,
Over the hoarse surging of the sea,
Or flitting from brier to brier by day,
I saw, I heard at intervals the remaining one, the he-bird,   50
The solitary guest from Alabama.

Blow! blow! blow!
Blow up sea-winds along Paumanok's shore;
I wait and I wait till you blow my mate to me.

Yes, when the stars glisten'd,   55
All night long on the prong of a moss-scallop'd stake,
Down almost amid the slapping waves,
Sat the lone singer wonderful causing tears.

He call'd on his mate,
He pour'd forth the meanings which I of all men know.   60

Yes my brother I know,
The rest might not, but I have treasur'd every note,
For more than once dimly down to the beach gliding,
Silent, avoiding the moonbeams, blending myself with the
    shadows,
Recalling now the obscure shapes, the echoes, the sounds and
    sights after their sorts,   65
The white arms out in the breakers tirelessly tossing,
I, with bare feet, a child, the wind wafting my hair,
Listen'd long and long.

Listen'd to keep, to sing, now translating the notes,
Following you my brother.   70

Soothe! soothe! soothe!
Close on its wave soothes the wave behind,
And again another behind embracing and lapping, every one
    close,
But my love soothes not me, not me.

Low hangs the moon, it rose late,   75
It is lagging—O I think it is heavy with love, with love.

O madly the sea pushes upon the land,
With love, with love.

O night! do I not see my love fluttering out among the breakers?
What is that little black thing I see there in the white?   80

Loud! loud! loud!
Loud I call to you, my love!
High and clear I shoot my voice over the waves,
Surely you must know who is here, is here,
You must know who I am, my love.   85

Low-hanging moon!
What is that dusky spot in your brown yellow?
O it is the shape, the shape of my mate!
O moon do not keep her from me any longer.

Land! land! O land! 90
Whichever way I turn, O I think you could give me my mate
    back again if you only would,
For I am almost sure I see her dimly whichever way I look.

O rising stars!
Perhaps the one I want so much will rise, will rise with some of
    you.

O throat! O trembling throat! 95
Sound clearer through the atmosphere!
Pierce the woods, the earth,
Somewhere listening to catch you must be the one I want.

Shake out carols!
Solitary here, the night's carols! 100
Carols of lonesome love! death's carols!
Carols under that lagging, yellow, waning moon!
O under that moon where she droops almost down into the sea!
O reckless despairing carols.

But soft! sink low! 105
Soft! let me just murmur,
And do you wait a moment you husky-nois'd sea,
For somewhere I believe I heard my mate responding to me,
So faint, I must be still, be still to listen,
But not altogether still, for then she might not come immediately
    to me. 110

Hither my love!
Here I am! here!
With this just-sustain'd note I announce myself to you,
This gentle call is for you my love, for you.

Do not be decoy'd elsewhere, 115
That is the whistle of the wind, it is not my voice,
That is the fluttering, the fluttering of the spray,
Those are the shadows of leaves.

O darkness! O in vain!
O I am very sick and sorrowful. 120

O brown halo in the sky near the moon, drooping upon the sea!
O troubled reflection in the sea!
O throat! O throbbing heart!
And I singing uselessly, uselessly all the night.

O past! O happy life! O songs of joy!   125
In the air, in the woods, over fields,
Loved! loved! loved! loved! loved!
But my mate no more, no more with me!
We two together no more.

The aria sinking,   130
All else continuing, the stars shining,
The winds blowing, the notes of the bird continuous echoing,
With angry moans the fierce old mother incessantly moaning,
On the sands of Paumanok's shore gray and rustling,
The yellow half-moon enlarged, sagging down, drooping, the
    face of the sea almost touching,   135
The boy ecstatic, with his bare feet the waves, with his hair the
    atmosphere dallying,
The love in the heart long pent, now loose, now at last tumultu-
    ously bursting,
The aria's meaning, the ears, the soul, swiftly depositing,
The strange tears down the cheeks coursing,
The colloquy there, the trio, each uttering,   140
The undertone, the savage old mother incessantly crying,
To the boy's soul's questions sullenly timing, some drown'd secret
    hissing,
To the outsetting bard.

Demon or bird! (said the boy's soul)
Is it indeed toward your mate you sing? or is it really to me?   145
For I, that was a child, my tongue's use sleeping, now I have
    heard you,
Now in a moment I know what I am for, I awake,
And already a thousand singers, a thousand songs, clearer,
    louder and more sorrowful than yours,
A thousand warbling echoes have started to life within me, never
    to die.

O you singer solitary, singing by yourself, projecting me, 150
O solitary me listening, never more shall I cease perpetuating
    you,
Never more shall I escape, never more the reverberations,
Never more the cries of unsatisfied love be absent from me,
Never again leave me to be the peaceful child I was before what
    there in the night,
By the sea under the yellow and sagging moon, 155
The messenger there arous'd, the fire, the sweet hell within,
The unknown want, the destiny of me.

O give me the clew! (it lurks in the night here somewhere)
O if I am to have so much, let me have more!

A word then (for I will conquer it), 160
The word final, superior to all,
Subtle, sent up—what is it?—I listen;
Are you whispering it, and have been all the time, you sea waves?
Is that it from your liquid rims and wet sands?

Whereto answering, the sea, 165
Delaying not, hurrying not,
Whisper'd me through the night, and very plainly before
    daybreak,
Lisp'd to me the low and delicious word death,
And again death, death, death, death,
Hissing melodious, neither like the bird nor like my arous'd
    child's heart, 170
But edging near as privately for me rustling at my feet,
Creeping thence steadily up to my ears and laving me softly all
    over,
Death, death, death, death, death.

Which I do not forget,
But fuse the song of my dusky demon and brother, 175
That he sang to me in the moonlight on Paumanok's gray beach,
With the thousand responsive songs at random,
My own songs awaked from that hour,
And with them the key, the word up from the waves,
The word of the sweetest song and all songs, 180

That strong and delicious word which, creeping to my feet,
(Or like some old crone rocking the cradle, swathed in sweet
    garments, bending aside)
The sea whisper'd me.

WHEN LILACS LAST IN THE
DOORYARD BLOOM'D

[1]

When lilacs last in the dooryard bloom'd,
And the great star early droop'd in the western sky in the night,
I mourn'd, and yet shall mourn with ever-returning spring.

Ever-returning spring, trinity sure to me you bring,
Lilac blooming perennial and drooping star in the west,   5
And thought of him I love.

[2]

O powerful western fallen star!
O shades of night—O moody, tearful night!
O great star disappear'd—O the black murk that hides the star!
O cruel hands that hold me powerless—O helpless soul of me!   10
O harsh surrounding cloud that will not free my soul.

[3]

In the dooryard fronting an old farmhouse near the white-wash'd
    palings,
Stands the lilac bush tall-growing with heart-shaped leaves of rich
    green,
With many a pointed blossom rising delicate, with the perfume
    strong I love,
With every leaf a miracle—and from this bush in the dooryard,   15
With delicate-color'd blossoms and heart-shaped leaves of rich
    green,
A sprig with its flower I break.

[4]

In the swamp in secluded recesses,
A shy and hidden bird is warbling a song.

Solitary the thrush, 20
The hermit withdrawn to himself, avoiding the settlements,
Sings by himself a song.

Song of the bleeding throat,
Death's outlet song of life (for well dear brother I know,
If thou wast not granted to sing thou would'st surely die). 25

[5]

Over the breast of the spring, the land, amid cities,
Amid lanes and through old woods, where lately the violets
    peep'd from the ground, spotting the gray debris,
Amid the grass in the fields each side of the lanes, passing the
    endless grass,
Passing the yellow-spear'd wheat, every grain from its shroud in
    the dark-brown fields uprisen,
Passing the apple tree blows of white and pink in the orchards, 30
Carrying a corpse to where it shall rest in the grave,
Night and day journeys a coffin.

[6]

Coffin that passes through lanes and streets,
Through day and night with the great cloud darkening the land,
With the pomp of the inloop'd flags with the cities draped in
    black, 35
With the show of the States themselves as of crape-veil'd women
    standing,
With processions long and winding and the flambeaus of the
    night,
With the countless torches lit, with the silent sea of faces and the
    unbared heads,
With the waiting depot, the arriving coffin, and the somber faces,
With dirges through the night, with the thousand voices rising
    strong and solemn, 40
With all the mournful voices of the dirges pour'd around the
    coffin,
The dim-lit churches and the shuddering organs—where amid
    these you journey,
With the tolling tolling bells' perpetual clang,

Here, coffin that slowly passes,
I give you my sprig of lilac.   45

[7]

(Nor for you, for one alone,
Blossoms and branches green to coffins all I bring,
For fresh as the morning, thus would I chant a song for you
    O sane and sacred death.

All over bouquets of roses,
O death, I cover you over with roses and early lilies,   50
But mostly and now the lilac that blooms the first,
Copious I break, I break the sprigs from the bushes,
With loaded arms I come, pouring for you,
For you and the coffins all of you O death.)

[8]

O western orb sailing the heaven,   55
Now I know what you must have meant as a month since I
    walk'd,
As I walk'd in silence the transparent shadowy night,
As I saw you had something to tell as you bent to me night after
    night,
As you droop'd from the sky low down as if to my side (while
    the other stars all look'd on),
As we wander'd together the solemn night (for something I know
    not what kept me from sleep),   60
As the night advanced, and I saw on the rim of the west how full
    you were of woe,
As I stood on the rising ground in the breeze in the cool trans-
    parent night,
As I watch'd where you pass'd and was lost in the netherward
    black of the night,
As my soul in its trouble dissatisfied sank, as where you sad orb,
Concluded, dropt in the night, and was gone.   65

[9]

Sing on there in the swamp,
O singer bashful and tender, I hear your notes, I hear your call,

I hear, I come presently, I understand you,
But a moment I linger, for the lustrous star has detain'd me,
The star my departing comrade holds and detains me.   70

[10]

O how shall I warble myself for the dead one there I loved?
And how shall I deck my song for the large sweet soul that has
    gone?
And what shall my perfume be for the grave of him I love?

Sea-winds blown from east and west,
Blown from the Eastern sea and blown from the Western sea,
    till there on the prairies meeting,   75
These and with these and the breath of my chant,
I'll perfume the grave of him I love.

[11]

O what shall I hang on the chamber walls?
And what shall the pictures be that I hang on the walls,
To adorn the burial-house of him I love?   80

Pictures of growing spring and farms and homes,
With the Fourth-month eve at sundown, and the gray smoke
    lucid and bright,
With floods of the yellow gold of the gorgeous, indolent, sinking
    sun, burning, expanding the air,
With the fresh sweet herbage under foot, and the pale green
    leaves of the trees prolific,
In the distance the flowing glaze, the breast of the river, with a
    wind-dapple here and there,   85
With ranging hills on the banks, with many a line against the
    sky, and shadows,
And the city at hand with dwellings so dense, and stacks of
    chimneys,
And all the scenes of life and the workshops, and the workmen
    homeward returning.

[12]

Lo, body and soul—this land,
My own Manhattan with spires, and the sparkling and hurrying
    tides, and the ships,   90

The varied and ample land, the South and the North in the light,
    Ohio's shores and flashing Missouri,
And ever the far-spreading prairies cover'd with grass and corn.

Lo, the most excellent sun so calm and haughty,
The violet and purple morn with just-felt breezes,
The gentle soft-born measureless light,   95
The miracle spreading bathing all, the fulfill'd noon,
The coming eve delicious, the welcome night and the stars,
Over my cities shining all, enveloping man and land.

[13]

Sing on, sing on you gray-brown bird,
Sing from the swamps, the recesses, pour your chant from the
    bushes,   100
Limitless out of the dusk, out of the cedars and pines.

Sing on dearest brother, warble your reedy song,
Loud human song, with voice of uttermost woe.

O liquid and free and tender!
O wild and loose to my soul—O wondrous singer!   105
You only I hear—yet the star holds me (but will soon depart),
Yet the lilac with mastering odor holds me.

[14]

Now while I sat in the day and look'd forth,
In the close of the day with its light and the fields of spring, and
    the farmers preparing their crops,
In the large unconscious scenery of my land with its lakes and
    forests,   110
In the heavenly aerial beauty (after the perturb'd winds and the
    storms),
Under the arching heavens of the afternoon swift passing, and
    the voices of children and women,
The many-moving sea-tides, and I saw the ships how they sail'd,
And the summer approaching with richness, and the fields all
    busy with labor,
And the infinite separate houses, how they all went on, each with
    its meals and minutia of daily usages,   115

And the streets how their throbbings throbb'd, and the cities
    pent—lo, then and there,
Falling upon them all and among them all, enveloping me with
    the rest,
Appear'd the cloud, appear'd the long black trail,
And I knew death, its thought, and the sacred knowledge of
    death.

Then with the knowledge of death as walking one side of me,   120
And the thought of death close-walking the other side of me,
And I in the middle as with companions, and as holding the
    hands of companions,
I fled forth to the hiding receiving night that talks not,
Down to the shores of the water, the path by the swamp in the
    dimness,
To the solemn shadowy cedars and ghostly pines so still.   125

And the singer so shy to the rest receiv'd me,
The gray-brown bird I know receiv'd us comrades three,
And he sang the carol of death, and a verse for him I love.

From deep secluded recesses,
From the fragrant cedars and the ghostly pines so still,   130
Came the carol of the bird.

And the charm of the carol rapt me,
As I held as if by their hands my comrades in the night,
And the voice of my spirit tallied the song of the bird.

Come lovely and soothing death,   135
Undulate round the world, serenely arriving, arriving,
In the day, in the night, to all, to each,
Sooner or later delicate death.

Prais'd be the fathomless universe,
For life and joy, and for objects and knowledge curious,   140
And for love, sweet love—but praise! praise! praise!
For the sure-enwinding arms of cool-enfolding death.

Dark mother always gliding near with soft feet,
Have none chanted for thee a chant of fullest welcome?

195

Then I chant it for thee, I glorify thee above all, 145
I bring thee a song that when thou must indeed come, come
    unfalteringly.

Approach strong deliveress,
When it is so, when thou hast taken them I joyously sing the
    dead,
Lost in the loving floating ocean of thee,
Laved in the flood of thy bliss O death. 150

From me to thee glad serenades,
Dances for thee I propose saluting thee, adornments and feastings
    for thee,
And the sights of the open landscape and the high-spread sky are
    fitting,
And life and the fields, and the huge and thoughtful night.

The night in silence under many a star, 155
The ocean shore and the husky whispering wave whose voice I
    know,
And the soul turning to thee O vast and well-veil'd death,
And the body gratefully nestling close to thee.

Over the tree tops I float thee a song,
Over the rising and sinking waves, over the myriad fields and the
    prairies wide, 160
Over the dense-pack'd cities all and the teeming wharves and
    ways,
I float this carol with joy, with joy to thee O death.

[15]

To the tally of my soul,
Loud and strong kept up the gray-brown bird,
With pure deliberate notes spreading filling the night. 165

Loud in the pines and cedars dim,
Clear in the freshness moist and the swamp-perfume,
And I with my comrades there in the night.

While my sight that was bound in my eyes unclosed,
As to long panoramas of visions. 170

And I saw askant the armies,
I saw as in noiseless dreams hundreds of battle-flags,
Borne through the smoke of the battles and pierc'd with missiles
    I saw them,
And caried hither and yon through the smoke, and torn and
    bloody,
And at last but a few shreds left on the staffs (and all in silence), 175
And the staffs all splinter'd and broken.

I saw battle-corpses, myriads of them,
And the white skeletons of young men, I saw them,
I saw the debris and debris of all the slain soldiers of the war,
But I saw they were not as was thought, 180
They themselves were fully at rest, they suffer'd not,
The living remain'd and suffer'd, the mother suffer'd,
And the wife and the child and the musing comrade suffer'd,
And the armies that remain'd suffer'd.

[16]

Passing the visions, passing the night, 185
Passing, unloosing the hold of my comrade's hands,
Passing the song of the hermit bird and the tallying song of my
    soul,
Victorious song, death's outlet song, yet varying ever-altering
    song,
As low and wailing, yet clear the notes, rising and falling, flood-
    ing the night,
Sadly sinking and fainting, as warning and warning, and yet
    again bursting with joy, 190
Covering the earth and filling the spread of heaven,
As that powerful psalm in the night I heard from recesses,
Passing, I leave thee lilac with heart-shaped leaves,
I leave thee there in the dooryard, blooming, returning with
    spring.

I cease from my song for thee, 195
From my gaze on thee in the west, fronting the west, communing
    with thee,
O comrade lustrous with silver face in the night.

Yet each to keep and all, retrievements out of the night,
The song, the wondrous chant of the gray-brown bird,
And the tallying chant, the echo arous'd in my soul,   200
With the lustrous and drooping star with the countenance full
 of woe,
With the holders holding my hand nearing the call of the bird,
Comrades mine and I in the midst, and their memory ever to
 keep, for the dead I loved so well,
For the sweetest, wisest soul of all my days and lands—and this
 for his dear sake,
Lilac and star and bird twined with the chant of my soul,   205
There in the fragrant pines and the cedars dusk and dim.

Matthew Arnold

THE FORSAKEN MERMAN

Come, dear children, let us away;
Down and away below!
Now my brothers call from the bay,
Now the great winds shoreward blow,
Now the salt tides seaward flow;   5
Now the wild white horses play,
Champ and chafe and toss in the spray.
Children dear, let us away!
This way, this way!

Call her once before you go—   10
Call once yet!
In a voice that she will know:
"Margaret! Margaret!"
Children's voices should be dear
(Call once more) to a mother's ear;   15
Children's voices, wild with pain—
Surely she will come again!

Call her once and come away;
This way, this way!
"Mother dear, we cannot stay!   20
The wild white horses foam and fret."
Margaret! Margaret!

　　Come, dear children, come away down;
Call no more!
One last look at the white-walled town,   25
And the little gray church on the windy shore,
Then come down!
She will not come though you call all day;
Come away, come away!

　　Children dear, was it yesterday   30
We heard the sweet bells over the bay?
In the caverns where we lay,
Through the surf and through the swell,
The far-off sound of a silver bell?
Sand-strewn caverns, cool and deep,   35
Where the winds are all asleep;
Where the spent lights quiver and gleam,
Where the salt weed sways in the stream,
Where the sea beasts, ranged all round,
Feed in the ooze of their pasture ground;   40
Where the sea snakes coil and twine,
Dry their mail and bask in the brine;
Where great whales come sailing by,
Sail and sail, with unshut eye,
Round the world for ever and aye?   45
When did music come this way?
Children dear, was it yesterday?

　　Children dear, was it yesterday
(Call yet once) that she went away?
Once she sate with you and me,   50
On a red gold throne in the heart of the sea,
And the youngest sate on her knee.
She combed its bright hair, and she tended it well,
When down swung the sound of a far-off bell.

She sighed, she looked up through the clear green sea;   55
She said: "I must go, for my kinsfolk pray
In the little gray church on the shore today.
'Twill be Easter time in the world—ah me!
And I lose my poor soul, Merman! here with thee."
I said: "Go up, dear heart, through the waves;   60
Say thy prayer, and come back to the kind sea caves!"
She smiled, she went up through the surf in the bay.
Children dear, was it yesterday?

   Children dear, were we long alone?
"The sea grows stormy, the little ones moan;   65
Long prayers," I said, "in the world they say;
Come!" I said; and we rose through the surf in the bay.
We went up the beach, by the sandy down
Where the sea stocks bloom, to the white-walled town;
Through the narrow paved streets, where all was still,   70
To the little gray church on the windy hill.
From the church came a murmur of folk at their prayers,
But we stood without in the cold blowing airs.
We climbed on the graves, on the stones worn with rains,
And we gazed up the aisle through the small leaded panes   75
She sate by the pillar; we saw her clear:
"Margaret, hist! come quick, we are here!
Dear heart," I said, "we are long alone;
The sea grows stormy, the little ones moan."
But, ah, she gave me never a look,   80
For her eyes were sealed to the holy book!
Loud prays the priest; shut stands the door.
Come away, children, call no more!
Come away, come down, call no more!

   Down, down, down!   85
Down to the depths of the sea!
She sits at her wheel in the humming town,
Singing most joyfully.
Hark what she sings: "O joy, O joy,
For the humming street, and the child with its toy!   90
For the priest, and the bell, and the holy well;
For the wheel where I spun,

And the blessed light of the sun!"
And so she sings her fill,
Singing most joyfully,   95
Till the spindle drops from her hand,
And the whizzing wheel stands still.
She steals to the window, and looks at the sand,
And over the sand at the sea;
And her eyes are set in a stare;   100
And anon there breaks a sigh,
And anon there drops a tear,
From a sorrow-clouded eye,
And a heart sorrow-laden,
A long, long sigh;   105
For the cold strange eyes of a little mermaiden
And the gleam of her golden hair.

Come away, away children;
Come children, come down!
The hoarse wind blows coldly;   110
Lights shine in the town.
She will start from her slumber
When gusts shake the door;
She will hear the winds howling,
Will hear the waves roar.   115
We shall see, while above us
The waves roar and whirl,
A ceiling of amber,
A pavement of pearl.
Singing: "Here came a mortal,   120
But faithless was she!
And alone dwell forever
The kings of the sea."

But, children, at midnight,
When soft the winds blow,   125
When clear falls the moonlight,
When spring tides are low;
When sweet airs come seaward
From heaths starred with broom,
And high rocks throw mildly   130

On the blanched sands a gloom;
Up the still, glistening beaches,
Up the creeks we will hie,
Over banks of bright seaweed
The ebb tide leaves dry.   135
We will gaze, from the sand hills,
At the white, sleeping town;
At the church on the hillside—
And then come back down.
Singing: "There dwells a loved one,   140
But cruel is she!
She left lonely forever
The kings of the sea."

THE BURIED LIFE

Light flows our war of mocking words, and yet,
Behold, with tears mine eyes are wet!
I feel a nameless sadness o'er me roll.
Yes, yes, we know that we can jest,
We know, we know that we can smile!   5
But there's a something in this breast,
To which thy light words bring no rest,
And thy gay smiles no anodyne.
Give me thy hand, and hush awhile,
And turn those limpid eyes on mine,   10
And let me read there, love! thy inmost soul.

Alas! is even love too weak
To unlock the heart, and let it speak?
Are even lovers powerless to reveal
To one another what indeed they feel?   15
I knew the mass of men concealed
Their thoughts, for fear that if revealed
They would by other men be met
With blank indifference, or with blame reproved;
I knew they lived and moved   20
Tricked in disguises, alien to the rest
Of men, and alien to themselves—and yet

The same heart beats in every human breast!
But we, my love!—doth a like spell benumb
Our hearts, our voices?—must we too be dumb?   25

Ah! well for us, if even we,
Even for a moment, can get free
Our heart, and have our lips unchained;
For that which seals them hath been deep-ordained!

Fate, which foresaw   30
How frivolous a baby man would be—
By what distractions he would be possessed,
How he would pour himself in every strife,
And well-nigh change his own identity—
That it might keep from his capricious play   35
His genuine self, and force him to obey
Even in his own despite his being's law,
Bade through the deep recesses of our breast
The unregarded river of our life
Pursue with indiscernible flow its way;   40
And that we should not see
The buried stream, and seem to be
Eddying at large in blind uncertainty,
Though driving on with it eternally.

But often, in the world's most crowded streets,   45
But often, in the din of strife,
There rises an unspeakable desire
After the knowledge of our buried life;
A thirst to spend our fire and restless force
In tracking out our true, original course;   50
A longing to inquire
Into the mystery of this heart which beats
So wild, so deep in us—to know
Whence our lives come and where they go.
And many a man in his own breast then delves,   55
But deep enough, alas! none ever mines.
And we have been on many thousand lines,
And we have shown, on each, spirit and power;
But hardly have we, for one little hour,
Been on our own line, have we been ourselves—   60

Hardly had skill to utter one of all
The nameless feelings that course through our breast,
But they course on forever unexpressed.
And long we try in vain to speak and act
Our hidden self, and what we say and do   65
Is eloquent, is well—but 'tis not true!
And then we will no more be racked
With inward striving, and demand
Of all the thousand nothings of the hour
Their stupefying power;   70
Ah yes, and they benumb us at our call!
Yet still, from time to time, vague and forlorn,
From the soul's subterranean depth upborne
As from an infinitely distant land,
Come airs, and floating echoes, and convey   75
A melancholy into all our day.

Only—but this is rare—
When a beloved hand is laid in ours,
When, jaded with the rush and glare
Of the interminable hours,   80
Our eyes can in another's eyes read clear,
When our world-deafened ear
Is by the tones of a loved voice caressed—
A bolt is shot back somewhere in our breast,
And a lost pulse of feeling stirs again.   85
The eye sinks inward, and the heart lies plain,
And what we mean, we say, and what we would, we know.
A man becomes aware of his life's flow,
And hears its winding murmur; and he sees
The meadows where it glides, the sun, the breeze.   90

And there arrives a lull in the hot race
Wherein he doth forever chase
That flying and elusive shadow, rest.
An air of coolness plays upon his face,
And an unwonted calm pervades his breast.   95
And then he thinks he knows
The hills where his life rose,
And the sea where it goes.

DOVER BEACH

The sea is calm tonight.
The tide is full, the moon lies fair
Upon the straits—on the French coast the light
Gleams and is gone; the cliffs of England stand,
Glimmering and vast, out in the tranquil bay.   5
Come to the window, sweet is the night air!
Only, from the long line of spray
Where the sea meets the moon-blanched land,
Listen! you hear the grating roar
Of pebbles which the waves draw back, and fling,   10
At their return, up the high strand,
Begin, and cease, and then again begin,
With tremulous cadence slow, and bring
The eternal note of sadness in.

Sophocles long ago   15
Heard it on the Aegean, and it brought
Into his mind the turbid ebb and flow
Of human misery; we
Find also in the sound a thought,
Hearing it by this distant northern sea.   20

The Sea of Faith
Was once, too, at the full, and round earth's shore
Lay like the folds of a bright girdle furled.
But now I only hear
Its melancholy, long, withdrawing roar,   25
Retreating, to the breath
Of the night wind, down the vast edges drear
And naked shingles of the world.

Ah, love, let us be true
To one another! for the world, which seems   30
To lie before us like a land of dreams,
So various, so beautiful, so new,
Hath really neither joy, nor love, nor light,
Nor certitude, nor peace, nor help for pain;
And we are here as on a darkling plain   35
Swept with confused alarms of struggle and flight,
Where ignorant armies clash by night.

George Meredith

LUCIFER IN STARLIGHT

On a starred night Prince Lucifer uprose.
Tired of his dark dominion, swung the fiend
Above the rolling ball, in cloud part screened,
Where sinners hugged their specter of repose.
Poor prey to his hot fit of pride were those.   5
And now upon his western wing he leaned,
Now his huge bulk o'er Afric's sands careened,
Now the black planet shadowed Arctic snows.
Soaring through wider zones that pricked his scars
With memory of the old revolt from awe,   10
He reached a middle height, and at the stars,
Which are the brain of heaven, he looked, and sank.
Around the ancient track marched, rank on rank,
The army of unalterable law.

Christina Rossetti

SONG

When I am dead, my dearest,
    Sing no sad songs for me;
Plant thou no roses at my head,
    Nor shady cypress tree.
Be the green grass above me   5
    With showers and dewdrops wet;
And if thou wilt, remember,
    And if thou wilt, forget.

I shall not see the shadows,
   I shall not feel the rain;   10
I shall not hear the nightingale
   Sing on as if in pain.
And dreaming through the twilight
   That doth not rise nor set,
Haply I may remember,   15
   And haply may forget.

Emily Dickinson *

THESE ARE THE DAYS WHEN BIRDS COME BACK

These are the days when Birds come back—
A very few—a Bird or two—
To take a backward look.

These are the days when skies resume
The old—old sophistries of June—   5
A blue and gold mistake.

Oh fraud that cannot cheat the Bee—
Almost thy plausibility
Induces my belief.

Till ranks of seeds their witness bear—   10
And softly thro' the altered air
Hurries a timid leaf.

---

* By direction of the Harvard University Press, the publisher, the poems of Emily Dickinson are reprinted exactly as printed in *The Poems of Emily Dickinson,* although this has meant reproducing the poet's oddities of spelling and punctuation. The editor of that edition suggests that Emily Dickinson would have expected such incidental eccentricities to be regularized had she published her poems.

7. *cannot cheat the Bee:* probably a reference to one of the apocryphal tales of Solomon, who is said to have introduced a bee into a room to distinguish between real and artificial flowers. The bee of course flew to the real flower.

Oh Sacrament of summer days,
Oh Last Communion in the Haze—
Permit a child to join.   15

Thy sacred emblems to partake—
Thy consecrated bread to take
And thine immortal wine!

THERE'S A CERTAIN SLANT OF LIGHT

There's a certain Slant of light,
Winter Afternoons—
That oppresses, like the Heft
Of Cathedral Tunes—

Heavenly Hurt, it gives us—   5
We can find no scar,
But internal difference,
Where the Meanings, are—

None may teach it—Any—
'Tis the Seal Despair—   10
An imperial affliction
Sent us of the Air—

When it comes, the Landscape listens—
Shadows—hold their breath—
When it goes, 'tis like the Distance   15
On the look of Death—

I FELT A FUNERAL, IN MY BRAIN

I felt a Funeral, in my Brain,
And Mourners to and fro
Kept treading—treading—till it seemed
That Sense was breaking through—

And when they all were seated,   5
A Service, like a Drum—
Kept beating—beating—till I thought
My Mind was going numb—

And then I heard them lift a Box
And creak across my Soul   10
With those same Boots of Lead, again,
Then Space—began to toll,

As all the Heavens were a Bell,
And Being, but an Ear,
And I, and Silence, some strange Race   15
Wrecked, solitary, here—

And then a Plank in Reason, broke,
And I dropped down, and down—
And hit a World, at every plunge,
And Finished knowing—then—   20

AFTER GREAT PAIN, A FORMAL FEELING COMES

After great pain, a formal feeling comes—
The Nerves sit ceremonious, like Tombs—
The stiff Heart questions was it He, that bore,
And Yesterday, or Centuries before?

The Feet, mechanical, go round—   5
A Wooden way
Of Ground, or Air, or Ought—
Regardless grown,
A Quartz contentment, like a stone-

This is the Hour of Lead—   10
Remembered, if outlived,
As Freezing persons, recollect the Snow—
First—Chill—then Stupor—then the letting go—

7. *Ought:* probably a misspelling for *aught.*

I HEARD A FLY BUZZ—WHEN I DIED

I heard a Fly buzz—when I died—
The Stillness in the Room
Was like the Stillness in the Air—
Between the Heaves of Storm—

The Eyes around—had wrung them dry— 5
And Breaths were gathering firm
For that last Onset—when the King
Be witnessed—in the Room—

I willed my Keepsakes—Signed away
What portion of me be 10
Assignable—and then it was
There interposed a Fly—

With Blue—uncertain stumbling Buzz—
Between the light—and me—
And then the Windows failed—and then 15
I could not see to see—

'TWAS WARM—AT FIRST—LIKE US

'Twas warm—at first—like Us—
Until there crept upon
A Chill—like frost upon a Glass—
Till all the scene—be gone.

The Forehead copied Stone— 5
The Fingers grew too cold
To ache—and like a Skater's Brook—
The busy eyes—congealed—

It straightened—that was all—
It crowded Cold to Cold— 10
It multiplied indifference—
As Pride were all it could—

And even when with Cords—
'Twas lowered, like a Weight—
It made no Signal, nor demurred, 15
But dropped like Adamant.

BECAUSE I COULD NOT STOP FOR DEATH

Because I could not stop for Death—
He kindly stopped for me—
The Carriage held but just Ourselves—
And Immortality.

We slowly drove—He knew no haste   5
And I had put away
My labor and my leisure too,
For His Civility—

We passed the School, where Children strove
At Recess—in the Ring—   10
We passed the Fields of Gazing Grain—
We passed the Setting Sun—

Or rather—He passed Us—
The Dews drew quivering and chill—
For only Gossamer, my Gown—   15
My Tippet—only Tulle—

We paused before a House that seemed
A Swelling of the Ground—
The Roof was scarcely visible—
The Cornice—in the Ground—   20

Since then—'tis Centuries—and yet
Feels shorter than the Day
I first surmised the Horses Heads
Were toward Eternity—

AND THIS OF ALL MY HOPES

And this of all my Hopes
This, is the silent end
Bountiful colored, my Morning rose
Early and sere, it's end

4. *it's:* no doubt a misspelling of *its.*

Never Bud from a Stem 5
Stepped with so gay a Foot
Never a Worm so confident
Bored at so brave a Root

FURTHER IN SUMMER THAN THE BIRDS

Further in Summer than the Birds
Pathetic from the Grass
A minor Nation celebrates
It's unobtrusive Mass.

No Ordinance be seen 5
So gradual the Grace
A pensive Custom it becomes
Enlarging Loneliness.

Antiquest felt at Noon
When August burning low 10
Arise this spectral Canticle
Repose to typify

Remit as yet no Grace
No Furrow on the Glow
Yet a Druidic Difference 15
Enhances Nature now

4. *it's:* no doubt a misspelling of *its.*
9. *Antiquest:* most antique.

THE LAST NIGHT THAT SHE LIVED

The last Night that She lived
It was a Common Night
Except the Dying—this to Us
Made Nature different

We noticed smallest things— 5
Things overlooked before
By this great light upon our Minds
Italicized—as 'twere.

As We went out and in
Between Her final Room   10
And Rooms where Those to be alive
Tomorrow were, a Blame

That Others could exist
While She must finish quite
A Jealousy for Her arose   15
So nearly infinite—

We waited while She passed—
It was a narrow time—
Too jostled were Our Souls to speak
At length the notice came.   20

She mentioned, and forgot—
Then lightly as a Reed
Bent to the Water, struggled scarce—
Consented, and was dead—

And We—We placed the Hair—   25
And drew the Head erect—
And then an awful leisure was
Belief to regulate—

A ROUTE OF EVANESCENCE *

A Route of Evanescence
With a revolving Wheel—
A Resonance of Emerald—
A Rush of Cochineal—
And every Blossom on the Bush   5
Adjusts it's tumbled Head—
The mail from Tunis, probably,
An easy Morning's Ride—

* In her correspondence, Emily Dickinson named the subject of this poem
"A Humming-Bird."
6. it's: no doubt a misspelling of its.
7. The mail from Tunis: probably a reference to Shakespeare's The Tempest
(II, i, 247–248), where it is reported that a person in Tunis is so distant
from Naples that she "can have no note, unless the sun were post."

AS IMPERCEPTIBLY AS GRIEF

As imperceptibly as Grief
The Summer lapsed away—
Too imperceptible at last
To seem like Perfidy—
A Quietness distilled   5
As Twilight long begun,
Or Nature spending with herself
Sequestered Afternoon—
The Dusk drew earlier in—
The Morning foreign shone—   10
A courteous, yet harrowing Grace,
As Guest, that would be gone—
And thus, without a Wing
Or service of a Keel
Our Summer made her light escape   15
Into the Beautiful.

Algernon Charles Swinburne

THE GARDEN OF PROSERPINE

Here, where the world is quiet;
  Here, where all trouble seems
Dead winds' and spent waves' riot
  In doubtful dreams of dreams;
I watch the green field growing   5
For reaping folk and sowing,
For harvest time and mowing,
  A sleepy world of streams.

I am tired of tears and laughter,
  And men that laugh and weep;   10
Of what may come hereafter
  For men that sow to reap;

I am weary of days and hours,
Blown buds of barren flowers,
Desires and dreams and powers 15
   And everything but sleep.

Here life has death for neighbor,
   And far from eye or ear
Wan waves and wet winds labor,
   Weak ships and spirits steer; 20
They drive adrift, and whither
They wot not who make thither;
But no such winds blow hither,
   And no such things grow here.

No growth of moor or coppice, 25
   No heather flower or vine,
But bloomless buds of poppies,
   Green grapes of Proserpine,
Pale beds of blowing rushes,
Where no leaf blooms or blushes 30
Save this whereout she crushes
   For dead men deadly wine.

Pale, without name or number,
   In fruitless fields of corn,
They bow themselves and slumber 35
   All night till light is born;
And like a soul belated,
In hell and heaven unmated,
By cloud and mist abated
   Comes out of darkness morn. 40

Though one were strong as seven,
   He too with death shall dwell,
Nor wake with wings in heaven,
   Nor weep for pains in hell;
Though one were fair as roses, 45
His beauty clouds and closes;
And well though love reposes,
   In the end it is not well.

Pale, beyond porch and portal,
   Crowned with calm leaves, she stands   50
Who gathers all things mortal
   With cold immortal hands;
Her languid lips are sweeter
Than love's who fears to greet her
To men that mix and meet her   55
   From many times and lands.

She waits for each and other,
   She waits for all men born;
Forgets the earth her mother,
   The life of fruits and corn;   60
And spring and seed and swallow
Take wing for her and follow
Where summer song rings hollow
   And flowers are put to scorn.

There go the loves that wither,   65
   The old loves with wearier wings;
And all dead years draw thither,
   And all disastrous things;
Dead dreams of days forsaken,
Blind buds that snows have shaken,   70
Wild leaves that winds have taken,
   Red strays of ruined springs.

We are not sure of sorrow,
   And joy was never sure;
Today will die tomorrow;   75
   Time stoops to no man's lure;
And love, grown faint and fretful,
With lips but half regretful
Sighs, and with eyes forgetful
   Weeps that no loves endure.   80

From too much love of living,
   From hope and fear set free,
We thank with brief thanksgiving
   Whatever gods may be
That no life lives forever;   85

That dead men rise up never;
That even the weariest river
   Winds somewhere safe to sea.

Then star nor sun shall waken,
   Nor any change of light: 90
Nor sound of waters shaken,
   Nor any sound or sight:
Nor wintry leaves nor vernal,
Nor days nor things diurnal;
Only the sleep eternal   95
   In an eternal night.

Thomas Hardy

THE DARKLING THRUSH

I leant upon a coppice gate
   When Frost was specter-gray,
And Winter's dregs made desolate
   The weakening eye of day.
The tangled bine-stems scored the sky   5
   Like strings of broken lyres,
And all mankind that haunted nigh
   Had sought their household fires.

The land's sharp features seemed to be
   The century's corpse outleant,   10
His crypt the cloudy canopy,
   The wind his death lament.
The ancient pulse of germ and birth
   Was shrunken hard and dry,
And every spirit upon earth   15
   Seemed fervorless as I.

At once a voice arose among
    The bleak twigs overhead
In a fullhearted evensong
    Of joy illimited;   20
An aged thrush, frail, gaunt, and small,
    In blast-beruffled plume,
Had chosen thus to fling his soul
    Upon the growing gloom.

CHANNEL FIRING

That night your great guns, unawares,
Shook all our coffins as we lay,
And broke the chancel window-squares,
We thought it was the Judgment Day

And sat upright. While drearisome   5
Arose the howl of wakened hounds:
The mouse let fall the altar-crumb,
The worms drew back into the mounds,

The glebe cow drooled. Till God called, "No;
It's gunnery practice out at sea   10
Just as before you went below;
The world is as it used to be:

"All nations striving strong to make
Red war yet redder. Mad as hatters
They do no more for Christès sake   15
Than you who are helpless in such matters.

"That this is not the judgment hour
For some of them's a blessed thing,
For if it were they'd have to scour
Hell's floor for so much threatening. . . .   20

"Ha, ha. It will be warmer when
I blow the trumpet (if indeed
I ever do; for you are men,
And rest eternal sorely need)."

So down we lay again. "I wonder,   25
Will the world ever saner be,"
Said one, "than when He sent us under
In our indifferent century!"

And many a skeleton shook his head.
"Instead of preaching forty year,"   30
My neighbor Parson Thirdly said,
"I wish I had stuck to pipes and beer."

Again the guns disturbed the hour,
Roaring their readiness to avenge,
As far inland as Stourton Tower,   35
And Camelot, and starlit Stonehenge.

35. *Stourton Tower:* a stone tower in southwest England, thought to be built for defensive purposes by Alfred the Great.

DURING WIND AND RAIN

They sing their dearest songs—
He, she, all of them—yea,
Treble and tenor and bass,
    And one to play;
With the candles mooning each face. . . .   5
    Ah, no; the years O!
How the sick leaves reel down in throngs!

They clear the creeping moss—
Elders and juniors—aye,
Making the pathways neat   10
    And the garden gay;
And they build a shady seat. . . .
    Ah, no; the years, the years;
See, the white stormbirds wing across!

They are blithely breakfasting all—   15
Men and maidens—yea,
Under the summer tree,
    With a glimpse of the bay,
While pet fowl come to the knee. . . .
    Ah, no; the years O!   20
And the rotten rose is ripped from the wall.

They change to a high new house,
He, she, all of them—aye,
Clocks and carpets and chairs
On the lawn all day,   25
And brightest things that are theirs. . . .
Ah, no; the years, the years;
Down their carved names the raindrop plows.

IN TIME OF "THE BREAKING OF NATIONS"

[1]

Only a man harrowing clods
In a slow silent walk
With an old horse that stumbles and nods
Half asleep as they stalk.

[2]

Only thin smoke without flame   5
From the heaps of crouch-grass;
Yet this will go onward the same
Though dynasties pass.

[3]

Yonder a maid and her wight
Come whispering by;   10
War's annals will cloud into night
Ere their story die.

AFTERWARDS

When the present has latched its postern behind my tremulous
    stay,
And the May month flaps its glad green leaves like wings,
Delicate-filmed as new-spun silk, will the neighbors say,
    "He was a man who used to notice such things"?

If it be in the dusk when, like an eyelid's soundless blink,   5
    The dewfall-hawk comes crossing the shades to alight
Upon the wind-warped upland thorn, a gazer may think,
    "To him this must have been a familiar sight."

If I pass during some nocturnal blackness, mothy and warm,
    When the hedgehog travels furtively over the lawn,   10
One may say, "He strove that such innocent creatures should
        come to no harm,
    But he could do little for them; and now he is gone."

If, when hearing that I have been stilled at last, they stand at
        the door,
    Watching the full-starred heavens that winter sees,
Will this thought rise on those who will meet my face no more,   15
    "He was one who had an eye for such mysteries"?

And will any say when my bell of quittance is heard in the
        gloom,
    And a crossing breeze cuts a pause in its outrollings,
Till they rise again, as they were a new bell's boom,
    "He hears it not now, but used to notice such things"?   20

Gerard Manley Hopkins

THE HABIT OF PERFECTION

    Elected silence, sing to me
    And beat upon my whorlèd ear,
    Pipe me to pastures still and be
    The music that I care to hear.

    Shape nothing, lips; be lovely-dumb: 5
    It is the shut, the curfew sent
    From there where all surrenders come
    Which only makes you eloquent.

Be shellèd, eyes, with double dark
And find the uncreated light: 10
This ruck and reel which you remark
Coils, keeps, and teases simple sight.

Palate, the hutch of tasty lust,
Desire not to be rinsed with wine:
The can must be so sweet, the crust   15
So fresh that come in fasts divine!

Nostrils, your careless breath that spend
Upon the stir and keep of pride,
What relish shall the censers send
Along the sanctuary side!   20

O feel-of-primrose hands, O feet
That want the yield of plushy sward,
But you shall walk the golden street
And you unhouse and house the Lord.

And, poverty, be thou the bride   25
And now the marriage feast begun,
And lily-colored clothes provide
Your spouse not labored-at nor spun.

GOD'S GRANDEUR

The world is charged with the grandeur of God.
  It will flame out, like shining from shook foil;
  It gathers to a greatness, like the ooze of oil
Crushed. Why do men then now not reck his rod?
Generations have trod, have trod, have trod;   5
  And all is seared with trade; bleared, smeared with toil;
  And wears man's smudge and shares man's smell: the soil
Is bare now, nor can foot feel, being shod.

And for all this, nature is never spent;
  There lives the dearest freshness deep down things;   10
And though the last lights off the black West went
  Oh, morning, at the brown brink eastward, springs—
Because the Holy Ghost over the bent
  World broods with warm breast and with ah! bright wings.

SPRING

Nothing is so beautiful as spring—
    When weeds, in wheels, shoot long and lovely and lush;
    Thrush's eggs look little low heavens, and thrush
Through the echoing timber does so rinse and wring
The ear, it strikes like lightnings to hear him sing;   5
    The glassy peartree leaves and blooms, they brush
    The descending blue; that blue is all in a rush
With richness; the racing lambs too have fair their fling.

What is all this juice and all this joy?
    A strain of the earth's sweet being in the beginning   10
In Eden garden.—Have, get, before it cloy,
    Before it cloud, Christ, lord, and sour with sinning,
Innocent mind and Mayday in girl and boy,
Most, O maid's child, thy choice and worthy the winning.

THE WINDHOVER

TO CHRIST OUR LORD

I caught this morning morning's minion, king-
    dom of daylight's dauphin, dapple-drawn-drawn Falcon, in
        his riding
Of the rolling level underneath him steady air, and striding
High there, how he rung upon the rein of a wimpling wing
In his ecstasy! then off, off forth on swing,   5
    As a skate's heel sweeps smooth on a bow-bend: the hurl and
        gliding
Rebuffed the big wind. My heart in hiding
Stirred for a bird,—the achieve of, the mastery of the thing!

Brute beauty and valor and act, oh, air, pride, plume here
    Buckle! AND the fire that breaks from thee then, a billion   10
Times told lovelier, more dangerous, O my chevalier!

No wonder of it: sheer plod makes plough down sillion
Shine, and blue-bleak embers, ah my dear,
    Fall, gall themselves, and gash gold-vermilion.

12. *sillion:* a ridge between plowed furrows.

NO WORST, THERE IS NONE

No worst, there is none. Pitched past pitch of grief,
More pangs will, schooled at forepangs, wilder wring.
Comforter, where, where is your comforting?
Mary, mother of us, where is your relief?

My cries heave, herds-long, huddle in a main, a chief   5
Woe, world-sorrow; on an age-old anvil wince and sing—
Then lull, then leave off. Fury had shrieked "No ling-
ering! Let me be fell: force I must be brief."

O the mind, mind has mountains; cliffs of fall
Frightful, sheer, no-man-fathomed. Hold them cheap   10
May who ne'er hung there. Nor does long our small
Durance deal with that steep or deep. Here! creep,
Wretch, under a comfort serves in a whirlwind: all
Life death does end and each day dies with sleep.

I WAKE AND FEEL THE FELL OF
DARK, NOT DAY

I wake and feel the fell of dark, not day.
What hours, O what black hoürs we have spent
This night! what sights you, heart, saw; ways you went!
And more must, in yet longer light's delay.
    With witness I speak this. But where I say   5
Hours I mean years, mean life. And my lament
Is cries countless, cries like dead letters sent
To dearest him that lives alas! away.

I am gall, I am heartburn. God's most deep decree
Bitter would have me taste: my taste was me;   10
Bones built in me, flesh filled, blood brimmed the curse.
    Selfyeast of spirit a dull dough sours. I see
The lost are like this, and their scourge to be
As I am mine, their sweating selves; but worse.

IN HONOR OF
ST. ALPHONSUS RODRIGUEZ

LAYBROTHER OF THE SOCIETY OF JESUS

Honor is flashed off exploit, so we say;
And those strokes once that gashed flesh or galled shield
Should tongue that time now, trumpet now that field,
And, on the fighter, forge his glorious day.
On Christ they do and on the martyr may;   5
But be the war within, the brand we wield
Unseen, the heroic breast not outward-steeled,
Earth hears no hurtle then from fiercest fray.

   Yet God (that hews mountain and continent,
Earth, all, out; who, with trickling increment,   10
Veins violets and tall trees makes more and more)
Could crowd career with conquest while there went
Those years and years by of world without event
That in Majorca Alfonso watched the door.

Robert Bridges

NIGHTINGALES

Beautiful must be the mountains whence ye come,
And bright in the fruitful valleys the streams wherefrom
    Ye learn your song:
Where are those starry woods? O might I wander there,
  Among the flowers, which in that heavenly air   5
    Bloom the year long!

Nay, barren are those mountains and spent the streams:
Our song is the voice of desire, that haunts our dreams,
    A throe of the heart,
Whose pining visions dim, forbidden hopes profound,   10
  No dying cadence nor long sigh can sound,
    For all our art.

Alone, aloud in the raptured ear of men
We pour our dark nocturnal secret; and then,
    As night is withdrawn 15
From these sweet-springing meads and bursting boughs of May,
  Dream, while the innumerable choir of day
    Welcome the dawn.

A PASSER-BY

Whither, O splendid ship, thy white sails crowding,
  Leaning across the bosom of the urgent West,
That fearest nor sea rising nor sky clouding,
  Whither away, fair rover, and what thy quest?
  Ah! soon, when winter has all our vales opprest, 5
When skies are cold and misty, and hail is hurling,
  Wilt thou glide on the blue Pacific, or rest
In a summer haven asleep, thy white sails furling.

I there before thee, in the country that well thou knowest,
  Already arrived am inhaling the odorous air: 10
I watch thee enter unerringly where thou goest,
  And anchor queen of the strange shipping there,
  Thy sails for awnings spread, thy masts bare;
Nor is aught from the foaming reef to the snow-capp'd, grandest
  Peak, that is over the feathery palms, more fair 15
Than thou, so upright, so stately, and still thou standest.

And yet, O splendid ship, unhail'd and nameless,
  I know not if, aiming a fancy, I rightly divine
That thou hast a purpose joyful, a courage blameless,
  Thy port assured in a happier land than mine. 20
  But for all I have given thee, beauty enough is thine,
As thou, aslant with trim tackle and shrouding,
  From the proud nostril curve of a prow's line
In the offing scatterest foam, thy white sails crowding.

LOW BAROMETER

The south-wind strengthens to a gale,
Across the moon the clouds fly fast,
The house is smitten as with a flail,
The chimney shudders to the blast.

On such a night, when air has loosed 5
Its guardian grasp on blood and brain,
Old terrors then of god or ghost
Creep from their caves to life again;

And reason kens he herits in
A haunted house. Tenants unknown 10
Assert their squalid lease of sin
With earlier title than his own.

Unbodied presences, the pack'd
Pollution and remorse of time,
Slipp'd from oblivion reenact 15
The horrors of unhouseled crime.

Some men would quell the thing with prayer
Whose sightless footsteps pad the floor,
Whose fearful trespass mounts the stair
Or bursts the lock'd forbidden door. 20

Some have seen corpses long inter'd
Escape from hallowing control,
Pale charnel forms—nay ev'n have heard
The shrilling of a troubled soul,

That wanders till the dawn hath cross'd 25
The dolorous dark, or earth hath wound
Closer her storm-spread cloke, and thrust
The baleful phantoms under ground.

A. E. Housman

EPITAPH ON AN ARMY OF MERCENARIES

These, in the day when heaven was falling,
   The hour when earth's foundations fled,
Followed their mercenary calling
   And took their wages and are dead.

Their shoulders held the sky suspended;   5
   They stood, and earth's foundations stay;
What God abandoned, these defended,
   And saved the sum of things for pay.

William Butler Yeats

TO A FRIEND WHOSE WORK HAS COME TO NOTHING

Now all the truth is out,
Be secret and take defeat
From any brazen throat,
For how can you compete,
Being honor bred, with one   5
Who, were it proved he lies,
Were neither shamed in his own
Nor in his neighbor's eyes?
Bred to a harder thing
Than triumph, turn away   10
And like a laughing string
Whereon mad fingers play
Amid a place of stone,
Be secret and exult,
Because of all things known   15
That is most difficult.

THE SECOND COMING

Turning and turning in the widening gyre
The falcon cannot hear the falconer;
Things fall apart; the center cannot hold;
Mere anarchy is loosed upon the world,
The blood-dimmed tide is loosed, and everywhere   5
The ceremony of innocence is drowned;
The best lack all conviction, while the worst
Are full of passionate intensity.

Surely some revelation is at hand;
Surely the Second Coming is at hand.   10
The Second Coming! Hardly are those words out
When a vast image out of *Spiritus Mundi*
Troubles my sight: somewhere in sands of the desert
A shape with lion body and the head of a man,
A gaze blank and pitiless as the sun,   15
Is moving its slow thighs, while all about it
Reel shadows of the indignant desert birds.
The darkness drops again; but now I know
That twenty centuries of stony sleep
Were vexed to nightmare by a rocking cradle,   20
And what rough beast, its hour come round at last,
Slouches towards Bethlehem to be born?

12. *Spiritus Mundi:* spirit of the world.

SAILING TO BYZANTIUM

[1]

That is no country for old men. The young
In one another's arms, birds in the trees
—Those dying generations—at their song,
The salmon-falls, the mackerel-crowded seas,
Fish, flesh, or fowl, commend all summer long   5
Whatever is begotten, born, and dies.
Caught in that sensual music all neglect
Monuments of unaging intellect.

[2]

An aged man is but a paltry thing,
A tattered coat upon a stick, unless   10
Soul clap its hands and sing, and louder sing
For every tatter in its mortal dress,
Nor is there singing school but studying
Monuments of its own magnificence;
And therefore I have sailed the seas and come   15
To the holy city of Byzantium.

[3]

O sages standing in God's holy fire   *purgatory*
As in the gold mosaic of a wall,   *Byzantine mosaic*
Come from the holy fire, perne in a gyre,
And be the singing-masters of my soul.   20
passion   Consume my heart away; sick with desire
And fastened to a dying animal   *The body*
It knows not what it is; and gather me
Into the artifice of eternity.

?

[4]

Once out of nature I shall never take   25
My bodily form from any natural thing,
But such a form as Grecian goldsmiths make
most durable   Of hammered gold and gold enameling
To keep a drowsy Emperor awake;
Or set upon a golden bough to sing   30
To lords and ladies of Byzantium
Of what is past, or passing, or to come.

19. *perne:* spin, revolve.   *art needs life for subject*

AMONG SCHOOL CHILDREN

[1]

I walk through the long schoolroom questioning;
A kind old nun in a white hood replies;
The children learn to cipher and to sing,
To study reading-books and history,

To cut and sew, be neat in everything   5
In the best modern way—the children's eyes
In momentary wonder stare upon
A sixty-year-old smiling public man.

[2]

I dream of a Ledaean body, bent
Above a sinking fire, a tale that she   10
Told of a harsh reproof, or trivial event
That changed some childish day to tragedy—
Told, and it seemed that our two natures blent
Into a sphere from youthful sympathy,
Or else, to alter Plato's parable,   15
Into the yolk and white of the one shell.

[3]

And thinking of that fit of grief or rage
I look upon one child or t'other there
And wonder if she stood so at that age—
For even daughters of the swan can share   20
Something of every paddler's heritage—
And had that color upon cheek or hair,
And thereupon my heart is driven wild:
She stands before me as a living child.

[4]

Her present image floats into the mind—   25
Did Quattrocento finger fashion it
Hollow of cheek as though it drank the wind
And took a mess of shadows for its meat?
And I though never of Ledaean kind
Had pretty plumage once—enough of that,   30
Better to smile on all that smile, and show
There is a comfortable kind of old scarecrow.

[5]

What youthful mother, a shape upon her lap
Honey of generation had betrayed,
And that must sleep, shriek, struggle to escape   35

231

As recollection or the drug decide,
Would think her son, did she but see that shape
With sixty or more winters on its head,
A compensation for the pang of his birth,
Or the uncertainty of his setting forth?   40

[6]

Plato thought nature but a spume that plays
Upon a ghostly paradigm of things;
Solider Aristotle played the taws
Upon the bottom of a king of kings;
World-famous golden-thighed Pythagoras   45
Fingered upon a fiddle-stick or strings
What a star sang and careless Muses heard:
Old clothes upon old sticks to scare a bird.

[7]

Both nuns and mothers worship images,
But those the candles light are not as those   50
That animate a mother's reveries,
But keep a marble or a bronze repose.
And yet they too break hearts—O Presences
That passion, piety, or affection knows,
And that all heavenly glory symbolize—   55
O self-born mockers of man's enterprise;

[8]

Labor is blossoming or dancing where
The body is not bruised to pleasure soul,
Nor beauty born out of its own despair,
Nor blear-eyed wisdom out of midnight oil.   60
O chestnut tree, great-rooted blossomer,
Are you the leaf, the blossom, or the bole?
O body swayed to music, O brightening glance,
How can we know the dancer from the dance?

FOR ANNE GREGORY

"Never shall a young man,
Thrown into despair
By those great honey-colored
Ramparts at your ear,
Love you for yourself alone   5
And not your yellow hair."

"But I can get a hair dye
And set such color there,
Brown, or black, or carrot,
That young men in despair   10
May love me for myself alone
And not my yellow hair."

"I heard an old religious man
But yesternight declare
That he had found a text to prove   15
That only God, my dear,
Could love you for yourself alone
And not your yellow hair."

LAPIS LAZULI

(FOR HARRY CLIFTON)

I have heard that hysterical women say
They are sick of the palette and fiddle bow,
Of poets that are always gay,
For everybody knows or else should know
That if nothing drastic is done   5
Aeroplane and zeppelin will come out,
Pitch like King Billy bomb-balls in
Until the town lie beaten flat.

All perform their tragic play,
There struts Hamlet, there is Lear,   10
That's Ophelia, that Cordelia;

7. *King Billy*: King William III, who suppressed an Irish rebellion in the
first years of his reign.

Yet they, should the last scene be there,
The great stage curtain about to drop,
If worthy their prominent part in the play,
Do not break up their lines to weep.   15
They know that Hamlet and Lear are gay;
Gaiety transfiguring all that dread.
All men have aimed at, found and lost;
Black out; Heaven blazing into the head:
Tragedy wrought to its uttermost.   20
Though Hamlet rambles and Lear rages,
And all the drop-scenes drop at once
Upon a hundred thousand stages,
It cannot grow by an inch or an ounce.

On their own feet they came, or on shipboard,   25
Camel-back, horse-back, ass-back, mule-back,
Old civilizations put to the sword.
Then they and their wisdom went to rack:
No handiwork of Callimachus,
   Who handled marble as if it were bronze,   30
Made draperies that seemed to rise
When sea wind swept the corner, stands;
His long lamp chimney shaped like the stem
Of a slender palm, stood but a day;
All things fall and are built again,   35
And those that build them again are gay.

Two Chinamen, behind them a third,
Are carved in lapis lazuli,
Over them flies a long-legged bird,
A symbol of longevity;   40
The third, doubtless a servingman,
Carries a musical instrument.

Every discoloration of the stone,
Every accidental crack or dent,
Seems a watercourse or an avalanche,   45
Or lofty slope where it still snows
Though doubtless plum or cherry branch

29. *Callimachus:* Greek sculptor of the 5th century B.C.

Sweeten the little halfway house
Those Chinamen climb towards, and I
Delight to imagine them seated there;   50
There, on the mountain and the sky,
On all the tragic scene they stare.
One asks for mournful melodies;
Accomplished fingers begin to play.
Their eyes mid many wrinkles, their eyes,   55
Their ancient, glittering eyes, are gay.

LONG-LEGGED FLY

That civilization may not sink,
Its great battle lost,
Quiet the dog, tether the pony
To a distant post;
Our master Caesar is in the tent   5
Where the maps are spread,
His eyes fixed upon nothing,
A hand under his head.
Like a long-legged fly upon the stream
His mind moves upon silence.   10

That the topless towers be burnt
And men recall that face,
Move most gently if move you must
In this lonely place.
She thinks, part woman, three parts a child,   15
That nobody looks; her feet
Practice a tinker shuffle
Picked up on a street.
Like a long-legged fly upon the stream
Her mind moves upon silence.   20

That girls at puberty may find
The first Adam in their thought,
Shut the door of the Pope's chapel,
Keep those children out.
There on that scaffolding reclines   25

Michelangelo.
With no more sound than the mice make
His hand moves to and fro.
Like a long-legged fly upon the stream
His mind moves upon silence.   30

Edwin Arlington Robinson

FOR A DEAD LADY

No more with overflowing light
Shall fill the eyes that now are faded,
Nor shall another's fringe with night
Their woman-hidden world as they did.
No more shall quiver down the days   5
The flowing wonder of her ways,
Whereof no language may requite
The shifting and the many-shaded.

The grace, divine, definitive,
Clings only as a faint forestalling;   10
The laugh that love could not forgive
Is hushed, and answers to no calling;
The forehead and the little ears
Have gone where Saturn keeps the years;
The breast where roses could not live   15
Has done with rising and with falling.

The beauty, shattered by the laws
That have creation in their keeping,
No longer trembles at applause,
Or over children that are sleeping;   20
And we who delve in beauty's lore
Know all that we have known before
Of what inexorable cause
Makes time so vicious in his reaping.

EROS TURANNOS

She fears him, and will always ask
   What fated her to choose him;
She meets in his engaging mask
   All reasons to refuse him;
But what she meets and what she fears   5
Are less than are the downward years,
Drawn slowly to the foamless weirs
   Of age, were she to lose him.

Between a blurred sagacity
   That once had power to sound him,   10
And Love, that will not let him be
   The Judas that she found him,
Her pride assuages her almost,
As if it were alone the cost.—
He sees that he will not be lost,   15
   And waits and looks around him.

A sense of ocean and old trees
   Envelops and allures him;
Tradition, touching all he sees,
   Beguiles and reassures him;   20
And all her doubts of what he says
Are dimmed with what she knows of days—
Till even prejudice delays
   And fades, and she secures him.

The falling leaf inaugurates   25
   The reign of her confusion
The pounding wave reverberates
   The dirge of her illusion;
And home, where passion lived and died,
Becomes a place where she can hide,   30
While all the town and harbor side
   Vibrate with her seclusion.

We tell you, tapping on our brows,
   The story as it should be,—

As if the story of a house   35
  Were told, or ever could be;
We'll have no kindly veil between
Her visions and those we have seen,—
As if we guessed what hers have been,
  Or what they are or would be.   40

Meanwhile we do no harm; for they
  That with a god have striven,
Not hearing much of what we say,
  Take what the god has given;
Though like waves breaking it may be,   45
Or like a changed familiar tree,
Or like a stairway to the sea
  Where down the blind are driven.

LUKE HAVERGAL

Go to the western gate, Luke Havergal,
There where the vines cling crimson on the wall,
And in the twilight wait for what will come.
The leaves will whisper there of her, and some,
Like flying words, will strike you as they fall;   5
But go, and if you listen she will call.
Go to the western gate, Luke Havergal—
Luke Havergal.

No, there is not a dawn in eastern skies
To rift the fiery night that's in your eyes;   10
But there, where western glooms are gathering,
The dark will end the dark, if anything:
God slays Himself with every leaf that flies,
And hell is more than half of paradise.
No, there is not a dawn in eastern skies—   15
In eastern skies.

Out of a grave I come to tell you this,
Out of a grave I come to quench the kiss
That flames upon your forehead with a glow
That blinds you to the way that you must go.   20

238

Yes, there is yet one way to where she is,
Bitter, but one that faith may never miss.
Out of a grave I come to tell you this—
To tell you this.

There is the western gate, Luke Havergal,   25
There are the crimson leaves upon the wall.
Go, for the winds are tearing them away,—
Nor think to riddle the dead words they say,
Nor any more to feel them as they fall;
But go, and if you trust her she will call.   30
There is the western gate, Luke Havergal—
Luke Havergal.

RICHARD CORY

Whenever Richard Cory went down town,
We people on the pavement looked at him:
He was a gentleman from sole to crown,
Clean favored, and imperially slim.

And he was always quietly arrayed,   5
And he was always human when he talked;
But still he fluttered pulses when he said,
"Good-morning," and he glittered when he walked.

And he was rich—yes, richer than a king—
And admirably schooled in every grace: 10
In fine, we thought that he was everything
To make us wish that we were in his place.

So on we worked, and waited for the light,
And went without the meat, and cursed the bread;
And Richard Cory, one calm summer night,   15
Went home and put a bullet through his head.

MINIVER CHEEVY

Miniver Cheevy, child of scorn,
  Grew lean while he assailed the seasons;
He wept that he was ever born,
  And he had reasons.

Miniver loved the days of old   5
  When swords were bright and steeds were prancing;
The vision of a warrior bold
  Would set him dancing.

Miniver sighed for what was not,
  And dreamed, and rested from his labors;   10
He dreamed of Thebes and Camelot,
  And Priam's neighbors.

Miniver mourned the ripe renown
  That made so many a name so fragrant;
He mourned Romance, now on the town,   15
  And Art, a vagrant.

Miniver loved the Medici,
  Albeit he had never seen one;
He would have sinned incessantly
  Could he have been one.   20

Miniver cursed the commonplace
  And eyed a khaki suit with loathing;
He missed the medieval grace
  Of iron clothing.

Miniver scorned the gold he sought,   25
  But sore annoyed was he without it;
Miniver thought, and thought, and thought,
  And thought about it.

Miniver Cheevy, born too late,
  Scratched his head and kept on thinking;   30
Miniver coughed, and called it fate,
  And kept on drinking.

BEWICK FINZER

Time was when his half million drew
    The breath of six per cent;
But soon the worm of what-was-not
    Fed hard on his content;
And something crumbled in his brain   5
    When his half million went.

Time passed, and filled along with his
    The place of many more;
Time came, and hardly one of us
    Had credence to restore,   10
From what appeared one day, the man
    Whom we had known before.

The broken voice, the withered neck,
    The coat worn out with care,
The cleanliness of indigence,   15
    The brilliance of despair,
The fond imponderable dreams
    Of affluence,—all were there.

Poor Finzer, with his dreams and schemes,
    Fares hard now in the race,   20
With heart and eye that have a task
    When he looks in the face
Of one who might so easily
    Have been in Finzer's place.

He comes unfailing for the loan   25
    We give and then forget;
He comes, and probably for years
    Will he be coming yet,—
Familiar as an old mistake,
    And futile as regret.   30

THE MILL

The miller's wife had waited long,
   The tea was cold, the fire was dead;
And there might yet be nothing wrong
   In how he went and what he said:
"There are no millers any more,"   5
   Was all that she had heard him say;
And he had lingered at the door
   So long that it seemed yesterday.

Sick with a fear that had no form
   She knew that she was there at last;   10
And in the mill there was a warm
   And mealy fragrance of the past.
What else there was would only seem
   To say again what he had meant;
And what was hanging from a beam   15
   Would not have heeded where she went.

And if she thought it followed her,
   She may have reasoned in the dark
That one way of the few there were
   Would hide her and would leave no mark: 20
Black water, smooth above the weir
   Like starry velvet in the night,
Though ruffled once, would soon appear
   The same as ever to the sight.

THE SHEAVES

Where long the shadows of the wind had rolled,
Green wheat was yielding to the change assigned;
And as by some vast magic undivined
The world was turning slowly into gold.
Like nothing that was ever bought or sold   5
It waited there, the body and the mind;
And with a mighty meaning of a kind
That tells the more the more it is not told.

So in a land where all days are not fair,
Fair days went on till on another day   10
A thousand golden sheaves were lying there,
Shining and still, but not for long to stay—
As if a thousand girls with golden hair
Might rise from where they slept and go away.

NEW ENGLAND

Here where the wind is always north-north-east
And children learn to walk on frozen toes,
Wonder begets an envy of all those
Who boil elsewhere with such a lyric yeast
Of love that you will hear them at a feast   5
Where demons would appeal for some repose,
Still clamoring where the chalice overflows
And crying wildest who have drunk the least.

Passion is here a soilure of the wits,
We're told, and Love a cross for them to bear;   10
Joy shivers in the corner where she knits
And Conscience always has the rocking-chair,
Cheerful as when she tortured into fits
The first cat that was ever killed by Care.

Robert Frost

AFTER APPLE-PICKING

My long two-pointed ladder's sticking through a tree
Toward heaven still,
And there's a barrel that I didn't fill
Beside it, and there may be two or three
Apples I didn't pick upon some bough.   5
But I am done with apple-picking now.

Essence of winter sleep is on the night,
The scent of apples: I am drowsing off.
I cannot rub the strangeness from my sight
I got from looking through a pane of glass   10
I skimmed this morning from the drinking trough
And held against the world of hoary grass.
It melted, and I let it fall and break.
But I was well
Upon my way to sleep before it fell,   15
And I could tell
What form my dreaming was about to take.
Magnified apples appear and disappear,
Stem end and blossom end,
And every fleck of russet showing clear.   20
My instep arch not only keeps the ache,
It keeps the pressure of a ladder-round.
I feel the ladder sway as the boughs bend.
And I keep hearing from the cellar bin
The rumbling sound   25
Of load on load of apples coming in.

For I have had too much
Of apple-picking: I am overtired
Of the great harvest I myself desired.
There were ten thousand thousand fruit to touch, 30
Cherish in hand, lift down, and not let fall.
For all
That struck the earth,
No matter if not bruised or spiked with stubble,
Went surely to the cider-apple heap   35
As of no worth.
One can see what will trouble
This sleep of mine, whatever sleep it is.
Were he not gone,
The woodchuck could say whether it's like his   40
Long sleep, as I describe its coming on,
Or just some human sleep.

THE OVEN BIRD

There is a singer everyone has heard,
Loud, a mid-summer and a mid-wood bird,
Who makes the solid tree trunks sound again.
He says that leaves are old and that for flowers
Mid-summer is to spring as one to ten.   5
He says the early petal-fall is past
When pear and cherry bloom went down in showers
On sunny days a moment overcast;
And comes that other fall we name the fall.
He says the highway dust is over all.   10
The bird would cease and be as other birds
But that he knows in singing not to sing.
The question that he frames in all but words
Is what to make of a diminished thing.

STOPPING BY WOODS ON A
SNOWY EVENING

Whose woods these are I think I know.
His house is in the village though;
He will not see me stopping here
To watch his woods fill up with snow.

My little horse must think it queer   5
To stop without a farmhouse near
Between the woods and frozen lake
The darkest evening of the year.

He gives his harness bells a shake
To ask if there is some mistake.   10
The only other sound's the sweep
Of easy wind and downy flake.

The woods are lovely, dark and deep,
But I have promises to keep,
And miles to go before I sleep,   15
And miles to go before I sleep.

FOR ONCE, THEN, SOMETHING

Others taunt me with having knelt at well-curbs
Always wrong to the light, so never seeing
Deeper down in the well than where the water
Gives me back in a shining surface picture
Me myself in the summer heaven godlike   5
Looking out of a wreath of fern and cloud puffs.
Once, when trying with chin against a well-curb,
I discerned, as I thought, beyond the picture,
Through the picture, a something white, uncertain,
Something more of the depths—and then I lost it.   10
Water came to rebuke the too clear water.
One drop fell from a fern, and lo, a ripple
Shook whatever it was lay there at bottom,
Blurred it, blotted it out. What was that whiteness?
Truth? A pebble of quartz? For once, then, something. 15

ACQUAINTED WITH THE NIGHT

I have been one acquainted with the night.
I have walked out in rain—and back in rain.
I have outwalked the furthest city light.

I have looked down the saddest city lane.
I have passed by the watchman on his beat   5
And dropped my eyes, unwilling to explain.

I have stood still and stopped the sound of feet
When far away an interrupted cry
Came over houses from another street,

But not to call me back or say good-by;   10
And further still at an unearthly height,
One luminary clock against the sky

Proclaimed the time was neither wrong nor right.
I have been one acquainted with the night.

DESERT PLACES

Snow falling and night falling fast, oh, fast
In a field I looked into going past,
And the ground almost covered smooth in snow,
But a few weeds and stubble showing last.

The woods around it have it—it is theirs.   5
All animals are smothered in their lairs.
I am too absent-spirited to count;
The loneliness includes me unawares.

And lonely as it is that loneliness
Will be more lonely ere it will be less—   10
A blanker whiteness of benighted snow
With no expression, nothing to express.

They cannot scare me with their empty spaces
Between stars—on stars where no human race is.
I have it in me so much nearer home   15
To scare myself with my own desert places.

NEVER AGAIN WOULD BIRDS' SONG
BE THE SAME

He would declare and could himself believe
That the birds there in all the garden round
From having heard the daylong voice of Eve
Had added to their own an oversound,
Her tone of meaning but without the words.   5
Admittedly an eloquence so soft
Could only have had an influence on birds
When call or laughter carried it aloft.
Be that as may be, she was in their song.
Moreover her voice upon their voices crossed   10
Had now persisted in the woods so long
That probably it never would be lost.
Never again would birds' song be the same.
And to do that to birds was why she came.

COME IN

As I came to the edge of the woods,
Thrush music—hark!
Now if it was dusk outside,
Inside it was dark.

Too dark in the woods for a bird   5
By sleight of wing
To better its perch for the night,
Though it still could sing.

The last of the light of the sun
That had died in the west   10
Still lived for one song more
In a thrush's breast.

Far in the pillared dark
Thrush music went—
Almost like a call to come in   15
To the dark and lament.

But no, I was out for stars:
I would not come in.
I meant not even if asked,
And I hadn't been.   20

DESIGN

I found a dimpled spider, fat and white,
On a white heal-all, holding up a moth
Like a white piece of rigid satin cloth—
Assorted characters of death and blight
Mixed ready to begin the morning right,   5
Like the ingredients of a witches' broth—
A snow-drop spider, a flower like froth,
And dead wings carried like a paper kite.

What had that flower to do with being white,
The wayside blue and innocent heal-all?   10

What brought the kindred spider to that height,
Then steered the white moth thither in the night?
What but design of darkness to appall?—
If design govern in a thing so small.

DIRECTIVE

Back out of all this now too much for us,
Back in a time made simple by the loss
Of detail, burned, dissolved, and broken off
Like graveyard marble sculpture in the weather,
There is a house that is no more a house   5
Upon a farm that is no more a farm
And in a town that is no more a town.
The road there, if you'll let a guide direct you
Who only has at heart your getting lost,
May seem as if it should been a quarry—   10
Great monolithic knees the former town
Long since gave up pretense of keeping covered.
And there's a story in a book about it:
Besides the wear of iron wagon wheels
The ledges show lines ruled southeast northwest,   15
The chisel work of an enormous Glacier
That braced his feet against the Arctic Pole.
You must not mind a certain coolness from him
Still said to haunt this side of Panther Mountain.
Nor need you mind the serial ordeal   20
Of being watched from forty cellar holes
As if by eye pairs out of forty firkins.
As for the woods' excitement over you
That sends light rustle rushes to their leaves,
Charge that to upstart inexperience.   25
Where were they all not twenty years ago?
They think too much of having shaded out
A few old pecker-fretted apple trees.
Make yourself up a cheering song of how
Someone's road home from work this once was,   30
Who may be just ahead of you on foot

Or creaking with a buggy load of grain.
The height of the adventure is the height
Of country where two village cultures faded
Into each other. Both of them are lost.   35
And if you're lost enough to find yourself
By now, pull in your ladder road behind you
And put a sign up CLOSED to all but me.
Then make yourself at home. The only field
Now left's no bigger than a harness gall.   40
First there's the children's house of make believe,
Some shattered dishes underneath a pine,
The playthings in the playhouse of the children.
Weep for what little things could make them glad.
Then for the house that is no more a house,   45
But only a belilaced cellar hole,
Now slowly closing like a dent in dough.
This was no playhouse but a house in earnest.
Your destination and your destiny's
A brook that was the water of the house,   50
Cold as a spring as yet so near its source,
Too lofty and original to rage.
(We know the valley streams that when aroused
Will leave their tatters hung on barb and thorn.)
I have kept hidden in the instep arch   55
Of an old cedar at the waterside
A broken drinking goblet like the Grail
Under a spell so the wrong ones can't find it,
So can't get saved, as Saint Mark says they mustn't.
(I stole the goblet from the children's playhouse.)   60
Here are your waters and your watering place.
Drink and be whole again beyond confusion.

Wallace Stevens

THE SNOW MAN

One must have a mind of winter
To regard the frost and the boughs
Of the pine-trees crusted with snow;

And have been cold a long time
To behold the junipers shagged with ice,   5
The spruces rough in the distant glitter

Of the January sun; and not to think
Of any misery in the sound of the wind,
In the sound of a few leaves,

Which is the sound of the land   10
Full of the same wind
That is blowing in the same bare place

For the listener, who listens in the snow,
And, nothing himself, beholds
Nothing that is not there and the nothing that is.   15

DISILLUSIONMENT OF TEN O'CLOCK

The houses are haunted
By white night-gowns.
None are green,
Or purple with green rings,
Or green with yellow rings,   5
Or yellow with blue rings,
None of them are strange,
With socks of lace
And beaded ceintures.
People are not going   10
To dream of baboons and periwinkles.
Only, here and there, an old sailor,

Drunk and asleep in his boots,
Catches tigers
In red weather.   15

SUNDAY MORNING

[1]

Complacencies of the peignoir, and late
Coffee and oranges in a sunny chair,
And the green freedom of a cockatoo
Upon a rug mingle to dissipate
The holy hush of ancient sacrifice.   5
She dreams a little, and she feels the dark
Encroachment of that old catastrophe,
As a calm darkens among water-lights.
The pungent oranges and bright, green wings
Seem things in some procession of the dead,   10
Winding across wide water, without sound.
The day is like wide water, without sound,
Stilled for the passing of her dreaming feet
Over the seas, to silent Palestine,
Dominion of the blood and sepulchre.   15

[2]

Why should she give her bounty to the dead?
What is divinity if it can come
Only in silent shadows and in dreams?
Shall she not find in comforts of the sun,
In pungent fruit and bright, green wings, or else   20
In any balm or beauty of the earth,
Things to be cherished like the thought of heaven?
Divinity must live within herself:
Passions of rain, or moods in falling snow;
Grievings in loneliness, or unsubdued   25
Elations when the forest blooms; gusty
Emotions on wet roads on autumn nights;
All pleasures and all pains, remembering
The bough of summer and the winter branch.
These are the measures destined for her soul.   30

[3]

Jove in the clouds had his inhuman birth.
No mother suckled him, no sweet land gave
Large-mannered motions to his mythy mind.
He moved among us, as a muttering king,
Magnificent, would move among his hinds,   35
Until our blood, commingling, virginal,
With heaven, brought such requital to desire
The very hinds discerned it, in a star.
Shall our blood fail? Or shall it come to be
The blood of paradise? And shall the earth   40
Seem all of paradise that we shall know?
The sky will be much friendlier then than now,
A part of labor and a part of pain,
And next in glory to enduring love,
Not this dividing and indifferent blue.   45

[4]

She says, "I am content when wakened birds,
Before they fly, test the reality
Of misty fields, by their sweet questionings;
But when the birds are gone, and their warm fields
Return no more, where, then, is paradise?"   50
There is not any haunt of prophecy,
Nor any old chimera of the grave,
Neither the golden underground, nor isle
Melodious, where spirits gat them home,
Nor visionary south, nor cloudy palm   55
Remote on heaven's hill, that has endured
As April's green endures; or will endure
Like her remembrance of awakened birds,
Or her desire for June and evening, tipped
By the consummation of the swallow's wings.   60

[5]

She says, "But in contentment I still feel
The need of some imperishable bliss."
Death is the mother of beauty; hence from her,
Alone, shall come fulfillment to our dreams

And our desires. Although she strews the leaves 65
Of sure obliteration on our paths,
The path sick sorrow took, the many paths
Where triumph rang its brassy phrase, or love
Whispered a little out of tenderness,
She makes the willow shiver in the sun 70
For maidens who were wont to sit and gaze
Upon the grass, relinquished to their feet.
She causes boys to pile new plums and pears
On disregarded plate. The maidens taste
And stray impassioned in the littering leaves. 75

[6]

Is there no change of death in paradise?
Does ripe fruit never fall? Or do the boughs
Hang always heavy in that perfect sky,
Unchanging, yet so like our perishing earth,
With rivers like our own that seek for seas 80
They never find, the same receding shores
That never touch with inarticulate pang?
Why set the pear upon those river-banks
Or spice the shores with odors of the plum?
Alas, that they should wear our colors there, 85
The silken weavings of our afternoons,
And pick the strings of our insipid lutes!
Death is the mother of beauty, mystical,
Within whose burning bosom we devise
Our earthly mothers waiting, sleeplessly. 90

[7]

Supple and turbulent, a ring of men
Shall chant in orgy on a summer morn
Their boisterous devotion to the sun,
Not as a god, but as a god might be,
Naked among them, like a savage source. 95
Their chant shall be a chant of paradise,
Out of their blood, returning to the sky;
And in their chant shall enter, voice by voice,
The windy lake wherein their lord delights,

The trees, like serafin, and echoing hills,   100
That choir among themselves long afterward.
They shall know well the heavenly fellowship
Of men that perish and of summer morn.
And whence they came and whither they shall go
The dew upon their feet shall manifest.   105

[8]

She hears, upon that water without sound,
A voice that cries, "The tomb in Palestine
Is not the porch of spirits lingering.
It is the grave of Jesus, where he lay."
We live in an old chaos of the sun,   110
Or old dependency of day and night,
Or island solitude, unsponsored, free,
Of that wide water, inescapable.
Deer walk upon our mountains, and the quail
Whistle about us their spontaneous cries;   115
Sweet berries ripen in the wilderness;
And, in the isolation of the sky,
At evening, casual flocks of pigeons make
Ambiguous undulations as they sink,
Downward to darkness, on extended wings.   120

PETER QUINCE AT THE CLAVIER*

[1]

Just as my fingers on these keys
Make music, so the self-same sounds
On my spirit make a music, too.

Music is feeling, then, not sound;
And thus it is that what I feel,   5
Here in this room, desiring you,

* *Peter Quince:* one of the clowns in *A Midsummer Night's Dream,* director
of the inept tragedy enacted within the play.

Thinking of your blue-shadowed silk,
Is music. It is like the strain
Waked in the elders by Susanna.

Of a green evening, clear and warm,   10
She bathed in her still garden, while
The red-eyed elders watching, felt

The basses of their beings throb
In witching chords, and their thin blood
Pulse pizzicati of Hosanna.   15

[2]

In the green water, clear and warm,
Susanna lay.
She searched
The touch of springs,
And found   20
Concealed imaginings.
She sighed,
For so much melody.

Upon the bank, she stood
In the cool   25
Of spent emotions.
She felt, among the leaves,
The dew
Of old devotions.

She walked upon the grass,   30
Still quavering.
The winds were like her maids,
On timid feet,
Fetching her woven scarves,
Yet wavering.   35

9. *Susanna:* in one of the Apocryphal books of the prophet Daniel, the virtuous Susanna is accosted by a group of elders. When she rejects them,
they accuse her of soliciting them. Daniel proves them guilty, and they are
executed.

A breath upon her hand
Muted the night.
She turned—
A cymbal crashed,
And roaring horns.   40

[3]

Soon, with a noise like tambourines,
Came her attendant Byzantines.

They wondered why Susanna cried
Against the elders by her side;

And as they whispered, the refrain   45
Was like a willow swept by rain.

Anon, their lamps' uplifted flame
Revealed Susanna and her shame.

And then, the simpering Byzantines
Fled, with a noise like tambourines.   50

[4]

Beauty is momentary in the mind—
The fitful tracing of a portal;
But in the flesh it is immortal.
The body dies; the body's beauty lives.
So evenings die, in their green going,   55
A wave, interminably flowing.
So gardens die, their meek breath scenting
The cowl of winter, done repenting.
So maidens die, to the auroral
Celebration of a maiden's choral.   60
Susanna's music touched the bawdy strings
Of those white elders; but, escaping,
Left only Death's ironic scraping.
Now, in its immortality, it plays
On the clear viol of her memory,   65
And makes a constant sacrament of praise.

THE DEATH OF A SOLDIER

Life contracts and death is expected,
As in a season of autumn.
The soldier falls.

He does not become a three-days personage,
Imposing his separation,   5
Calling for pomp.

Death is absolute and without memorial,
As in a season of autumn,
When the wind stops,

When the wind stops and, over the heavens,   10
The clouds go, nevertheless,
In their direction.

THE IDEA OF ORDER AT KEY WEST

She sang beyond the genius of the sea.
The water never formed to mind or voice,
Like a body wholly body, fluttering
Its empty sleeves; and yet its mimic motion
Made constant cry, caused constantly a cry,   5
That was not ours although we understood,
Inhuman, of the veritable ocean.

The sea was not a mask. No more was she.
The song and water were not medleyed sound
Even if what she sang was what she heard,   10
Since what she sang was uttered word by word.
It may be that in all her phrases stirred
The grinding water and the gasping wind;
But it was she and not the sea we heard.

For she was the maker of the song she sang.   15
The ever-hooded, tragic-gestured sea
Was merely a place by which she walked to sing.
Whose spirit is this? we said, because we knew
It was the spirit that we sought and knew
That we should ask this often as she sang.   20

If it was only the dark voice of the sea
That rose, or even colored by many waves;
If it was only the outer voice of sky
And cloud, of the sunken coral water-walled,
However clear, it would have been deep air,   25
The heaving speech of air, a summer sound
Repeated in a summer without end
And sound alone. But it was more than that,
More even than her voice, and ours, among
The meaningless plungings of water and the wind,   30
Theatrical distances, bronze shadows heaped
On high horizons, mountainous atmospheres
Of sky and sea.
                It was her voice that made
The sky acutest at its vanishing.
She measured to the hour its solitude.   35
She was the single artificer of the world
In which she sang. And when she sang, the sea,
Whatever self it had, became the self
That was her song, for she was the maker. Then we,
As we beheld her striding there alone,   40
Knew that there never was a world for her
Except the one she sang and, singing, made.

Ramon Fernandez, tell me, if you know,
Why, when the singing ended and we turned
Toward the town, tell why the glassy lights,   45
The lights in the fishing boats at anchor there,
As the night descended, tilting in the air,
Mastered the night and portioned out the sea,
Fixing emblazoned zones and fiery poles,
Arranging, deepening, enchanting night.   50

Oh! Blessed rage for order, pale Ramon,
The maker's rage to order words of the sea,
Words of the fragrant portals, dimly-starred,
And of ourselves and of our origins,
In ghostlier demarcations, keener sounds.   55

43. *Ramon Fernandez*: French novelist and critic, 1894–1944.

THE COURSE OF A PARTICULAR

Today the leaves cry, hanging on branches swept by wind,
Yet the nothingness of winter becomes a little less.
It is still full of icy shades and shapen snow.

The leaves cry . . . One holds off and merely hears the cry.
It is a busy cry, concerning someone else.   5
And though one says that one is part of everything,

There is a conflict, there is a resistance involved;
And being part is an exertion that declines:
One feels the life of that which gives life as it is.

The leaves cry. It is not a cry of divine attention,   10
Nor the smoke-drift of puffed-out heroes, nor human cry.
It is the cry of leaves that do not transcend themselves,

In the absence of fantasia, without meaning more
Than they are in the final finding of the ear, in the thing
Itself, until, at last, the cry concerns no one at all.   15

William Carlos Williams

DANSE RUSSE

If when my wife is sleeping
and the baby and Kathleen
are sleeping
and the sun is a flame-white disc
in silken mists   5
above shining trees,—
if I in my north room
dance naked, grotesquely
before my mirror
waving my shirt round my head   10
and singing softly to myself:

"I am lonely, lonely.
I was born to be lonely,
I am best so!"
If I admire my arms, my face,   15
my shoulders, flanks, buttocks
against the yellow drawn shades,—

Who shall say I am not
the happy genius of my household?

THE WIDOW'S LAMENT IN SPRINGTIME

Sorrow is my own yard
where the new grass
flames as it has flamed
often before but not
with the cold fire   5
that closes round me this year.
Thirtyfive years
I lived with my husband.
The plumtree is white today
with masses of flowers.   10
Masses of flowers
load the cherry branches
and color some bushes
yellow and some red
but the grief in my heart   15
is stronger than they
for though they were my joy
formerly, today I notice them
and turned away forgetting.
Today my son told me   20
that in the meadows,
at the edge of the heavy woods
in the distance, he saw
trees of white flowers.
I feel that I would like   25
to go there
and fall into those flowers
and sink into the marsh near them.

WILLIAM CARLOS WILLIAMS

SPRING AND ALL

By the road to the contagious hospital
under the surge of the blue
mottled clouds driven from the
northeast—a cold wind. Beyond, the
waste of broad, muddy fields   5
brown with dried weeds, standing and fallen

patches of standing water
the scattering of tall trees

All along the road the reddish
purplish, forked, upstanding, twiggy   10
stuff of bushes and small trees
with dead, brown leaves under them
leafless vines—

Lifeless in appearance, sluggish
dazed spring approaches—   15

They enter the new world naked,
cold, uncertain of all
save that they enter. All about them
the cold, familiar wind—

Now the grass, tomorrow   20
The stiff curl of wildcarrot leaf
One by one objects are defined—
It quickens: clarity, outline of leaf

But now the stark dignity of
entrance—Still, the profound change   25
has come upon them: rooted, they
grip down and begin to awaken

THE RED WHEELBARROW

so much depends
upon

a red wheel
barrow

what does he mean?

262

glazed with rain   5
water

beside the white
chickens.

THIS IS JUST TO SAY

I have eaten
the plums
that were in
the icebox

and which   5
you were probably
saving
for breakfast

Forgive me
they were delicious   10
so sweet
and so cold

Ezra Pound

PORTRAIT D'UNE FEMME

Your mind and you are our Sargasso Sea,
London has swept about you this score years
And bright ships left you this or that in fee:
Ideas, old gossip, oddments of all things,
Strange spars of knowledge and dimmed wares of price.   5
Great minds have sought you—lacking someone else.
You have been second always. Tragical?
No. You preferred it to the usual thing:
One dull man, dulling and uxorious,

One average mind—with one thought less, each year.   10
Oh, you are patient, I have seen you sit
Hours, where something might have floated up.
And now you pay one. Yes, you richly pay.
You are a person of some interest, one comes to you
And takes strange gain away: 15
Trophies fished up; some curious suggestion;
Fact that leads nowhere; and a tale for two,
Pregnant with mandrakes, or with something else
That might prove useful and yet never proves,
That never fits a corner or shows use,   20
Or finds its hour upon the loom of days:
The tarnished, gaudy, wonderful old work;
Idols and ambergris and rare inlays,
These are your riches, your great store; and yet
For all this sea-hoard of deciduous things,   25
Strange woods half sodden, and new brighter stuff:
In the slow float of differing light and deep,
No! there is nothing! In the whole and all,
Nothing that's quite your own.
                    Yet this is you.   30

AN IMMORALITY

Sing we for love and idleness,
Naught else is worth the having.

Though I have been in many a land,
There is naught else in living.

And I would rather have my sweet,   5
Though rose-leaves die of grieving,

Than do high deeds in Hungary
To pass all men's believing.

IN A STATION OF THE METRO

The apparition of these faces in the crowd;
Petals on a wet, black bough.

Marianne Moore

A GRAVE

Man looking into the sea,
taking the view from those who have as much right to it as you
     have to it yourself,
it is human nature to stand in the middle of a thing,
but you cannot stand in the middle of this;
the sea has nothing to give but a well excavated grave. 5
The firs stand in a procession, each with an emerald turkey-foot
     at the top,
reserved as their contours, saying nothing;
repression, however, is not the most obvious characteristic of the
     sea;
the sea is a collector, quick to return a rapacious look.
There are others besides you who have worn that look— 10
whose expression is no longer a protest; the fish no longer in-
     vestigate them
for their bones have not lasted:
men lower nets, unconscious of the fact that they are desecrat-
     ing a grave,
and row quickly away—the blades of the oars
moving together like the feet of water-spiders as if there were
     no such thing as death. 15
The wrinkles progress among themselves in a phalanx—beau-
     tiful under networks of foam,
and fade breathlessly while the sea rustles in and out of the
     seaweed;
the birds swim through the air at top speed, emitting cat-calls as
     heretofore—
the tortoise-shell scourges about the feet of the cliffs, in motion
     beneath them;
and the ocean, under the pulsation of lighthouses and noise of
     bell-buoys, 20
advances as usual, looking as if it were not that ocean in which
     dropped things are bound to sink—
in which if they turn and twist, it is neither with volition nor
     consciousness.

WHAT ARE YEARS?

What is our innocence,
what is our guilt? All are
   naked, none is safe. And whence
is courage: the unanswered question,
the resolute doubt,—   5
dumbly calling, deafly listening—that
in misfortune, even death,
      encourages others
      and in its defeat, stirs

   the soul to be strong? He   10
sees deep and is glad, who
   accedes to mortality
and in his imprisonment rises
upon himself as
the sea in a chasm, struggling to be   15
free and unable to be,
      in its surrendering
      finds its continuing.

   So he who strongly feels,
behaves. The very bird,   20
   grown taller as he sings, steels
his form straight up. Though he is captive,
his mighty singing
says, satisfaction is a lowly
thing, how pure a thing is joy.   25
      This is mortality.
      this is eternity.

NEVERTHELESS

you've seen a strawberry
     that's had a struggle; yet
     was, where the fragments met,

a hedgehog or a star-
        fish for the multitude   5
        of seeds. What better food

than apple-seeds—the fruit
        within the fruit—locked in
        like counter-curved twin

hazel-nuts? Frost that kills   10
        the little rubber-plant-
        leaves of *kok-saghyz*-stalks, can't

harm the roots; they still grow
        in frozen ground. Once where
        there was a prickly-pear-   15

leaf clinging to barbed wire,
        a root shot down to grow
        in earth two feet below;

as carrots form mandrakes
        or a ram's-horn root some-   20
        times. Victory won't come

to me unless I go
        to it; a grape-tendril
        ties a knot in knots till

knotted thirty times,—so   25
        the bound twig that's under-
        gone and over-gone, can't stir.

The weak overcomes its
        menace, the strong over-
        comes itself. What is there   30

like fortitude! What sap
        went through that little thread
        to make the cherry red!

John Crowe Ransom

HERE LIES A LADY

Here lies a lady of beauty and high degree.
Of chills and fever she died, of fever and chills,
The delight of her husband, her aunts, an infant of three,
And of medicos marveling sweetly on her ills.

For either she burned, and her confident eyes would blaze,   5
And her fingers fly in a manner to puzzle their heads—
What was she making? Why, nothing; she sat in a maze
Of old scraps of laces, snipped into curious shreds—

Or this would pass, and the light of her fire decline
Till she lay discouraged and cold as a thin stalk white and blown,   10
And would not open her eyes, to kisses, to wine.
The sixth of these states was her last; the cold settled down.

Sweet ladies, long may ye bloom, and toughly I hope ye may
      thole,
But was she not lucky? In flowers and lace and mourning,
In love and great honor we bade God rest her soul   15
After six little spaces of chill, and six of burning.

JANET WAKING

Beautifully Janet slept
Till it was deeply morning. She woke then
And thought about her dainty-feathered hen,
To see how it had kept.

One kiss she gave her mother,   5
Only a small one gave she to her daddy
Who would have kissed each curl of his shining baby;
No kiss at all for her brother.

"Old Chucky, Old Chucky!" she cried,
Running on little pink feet upon the grass   10

To Chucky's house, and listening. But alas,
Her Chucky had died.

It was a transmogrifying bee
Came droning down on Chucky's old bald head
And sat and put the poison. It scarcely bled,   15
But how exceedingly

And purply did the knot
Swell with the venom and communicate
Its rigor! Now the poor comb stood up straight
But Chucky did not.   20

So there was Janet
Kneeling on the wet grass, crying her brown hen
(Translated far beyond the daughters of men)
To rise and walk upon it.

And weeping fast as she had breath   25
Janet implored us, "Wake her from her sleep!"
And would not be instructed in how deep
Was the forgetful kingdom of death.

T. S. Eliot

PORTRAIT OF A LADY

Thou hast committed—
Fornication: but that was in another country,
And besides, the wench is dead.
                    The Jew of Malta

[1]

Among the smoke and fog of a December afternoon
You have the scene arrange itself—as it will seem to do—
With "I have saved this afternoon for you";
And four wax candles in the darkened room,
Four rings of light upon the ceiling overhead,   5
An atmosphere of Juliet's tomb

269

Prepared for all the things to be said, or left unsaid.
We have been, let us say, to hear the latest Pole
Transmit the Preludes, through his hair and fingertips.
"So intimate, this Chopin, that I think his soul   10
Should be resurrected only among friends
Some two or three, who will not touch the bloom
That is rubbed and questioned in the concert room."
—And so the conversation slips
Among velleities and carefully caught regrets   15
Through attenuated tones of violins
Mingled with remote cornets
And begins.
"You do not know how much they mean to me, my friends,
And how, how rare and strange it is, to find   20
In a life composed so much, so much of odds and ends,
[For indeed I do not love it . . . you knew? you are not blind!
How keen you are!]
To find a friend who has these qualities,
Who has, and gives   25
Those qualities upon which friendship lives.
How much it means that I say this to you—
Without these friendships—life, what *cauchemar!*"

Among the windings of the violins
And the ariettes   30
Of cracked cornets
Inside my brain a dull tom-tom begins
Absurdly hammering a prelude of its own,
Capricious monotone
That is at least one definite "false note."   35
—Let us take the air, in a tobacco trance,
Admire the monuments,
Discuss the late events,
Correct our watches by the public clocks.
Then sit for half an hour and drink our bocks.   40
                        [2]
Now that lilacs are in bloom
She has a bowl of lilacs in her room

28. *cauchemar:* Fr., nightmare.

And twists one in her fingers while she talks.
"Ah, my friend, you do not know, you do not know
What life is, you who hold it in your hands";   45
(Slowly twisting the lilac stalks)
"You let it flow from you, you let it flow,
And youth is cruel, and has no remorse
And smiles at situations which it cannot see."
I smile, of course,   50
And go on drinking tea.
"Yet with these April sunsets, that somehow recall
My buried life, and Paris in the spring,
I feel immeasurably at peace, and find the world
To be wonderful and youthful after all."   55

The voice returns like the insistent out-of-tune
Of a broken violin on an August afternoon:
"I am always sure that you understand
My feelings, always sure that you feel,
Sure that across the gulf you reach your hand.   60

You are invulnerable, you have no Achilles' heel.
You will go on, and when you have prevailed
You can say: at this point many a one has failed.
But what have I, but what have I, my friend,
To give you, what can you receive from me?   65
Only the friendship and the sympathy
Of one about to reach her journey's end.

I shall sit here, serving tea to friends. . . ."

I take my hat: how can I make a cowardly amends
For what she has said to me?   70
You will see me any morning in the park
Reading the comics and the sporting page.
Particularly I remark
An English countess goes upon the stage.
A Greek was murdered at a Polish dance,   75
Another bank defaulter has confessed.
I keep my countenance,
I remain self-possessed
Except when a street piano, mechanical and tired,

Reiterates some worn-out common song 80
With the smell of hyacinths across the garden
Recalling things that other people have desired.
Are these ideas right or wrong?

[3]

The October night comes down; returning as before
Except for a slight sensation of being ill at ease 85
I mount the stairs and turn the handle of the door
And feel as if I had mounted on my hands and knees.
"And so you are going abroad; and when do you return?
But that's a useless question.
You hardly know when you are coming back, 90
You will find so much to learn."
My smile falls heavily among the bric-à-brac.

"Perhaps you can write to me."
My self-possession flares up for a second;
This is as I had reckoned. 95
"I have been wondering frequently of late
(But our beginnings never know our ends!)
Why we have not developed into friends."
I feel like one who smiles, and turning shall remark
Suddenly, his expression in a glass. 100
My self-possession gutters; we are really in the dark.

"For everybody said so, all our friends,
They all were sure our feelings would relate
So closely! I myself can hardly understand.
We must leave it now to fate. 105
You will write, at any rate.
Perhaps it is not too late.
I shall sit here, serving tea to friends."
And I must borrow every changing shape
To find expression . . . dance, dance 110
Like a dancing bear,
Cry like a parrot, chatter like an ape.
Let us take the air, in a tobacco trance—

Well! and what if she should die some afternoon,
Afternoon gray and smoky, evening yellow and rose; 115

Should die and leave me sitting pen in hand
With the smoke coming down above the housetops;
Doubtful, for a while
Not knowing what to feel or if I understand
Or whether wise or foolish, tardy or too soon . . .   120
Would she not have the advantage, after all?
This music is successful with a "dying fall"
Now we talk of dying—
And should I have the right to smile?

contrast c̄ tragedy

THE LOVE SONG OF
J. ALFRED PRUFROCK

*Man in Hell
to Dante (poet)*

to Eliot

> S'io credesse che mia risposta fosse
> A persona che mai tornasse al mondo,
> Questa fiamma staria senza piu scosse.
> Ma perciocche giammai di questo fondo
> Non torno vivo alcun, s'i odo il vero,
> Senza tema d'infamia ti rispondo.*

Let us go then, you and I,
When the evening is spread out against the sky
Like a patient etherized upon a table;
Let us go, through certain half-deserted streets,
The muttering retreats   5
Of restless nights in one-night cheap hotels
And sawdust restaurants with oyster-shells:
Streets that follow like a tedious argument
Of insidious intent
To lead you to an overwhelming question. . .   10
Oh, do not ask, "What is it?"
Let us go and make our visit.

In the room the women come and go
Talking of Michelangelo.

The yellow fog that rubs its back upon the window-panes,   15
The yellow smoke that rubs its muzzle on the window-panes

* From Dante's *Inferno*, XXVII, 61–66. The speaker feels free to talk about
his sins without fear for his reputation on earth, because he knows no
listener in hell can return to the world of the living.

273

Licked its tongue into the corners of the evening,
Lingered upon the pools that stand in drains,
Let fall upon its back the soot that falls from chimneys,
Slipped by the terrace, made a sudden leap,   20
And seeing that it was a soft October night,
Curled once about the house, and fell asleep.

And indeed there will be time
For the yellow smoke that slides along the street,
Rubbing its back upon the window-panes;   25
There will be time, there will be time
To prepare a face to meet the faces that you meet;
There will be time to murder and create,
And time for all the works and days of hands
That lift and drop a question on your plate;   30
Time for you and time for me,
And time yet for a hundred indecisions,
And for a hundred visions and revisions,
Before the taking of a toast and tea.

In the room the women come and go   35
Talking of Michelangelo.

And indeed there will be time
To wonder, "Do I dare?" and, "Do I dare?"
Time to turn back and descend the stair,
With a bald spot in the middle of my hair—   40
[They will say: "How his hair is growing thin!"]
My morning coat, my collar mounting firmly to the chin,
My necktie rich and modest, but asserted by a simple pin—
[They will say: "But how his arms and legs are thin!"]
Do I dare   45
Disturb the universe?
In a minute there is time
For decisions and revisions which a minute will reverse.

For I have known them all already, known them all:—
Have known the evenings, mornings, afternoons,   50
I have measured out my life with coffee spoons;
I know the voices dying with a dying fall

274

Beneath the music from a farther room.
   So how should I presume?

And I have known the eyes already, known them all—   55
The eyes that fix you in a formulated phrase,
And when I am formulated, sprawling on a pin,
When I am pinned and wriggling on the wall,
Then how should I begin
To spit out all the butt-ends of my days and ways?   60
   And how should I presume?

And I have known the arms already, known them all—
Arms that are braceleted and white and bare
(But in the lamplight, downed with light brown hair!)
Is it perfume from a dress   65
That makes me so digress?
Arms that lie along a table, or wrap about a shawl.
   And should I then presume?
   And how should I begin?

     .   .   .   .

Shall I say, I have gone at dusk through narrow streets   70
And watched the smoke that rises from the pipes
Of lonely men in shirt-sleeves, leaning out of windows? . . .

I should have been a pair of ragged claws
Scuttling across the floors of silent seas.

     .   .   .   .

And the afternoon, the evening, sleeps so peacefully!   75
Smoothed by long fingers,
Asleep . . . tired . . . or it malingers,
Stretched on the floor, here beside you and me.
Should I, after tea and cakes and ices,
Have the strength to force the moment to its crisis?   80
But though I have wept and fasted, wept and prayed,
Though I have seen my head (grown slightly bald) brought in
   upon a platter,
I am no prophet—and here's no great matter;
I have seen the moment of my greatness flicker,
And I have seen the eternal Footman hold my coat, and snicker,   85
And in short, I was afraid.

And would it have been worth it, after all,
After the cups, the marmalade, the tea,
Among the porcelain, among some talk of you and me,
Would it have been worth while,   90
To have bitten off the matter with a smile,
To have squeezed the universe into a ball
To roll it toward some overwhelming question,
To say: "I am Lazarus, come from the dead,
Come back to tell you all, I shall tell you all"—   95
If one, settling a pillow by her head,
     Should say: "That is not what I meant at all.
     That is not it, at all."

And would it have been worth it, after all,
Would it have been worth while,   100
After the sunsets and the dooryards and the sprinkled streets,
After the novels, after the teacups, after the skirts that trail along
        the floor—
And this, and so much more?—
It is impossible to say just what I mean!
But as if a magic lantern threw the nerves in patterns on a screen: 105
Would it have been worth while
If one, settling a pillow or throwing off a shawl,
And turning toward the window, should say:
     "That is not it at all,
     That is not what I meant, at all."   110

          .   .   .   .

No! I am not Prince Hamlet, nor was meant to be;
Am an attendant lord, one that will do
To swell a progress, start a scene or two,
Advise the prince; no doubt, an easy tool,
Deferential, glad to be of use,   115
Politic, cautious, and meticulous;
Full of high sentence, but a bit obtuse;
At times, indeed, almost ridiculous—
Almost, at times, the Fool.

I grow old . . . I grow old . . .   120
I shall wear the bottoms of my trousers rolled.

276

Shall I part my hair behind? Do I dare to eat a peach? *indecision over detail*
I shall wear white flannel trousers, and walk upon the beach.
I have heard the mermaids singing, each to each.

I do not think that they will sing to me. *lack o confdnc* 125

I have seen them riding seaward on the waves
Combing the white hair of the waves blown back
When the wind blows the water white and black.

We have lingered in the chambers of the sea
By sea-girls wreathed with seaweed red and brown 130
Till human voices wake us, and we drown. *fantasy vs fact*

his longing vis a vis his unbelief in self

GERONTION

> *Thou has nor youth nor age*
> *But as it were an after dinner sleep*
> *Dreaming of both.**

Here I am, an old man in a dry month,
Being read to by a boy, waiting for rain.
I was neither at the hot gates
Nor fought in the warm rain
Nor knee deep in the salt marsh, heaving a cutlass, 5
Bitten by flies, fought.
My house is a decayed house,
And the jew squats on the window sill, the owner,
Spawned in some estaminet of Antwerp,
Blistered in Brussels, patched and peeled in London. 10
The goat coughs at night in the field overhead;
Rocks, moss, stonecrop, iron, merds.
The woman keeps the kitchen, makes tea,
Sneezes at evening, poking the peevish gutter.

                                    I an old man,
A dull head among windy spaces. 15

Signs are taken for wonders. "We would see a sign":
The word within a word, unable to speak a word,

* From *Measure for Measure*, III, 1.

277

Swaddled with darkness. In the juvescence of the year
Came Christ the tiger

In depraved May, dogwood and chestnut, flowering judas,   20
To be eaten, to be divided, to be drunk
Among whispers; by Mr. Silvero
With caressing hands, at Limoges
Who walked all night in the next room;

By Hakagawa, bowing among the Titians;   25
By Madame de Tornquist, in the dark room
Shifting the candles; Fräulein von Kulp
Who turned in the hall, one hand on the door. Vacant shuttles
Weave the wind. I have no ghosts,
An old man in a draughty house   30
Under a windy knob.

After such knowledge, what forgiveness? Think now
History has many cunning passages, contrived corridors
And issues, deceives with whispering ambitions,
Guides us by vanities. Think now   35
She gives when our attention is distracted
And what she gives, gives with such supple confusions
That the giving famishes the craving. Gives too late
What's not believed in, or if still believed,
In memory only, reconsidered passion. Gives too soon   40
Into weak hands, what's thought can be dispensed with
Till the refusal propagates a fear. Think
Neither fear nor courage saves us. Unnatural vices
Are fathered by our heroism. Virtues
Are forced upon us by our impudent crimes.   45
These tears are shaken from the wrath-bearing tree.

The tiger springs in the new year. Us he devours.
   Think at last
We have not reached conclusion, when I
Stiffen in a rented house. Think at last   50
I have not made this show purposelessly
And it is not by any concitation
Of the backward devils.
I would meet you upon this honestly.

I that was near your heart was removed therefrom   55
To lose beauty in terror, terror in inquisition.
I have lost my passion: why should I need to keep it
Since what is kept must be adulterated?
I have lost my sight, smell, hearing, taste and touch:
How should I use them for your closer contact?   60

These with a thousand small deliberations
Protract the profit of their chilled delirium,
Excite the membrane, when the sense has cooled,
With pungent sauces, multiply variety
In a wilderness of mirrors. What will the spider do,   65
Suspend its operations, will the weevil
Delay? De Bailhache, Fresca, Mrs. Cammel, whirled
Beyond the circuit of the shuddering Bear
In fractured atoms. Gull against the wind, in the windy straits
Of Belle Isle, or running on the Horn,   70
White feathers in the snow, the Gulf claims,
And an old man driven by the Trades
To a sleepy corner.
                    Tenants of the house,
Thoughts of a dry brain in a dry season.

THE HOLLOW MEN

*A penny for the Old Guy.**

[1]

We are the hollow men
We are the stuffed men
Leaning together
Headpiece filled with straw. Alas!
Our dried voices, when   5
We whisper together
Are quiet and meaningless
As wind in dry grass
Or rats' feet over broken glass
In our dry cellar   10

* Phrase used by English children begging money to buy fireworks for Guy
Fawkes Day.

Shape without form, shade without color,
Paralyzed force, gesture without motion;

Those who have crossed
With direct eyes, to death's other Kingdom
Remember us—if at all—not as lost   15
Violent souls, but only
As the hollow men
The stuffed men.

[2]

Eyes I dare not meet in dreams
In death's dream kingdom   20
These do not appear:
There, the eyes are
Sunlight on a broken column
There, is a tree swinging
And voices are   25
In the wind's singing
More distant and more solemn
Than a fading star.

Let me be no nearer
In death's dream kingdom   30
Let me also wear
Such deliberate disguises
Rat's coat, crowskin, crossed staves
In a field
Behaving as the wind behaves   35
No nearer—

Not that final meeting
In the twilight kingdom

[3]

This is the dead land
This is cactus land   40
Here the stone images
Are raised, here they receive
The supplication of a dead man's hand
Under the twinkle of a fading star.

Is it like this   45
In death's other kingdom
Waking alone
At the hour when we are
Trembling with tenderness
Lips that would kiss   50
Form prayers to broken stone.

[4]

The eyes are not here
There are no eyes here
In this valley of dying stars
In this hollow valley   55
This broken jaw of our lost kingdoms

In this last of meeting places
We grope together
And avoid speech
Gathered on this beach of the tumid river   60

Sightless, unless
The eyes reappear
As the perpetual star
Multifoliate rose
Of death's twilight kingdom   65
The hope only
Of empty men.

[5]

Here we go round the prickly pear
Prickly pear prickly pear
Here we go round the prickly pear   70
At five o'clock in the morning.

Between the idea
And the reality
Between the motion
And the act   75
Falls the Shadow

For Thine is the Kingdom

Between the conception
And the creation

Between the emotion 80
And the response
Falls the Shadow

Life is very long

Between the desire
And the spasm 85
Between the potency
And the existence
Between the essence
And the descent
Falls the Shadow 90

For Thine is the Kingdom

For Thine is
Life is
For Thine is the

This is the way the world ends 95
This is the way the world ends
This is the way the world ends
Not with a bang but a whimper.

Robert Graves

RECALLING WAR

Entrance and exit wounds are silvered clean,
The track aches only when the rain reminds.
The one-legged man forgets his leg of wood,
The one-armed man his jointed wooden arm.
The blinded man sees with his ears and hands 5
As much or more than once with both his eyes.
Their war was fought these twenty years ago
And now assumes the nature-look of time,

As when the morning traveler turns and views
His wild night-stumbling carved into a hill. 10

What, then, was war? No mere discord of flags
But an infection of the common sky
That sagged ominously upon the earth
Even when the season was the airiest May.
Down pressed the sky, and we, oppressed, thrust out 15
Boastful tongue, clenched fist and valiant yard.
Natural infirmities were out of mode,
For Death was young again: patron alone
Of healthy dying, premature fate-spasm.

Fear made fine bed-fellows. Sick with delight 20
At life's discovered transitoriness,
Our youth became all-flesh and waived the mind.
Never was such antiqueness of romance,
Such tasty honey oozing from the heart.
And old importances came swimming back— 25
Wine, meat, log-fires, a roof over the head,
A weapon at the thigh, surgeons at call.
Even there was a use again for God—
A word of rage in lack of meat, wine, fire,
In ache of wounds beyond all surgeoning. 30

War was return of earth to ugly earth,
War was foundering of sublimities,
Extinction of each happy art and faith
By which the world had still kept head in air,
Protesting logic or protesting love, 35
Until the unendurable moment struck—
The inward scream, the duty to run mad.

And we recall the merry ways of guns—
Nibbling the walls of factory and church
Like a child, piecrust; felling groves of trees 40
Like a child, dandelions with a switch.
Machine-guns rattle toy-like from a hill,
Down in a row the brave tin-soldiers fall:
A sight to be recalled in elder days
When learnedly the future we devote 45
To yet more boastful visions of despair.

Hart Crane

REPOSE OF RIVERS

The willows carried a slow sound,
A sarabande the wind mowed on the mead.
I could never remember
That seething, steady leveling of the marshes
Till age had brought me to the sea.   5

Flags, weeds. And remembrance of steep alcoves
Where cypresses shared the noon's
Tyranny; they drew me into hades almost.
And mammoth turtles climbing sulphur dreams
Yielded, while sun-silt rippled them   10
Asunder . . .

How much I would have bartered! the black gorge
And all the singular nestings in the hills
Where beavers learn stitch and tooth.
The pond I entered once and quickly fled—   15
I remember now its singing willow rim.

And finally, in that memory all things nurse;
After the city that I finally passed
With scalding unguents spread and smoking darts
The monsoon cut across the delta   20
At gulf gates . . . There, beyond the dykes

I heard wind flaking sapphire, like this summer,
And willows could not hold more steady sound.

VOYAGES: I

Above the fresh ruffles of the surf
Bright striped urchins flay each other with sand.
They have contrived a conquest for shell shucks,
And their fingers crumble fragments of baked weed
Gaily digging and scattering.   5

And in answer to their treble interjections
The sun beats lightning on the waves,
The waves fold thunder on the sand;
And could they hear me I would tell them:

O brilliant kids, frisk with your dog,   10
Fondle your shells and sticks, bleached
By time and the elements; but there is a line
You must not cross nor ever trust beyond it
Spry cordage of your bodies to caresses
Too lichen-faithful from too wide a breast.   15
The bottom of the sea is cruel.

VOYAGES: II

—And yet this great wink of eternity,
Of rimless floods, unfettered leewardings,
Samite sheeted and processioned where
Her undinal vast belly moonward bends,
Laughing the wrapt inflections of our love;   5

Take this Sea, whose diapason knells
On scrolls of silver snowy sentences,
The sceptered terror of whose sessions rends
As her demeanors motion well or ill,
All but the pieties of lovers' hands.   10

And onward, as bells off San Salvador
Salute the crocus lusters of the stars,
In these poinsettia meadows of her tides,—
Adagios of islands, O my Prodigal,
Complete the dark confessions her veins spell.   15

Mark how her turning shoulders wind the hours,
And hasten while her penniless rich palms
Pass superscription of bent foam and wave,—
Hasten, while they are true,—sleep, death, desire,
Close round one instant in one floating flower.   20

Bind us in time, O seasons clear, and awe.
O minstrel galleons of Carib fire,

Bequeath us to no earthly shore until
Is answered in the vortex of our grave
The seal's wide spindrift gaze toward paradise.   25

VOYAGES: III

Infinite consanguinity it bears—
This tendered theme of you that light
Retrieves from sea plains where the sky
Resigns a breast that every wave enthrones;
While ribboned water lanes I wind   5
Are laved and scattered with no stroke
Wide from your side, whereto this hour
The sea lifts, also, reliquary hands.

And so, admitted through black swollen gates
That must arrest all distance otherwise,—   10
Past whirling pillars and lithe pediments,
Light wrestling there incessantly with light,
Star kissing star through wave on wave unto
Your body rocking!
                          and where death, if shed,
Presumes no carnage, but this single change,—   15
Upon the steep floor flung from dawn to dawn
The silken skilled transmemberment of song;

Permit me voyage, love, into your hands . . .

TO EMILY DICKINSON

You who desired so much—in vain to ask—
Yet fed your hunger like an endless task,
Dared dignify the labor, bless the quest—
Achieved that stillness ultimately best,

Being, of all, least sought for: Emily, hear!   5
O sweet, dead Silencer, most suddenly clear
When singing that Eternity possessed
And plundered momently in every breast;

—Truly no flower yet withers in your hand,
The harvest you descried and understand   10
Needs more than wit to gather, love to bind.
Some reconcilement of remotest mind—

Leaves Ormus rubyless, and Ophir chill.
Else tears heap all within one clay-cold hill.

13. *Ormus . . . Ophir:* ancient Eastern cities, one real and one legendary, renowned for their riches; both figure in Emily Dickinson poems.

Yvor Winters

THE SLOW PACIFIC SWELL

Far out of sight forever stands the sea,
Bounding the land with pale tranquillity.
When a small child, I watched it from a hill
At thirty miles or more. The vision still
Lies in the eye, soft blue and far away: 5
The rain has washed the dust from April day;
Paint-brush and lupine lie against the ground;
The wind above the hill-top has the sound
Of distant water in unbroken sky;
Dark and precise the little steamers ply—   10
Firm in direction they seem not to stir.
That is illusion. The artificer
Of quiet, distance holds me in a vise
And holds the ocean steady to my eyes.

Once when I rounded Flattery, the sea   15
Hove its loose weight like sand to tangle me
Upon the washing deck, to crush the hull;
Subsiding, dragged flesh at the bone. The skull
Felt the retreating wash of dreaming hair.

15. *Flattery:* Cape Flattery, the northwest extremity of the State of Washington.

Half drenched in dissolution, I lay bare.   20
I scarcely pulled myself erect; I came
Back slowly, slowly knew myself the same.
That was the ocean. From the ship we saw
Gray whales for miles: the long sweep of the jaw,
The blunt head plunging clean above the wave.   25
And one rose in a tent of sea and gave
A darkening shudder; water fell away;
The whale stood shining, and then sank in spray.

A landsman, I. The sea is but a sound.
I would be near it on a sandy mound,   30
And hear the steady rushing of the deep
While I lay stinging in the sand with sleep.
I have lived inland long. The land is numb.
It stands beneath the feet, and one may come
Walking securely, till the sea extends   35
Its limber margin, and precision ends.
By night a chaos of commingling power,
The whole Pacific hovers hour by hour.
The slow Pacific swell stirs on the sand,
Sleeping to sink away, withdrawing land,   40
Heaving and wrinkled in the moon, and blind;
Or gathers seaward, ebbing out of mind.

TO THE HOLY SPIRIT

from a deserted graveyard
in the Salinas Valley

Immeasurable haze:
The desert valley spreads
Up golden river-beds
As if in other days.
Trees rise and thin away,   5
And past the trees, the hills,
Pure line and shade of dust,
Bear witness to our wills:
We see them, for we must;
Calm in deceit, they stay.   10

High noon returns the mind
Upon its local fact:
Dry grass and sand; we find
No vision to distract.
Low in the summer heat,   15
Naming old graves, are stones
Pushed here and there, the seat
Of nothing, and the bones
Beneath are similar:
Relics of lonely men,   20
Brutal and aimless, then,
As now, irregular.

These are thy fallen sons,
Thou whom I try to reach.
Thou whom the quick eye shuns,   25
Thou dost elude my speech.
Yet when I go from sense
And trace thee down in thought,
I meet thee, then, intense,
And know thee as I ought.   30
But thou art mind alone,
And I, alas, am bound
Pure mind to flesh and bone,
And flesh and bone to ground.

These had no thought: at most   35
Dark faith and blinding earth.
Where is the trammeled ghost?
Was there another birth?
Only one certainty
Beside thine unfleshed eye,   40
Beside the spectral tree,
Can I discern: these die.
All of this stir of age,
Though it elude my sense
Into what heritage   45
I know not, seems to fall,
Quiet beyond recall,
Into irrelevance.

AT THE SAN FRANCISCO AIRPORT

To my daughter, 1954

This is the terminal: the light
Gives perfect vision, false and hard;
The metal glitters, deep and bright.
Great planes are waiting in the yard—
They are already in the night.   5

And you are here beside me, small,
Contained and fragile, and intent
On things that I but half recall—
Yet going whither you are bent.
I am the past, and that is all.   10

But you and I in part are one:
The frightened brain, the nervous will,
The knowledge of what must be done,
The passion to acquire the skill
To face that which you dare not shun.   15

The rain of matter upon sense
Destroys me momently. The score:
There comes what will come. The expense
Is what one thought, and something more—
One's being and intelligence.   20

This is the terminal, the break.
Beyond this point, on lines of air,
You take the way that you must take;
And I remain in light and stare—
In light, and nothing else, awake.   25

William Empson

MISSING DATES

Slowly the poison the whole blood stream fills.
It is not the effort nor the failure tires.
The waste remains, the waste remains and kills.

It is not your system or clear sight that mills
Down small to the consequence a life requires;   5
Slowly the poison the whole blood stream fills.

They bled an old dog dry yet the exchange rills
Of young dog blood gave but a month's desires;
The waste remains, the waste remains and kills.

It is the Chinese tombs and the slag hills   10
Usurp the soil, and not the soil retires.
Slowly the poison the whole blood stream fills.

Not to have fire is to be a skin that shrills.
The complete fire is death. From partial fires
The waste remains, the waste remains and kills.   15

It is the poems you have lost, the ills
From missing dates, at which the heart expires.
Slowly the poison the whole blood stream fills.
The waste remains, the waste remains and kills.

W. H. Auden

SEPTEMBER 1, 1939

I sit in one of the dives
On Fifty-second Street
Uncertain and afraid

As the clever hopes expire
Of a low dishonest decade: 5
Waves of anger and fear
Circulate over the bright
And darkened lands of the earth,
Obsessing our private lives;
The unmentionable odor of death   10
Offends the September night.

Accurate scholarship can
Unearth the whole offense
From Luther until now
That has driven a culture mad,   15
Find what occurred at Linz,
What huge imago made
A psychopathic god:
I and the public know
What all schoolchildren learn,   20
Those to whom evil is done
Do evil in return.

Exiled Thucydides knew
All that a speech can say
About Democracy,   25
And what dictators do,
The elderly rubbish they talk
To an apathetic grave;
Analyzed all in his book,
The enlightenment driven away,   30
The habit-forming pain,
Mismanagement and grief:
We must suffer them all again.

Into this neutral air
Where blind skyscrapers use   35
Their full height to proclaim
The strength of Collective Man,
Each language pours its vain
Competitive excuse:
But who can live for long   40

In an euphoric dream;
Out of the mirror they stare,
Imperialism's face
And the international wrong.

Faces along the bar   45
Cling to their average day:
The lights must never go out,
The music must always play,
All the conventions conspire
To make this fort assume   50
The furniture of home;
Lest we should see where we are,
Lost in a haunted wood,
Children afraid of the night
Who have never been happy or good.   55

The windiest militant trash
Important Persons shout
Is not so crude as our wish:
What mad Nijinsky wrote
About Diaghilev   60
Is true of the normal heart;
For the error bred in the bone
Of each woman and each man
Craves what it cannot have,
Not universal love   65
But to be loved alone.

From the conservative dark
Into the ethical life
The dense commuters come,
Repeating their morning vow;   70
"I *will* be true to the wife,
I'll concentrate more on my work,"
And helpless governors wake
To resume their compulsory game:
Who can release them now,   75
Who can reach the deaf,
Who can speak for the dumb?

All I have is a voice
To undo the folded lie,
The romantic lie in the brain   80
Of the sensual man-in-the-street
And the lie of Authority
Whose buildings grope the sky:
There is no such thing as the State
And no one exists alone;   85
Hunger allows no choice
To the citizen or the police;
We must love one another or die.

Defenseless under the night
Our world in stupor lies;   90
Yet, dotted everywhere,
Ironic points of light
Flash out wherever the Just
Exchange their messages:
May I, composed like them   95
Of Eros and of dust,
Beleaguered by the same
Negation and despair,
Show an affirming flame.

MUSÉE DES BEAUX ARTS

About suffering they were never wrong,
The Old Masters: how well they understood
Its human position; how it takes place
While someone else is eating or opening a window or just walking
   · dully along;
How, when the aged are reverently, passionately waiting   5
For the miraculous birth, there always must be
Children who did not specially want it to happen, skating
On a pond at the edge of the wood:
They never forgot
That even the dreadful martyrdom must run its course   10
Anyhow in a corner, some untidy spot

Where the dogs go on with their doggy life and the torturer's
    horse
Scratches its innocent behind on a tree.

In Brueghel's *Icarus,* for instance: how everything turns away
Quite leisurely from the disaster; the plowman may   15
Have heard the splash, the forsaken cry,
But for him it was not an important failure; the sun shone
As it had to on the white legs disappearing into the green
Water; and the expensive delicate ship that must have seen
Something amazing, a boy falling out of the sky,   20
Had somewhere to get to and sailed calmly on.

J. V. Cunningham

MEDITATION ON
STATISTICAL METHOD

Plato, despair!
We prove by norms
How numbers bear
Empiric forms,

How random wrong   5
Will average right
If time be long
And error slight,

But in our hearts
Hyperbole   10
Curves and departs
To infinity.

Error is boundless.
Nor hope nor doubt,
Though both be groundless,   15
Will average out.

Robert Lowell

AS A PLANE TREE BY THE WATER

Darkness has called to darkness, and disgrace
Elbows about our windows in this planned
Babel of Boston where our money talks
And multiplies the darkness of a land
Of preparation where the Virgin walks   5
And roses spiral her enameled face
Or fall to splinters on unwatered streets.
Our Lady of Babylon, go by, go by,
I was once the apple of your eye;
Flies, flies are on the plane tree, on the streets.   10

The flies, the flies, the flies of Babylon
Buzz in my ear drums while the devil's long
Dirge of the people detonates the hour
For floating cities where his golden tongue
Enchants the masons of the Babel Tower   15
To raise tomorrow's city to the sun
That never sets upon these hell-fire streets
Of Boston, where the sunlight is a sword
Striking at the withholder of the Lord:
Flies, flies are on the plane tree, on the streets.   20

Flies strike the miraculous waters of the iced
Atlantic and the eyes of Bernadette
Who saw Our Lady standing in the cave
At Massabielle, saw her so squarely that
Her vision put out reason's eyes. The grave   25
Is open-mouthed and swallowed up in Christ.
O walls of Jericho! And all the streets
To our Atlantic wall are singing: "Sing,
Sing for the resurrection of the King."
Flies, flies are on the plane tree, on the streets.   30

MY LAST AFTERNOON WITH
UNCLE DEVEREUX WINSLOW

1922: the stone porch of my Grandfather's summer house

[1]

"I won't go with you. I want to stay with Grandpa!"
That's how I threw cold water
on my Mother and Father's
watery martini pipe dreams at Sunday dinner.
. . . Fontainebleau, Mattapoisett, Puget Sound. . . .   5
Nowhere was anywhere after a summer
at my Grandfather's farm.
Diamond-pointed, athirst and Norman,
its alley of poplars
paraded from Grandmother's rose garden   10
to a scarey stand of virgin pine,
scrub, and paths forever pioneering.

One afternoon in 1922,
I sat on the stone porch, looking through
screens as black-grained as drifting coal.   15
Tockytock, tockytock
clumped our Alpine, Edwardian cuckoo clock,
slung with strangled, wooden game.
Our farmer was cementing a root-house under the hill.
One of my hands was cool on a pile   20
of black earth, the other warm
on a pile of lime. All about me
were the works of my Grandfather's hands:
snapshots of his *Liberty Bell* silver mine;
his high school at *Stukkert am Neckar;*   25
stogie-brown beams; fools'-gold nuggets;
octagonal red tiles,
sweaty with a secret dank, crummy with ant-stale;
a Rocky Mountain chaise longue,
its legs, shellacked saplings.   30
A pastel-pale Huckleberry Finn
fished with a broom straw in a basin
hollowed out of a millstone.

Like my Grandfather, the décor
was manly, comfortable,   35
overbearing, disproportioned.

What were those sunflowers? Pumpkins floating shoulder-high?
It was sunset, Sadie and Nellie
bearing pitchers of ice-tea,
oranges, lemons, mint, and peppermints,   40
and the jug of shandygaff,
which Grandpa made by blending half and half
yeasty, wheezing homemade sarsaparilla with beer.
The farm, entitled *Char-de-sa*
in the Social Register,   45
was named for my Grandfather's children:
Charlotte, Devereux, and Sarah.
No one had died there in my lifetime . . .
Only Cinder, our Scottie puppy
paralyzed from gobbling toads.   50
I sat mixing black earth and lime.

[2]

I was five and a half.
My formal pearl gray shorts
had been worn for three minutes.
My perfection was the Olympian   55
poise of my models in the imperishable autumn
display windows
of Rogers Peet's boys' store below the State House
in Boston. Distorting drops of water
pinpricked my face in the basin's mirror.   60
I was a stuffed toucan
with a bibulous, multicolored beak.

[3]

Up in the air
by the lakeview window in the billiards-room,
lurid in the doldrums of the sunset hour,   65
my Great Aunt Sarah
was learning *Samson and Delilah*.

She thundered on the keyboard of her dummy piano,
with gauze curtains like a boudoir table,
accordionlike yet soundless.   70
It had been bought to spare the nerves
of my Grandmother,
tone-deaf, quick as a cricket,
now needing a fourth for "Auction,"
and casting a thirsty eye   75
on Aunt Sarah, risen like the phoenix
from her bed of troublesome snacks and Tauchnitz classics.

Forty years earlier,
twenty, auburn headed,
grasshopper notes of genius!   80
Family gossip says Aunt Sarah
tilted her Athenian nose
and jilted an Astor.
Each morning she practiced
on the grand piano at Symphony Hall,   85
deathlike in the off-season summer—
its naked Greek statues draped with purple
like the saints in Holy Week. . . .
On the recital day, she failed to appear.

[4]

I picked with a clean finger nail at the blue anchor   90
on my sailor blouse washed white as a spinnaker.
What in the world was I wishing?
. . . A sail-colored horse browsing in the bullrushes . . .
A fluff of the west wind puffing
my blouse, kiting me over our seven chimneys,   95
troubling the waters. . . .
As small as sapphires were the ponds: *Quittacus, Snippituit,*
and *Assawompset,* halved by "the Island,"
where my Uncle's duck blind
floated in a barrage of smoke-clouds.   100
Double-barreled shotguns
stuck out like bundles of baby crow-bars.
A single sculler in a camouflaged kayak

was quacking to the decoys. . . .
At the cabin between the waters,   105
the nearest windows were already boarded.
Uncle Devereux was closing camp for the winter.
As if posed for "the engagement photograph,"
he was wearing his severe
war-uniform of a volunteer Canadian officer.   110
Daylight from the doorway riddled his student posters,
tacked helter-skelter on walls as raw as a board-walk.
Mr. Punch, a water melon in hockey tights,
was tossing off a decanter of Scotch.
La Belle France in a red, white and blue toga   115
was accepting the arm of her "protector,"
the ingenu and porcine Edward VII.
The pre-war music hall belles
had goose necks, glorious signatures, beauty-moles,
and coils of hair like rooster tails.   120
The finest poster was two or three young men in khaki kilts
being bushwacked on the veldt—
They were almost life-size. . . .

My Uncle was dying at twenty-nine.
"You are behaving like children,"   125
said my Grandfather,
when my Uncle and Aunt left their three baby daughters,
and sailed for Europe on a last honeymoon . . .
I cowered in terror.
I wasn't a child at all—   130
unseen and all-seeing, I was Agrippina
in the Golden House of Nero. . . .

Near me was the white measuring-door
my Grandfather had penciled with my Uncle's heights.
In 1911, he had stopped growing at just six feet.   135
While I sat on the tiles,
and dug at the anchor on my sailor blouse,
Uncle Devereux stood behind me.
He was as brushed as Bayard, our riding horse.

131. *Agrippina*: mother of the Roman Emperor Nero, put to death by him
after pursuing a long career of intrigue.

His face was putty.   140
His blue coat and white trousers
grew sharper and straighter.
His coat was a blue jay's tail,
his trousers were solid cream from the top of the bottle.
He was animated, hierarchical,   145
like a ginger snap man in a clothes-press.
He was dying of the incurable Hodgkin's disease. . . .
My hands were warm, then cool, on the piles
of earth and lime,
a black pile and a white pile. . . .   150
Come winter,
Uncle Devereux would blend to the one color.

Richard Wilbur

THE DEATH OF A TOAD

A toad the power mower caught,
Chewed and clipped of a leg, with a hobbling hop has got
   To the garden verge, and sanctuaried him
   Under the cineraria leaves, in the shade
     Of the ashen heartshaped leaves, in a dim,   5
       Low, and a final glade.

The rare original heartsblood goes,
Spends on the earthen hide, in the folds and wizenings, flows
   In the gutters of the banked and staring eyes. He lies
   As still as if he would return to stone,   10
     And soundlessly attending, dies
       Toward some deep monotone,

   Toward misted and ebullient seas
And cooling shores, toward lost Amphibia's emperies.
   Day dwindles, drowning, and at length is gone   15
   In the wide and antique eyes, which still appear

To watch, across the castrate lawn,
    The haggard daylight steer.

MIND

Mind in its purest play is like some bat
That beats about in caverns all alone,
Contriving by a kind of senseless wit
Not to conclude against a wall of stone.

It has no need to falter or explore;   5
Darkly it knows what obstacles are there,
And so may weave and flitter, dip and soar
In perfect courses through the blackest air.

And has this simile a like perfection?
The mind is like a bat. Precisely. Save   10
That in the very happiest intellection
A graceful error may correct the cave.

Philip Larkin

CHURCH GOING

Once I am sure there's nothing going on
I step inside, letting the door thud shut.
Another church: matting, seats, and stone,
And little books; sprawlings of flowers, cut
For Sunday, brownish now; some brass and stuff   5
Up at the holy end; the small neat organ;
And a tense, musty, unignorable silence,
Brewed God knows how long. Hatless, I take off
My cycle-clips in awkward reverence,

Move forward, run my hand around the font.   10
From where I stand, the roof looks almost new—

Cleaned, or restored? Someone would know: I don't.
Mounting the lectern, I peruse a few
Hectoring large-scale verses, and pronounce
"Here endeth" much more loudly than I'd meant.   15
The echoes snigger briefly. Back at the door
I sign the book, donate an Irish sixpence,
Reflect the place was not worth stopping for.

Yet stop I did: in fact I often do,
And always end much at a loss like this,   20
Wondering what to look for; wondering, too,
When churches fall completely out of use
What we shall turn them into, if we shall keep
A few cathedrals chronically on show,
Their parchment, plate and pyx in locked cases,   25
And let the rest rent-free to rain and sheep.
Shall we avoid them as unlucky places?

Or, after dark, will dubious women come
To make their children touch a particular stone;
Pick simples for a cancer; or on some   30
Advised night see walking a dead one?
Power of some sort or other will go on
In games, in riddles, seemingly at random;
But superstition, like belief, must die,
And what remains when disbelief has gone?   35
Grass, weedy pavement, brambles, buttress, sky,

A shape less recognizable each week,
A purpose more obscure. I wonder who
Will be the last, the very last, to seek
This place for what it was; one of the crew   40
That tap and jot and know what rood-lofts were?
Some ruin-bibber, randy for antique,
Or Christmas-addict, counting on a whiff
Of gown-and-bands and organ-pipes and myrrh?
Or will he be my representative,   45

Bored, uninformed, knowing the ghostly silt
Dispersed, yet tending to this cross of ground
Through suburb scrub because it held unspilt

So long and equably what since is found
Only in separation—marriage, and birth,   50
And death, and thoughts of these—for which was built
This special shell? For, though I've no idea
What this accoutred frowsty barn is worth,
It pleases me to stand in silence here;

A serious house on serious earth it is,   55
In whose blent air all our compulsions meet,
Are recognized, and robed as destinies.
And that much never can be obsolete,
Since someone will forever be surprising
A hunger in himself to be more serious,   60
And gravitating with it to this ground,
Which, he once heard, was proper to grow wise in,
If only that so many dead lie round.

TOADS

Why should I let the toad *work*
    Squat on my life?
Can't I use my wit as a pitchfork
    And drive the brute off?

Six days of the week it soils   5
    With its sickening poison—
Just for paying a few bills!
    That's out of proportion.

Lots of folk live on their wits:
    Lecturers, lispers,   10
Losels, loblolly-men, louts—
    They don't end as paupers;

Lots of folk live up lanes
    With fires in a bucket,
Eat windfalls and tinned sardines—   15
    They seem to like it.

Their nippers have got bare feet,
    Their unspeakable wives

Are skinny as whippets—and yet
    No one actually *starves*.   20

Ah, were I courageous enough
    To shout *Stuff your pension!*
But I know, all too well, that's the stuff
    That dreams are made on:

For something sufficiently toad-like   25
    Squats in me, too;
Its hunkers are heavy as hard luck,
    And cold as snow,

And will never allow me to blarney
    My way to getting   30
The fame and the girl and the money
    All at one sitting.

I don't say, one bodies the other
    One's spiritual truth;
But I do say it's hard to lose either,   35
    When you have both.

Thom Gunn

ON THE MOVE

"Man, you gotta Go."

The blue jay scuffling in the bushes follows
Some hidden purpose, and the gust of birds
That spurts across the field, the wheeling swallows,
Have nested in the trees and undergrowth.
Seeking their instinct, or their poise, or both,   5
One moves with an uncertain violence
Under the dust thrown by a baffled sense
Or the dull thunder of approximate words.

On motorcycles, up the road, they come:
Small, black, as flies hanging in heat, the Boys,   10
Until the distance throws them forth, their hum
Bulges to thunder held by calf and thigh.
In goggles, donned impersonality,
In gleaming jackets trophied with dust,
They strap in doubt—by hiding it, robust—   15
And almost hear a meaning in their noise.

Exact conclusion of their hardiness
Has no shape yet, but from known whereabouts
They ride, direction where the tires press.
They scare a flight of birds across the field: 20
Much that is natural, to the will must yield.
Men manufacture both machine and soul,
And use what they imperfectly control
To dare a future from the taken routes.

It is a part solution, after all.   25
One is not necessarily discord
On earth; or damned because, half animal,
One lacks direct instinct, because one wakes
Afloat on movement that divides and breaks.
One joins the movement in a valueless world,   30
Choosing it, till, both hurler and the hurled,
One moves as well, always toward, toward.

A minute holds them, who have come to go:
The self-defined, astride the created will
They burst away; the towns they travel through   35
Are home for neither bird nor holiness,
For birds and saints complete their purposes.
At worst, one is in motion; and at best,
Reaching no absolute, in which to rest,
One is always nearer by not keeping still.   40

THE UNSETTLED MOTORCYCLIST'S
VISION OF HIS DEATH

Across the open countryside,
Into the walls of rain I ride.
It beats my cheek, drenches my knees,
But I am being what I please.

The firm heath stops, and marsh begins.   5
Now we're at war: whichever wins
My human will cannot submit
To nature, though brought out of it.
The wheels sink deep; the clear sound blurs:
Still, bent on the handle-bars,   10
I urge my chosen instrument
Against the mere embodiment.
The front wheel wedges fast between
Two shrubs of glazed insensate green
—Gigantic order in the rim   15
Of each flat leaf. Black eddies brim
Around my heel which, pressing deep,
Accelerates the waiting sleep.

I used to live in sound, and lacked
Knowledge of still or creeping fact,   20
But now the stagnant strips my breath,
Leant on my cheek in weight of death.
Though so oppressed I find I may
Through substance move. I pick my way,
Where death and life in one combine,   25
Through the dark earth that is not mine,
Crowded with fragments, blunt, unformed;
While past my ear where noises swarmed
The marsh plant's white extremities,
Slow without patience, spread at ease   30
Invulnerable and soft, extend
With a quiet grasping toward their end.

And though the tubers, once I rot,
Reflesh my bones with pallid knot,

Till swelling out my clothes they feign   35
This dummy is a man again,
It is as servants they insist,
Without volition that they twist;
And habit does not leave them tired,
By men laboriously acquired.   40
Cell after cell the plants convert
My special richness in the dirt:
All that they get, they get by chance.

And multiply in ignorance.

Ellen Kay

TO A BLUE HIPPOPOTAMUS

Egyptian, c. 1950 B.C.

Millions who pass you see
But incongruity;
Fail now to reconcile
The river horse, the Nile
Your pasture, rapid, blue,   5
With that bare dungeoned zoo
Where your descendants dwell,
Mocked in their three-walled hell.

None have observed your pace,
Swift underwater grace,   10
Or rest like river gods
Feeding on sacred pods
In shallows by the bank.
They picture but the rank
Straw, the abrupt cement,   15
Nutshells and excrement.

Who know but cramp and noise,
Smile at your easy poise;
Who have not seen you swim
Can only damn as whim   20
That you, instead of mud,
Wear lotus, bloom and bud;
Who rush past will not span
Four thousand years of man.

Yet some Egyptian youth   25
Saw, not in whim but truth,
The river horse submerge
Under cerulean surge
Prisoned in lotus. We
Who condescendingly   30
Smile at the primitive,
The simplified, who live

Magnified incidents;
Which of us has the sense,
Perspective, or the power   35
To cast beast, river, flower—
One moment's entity—
In such simplicity
Of whole, perfect with part;
In such immobile art?   40

Biographical Notes

MATTHEW ARNOLD (p. 198), 1822–1888. Arnold was the son of the famous headmaster of Rugby, and spent most of his lifetime involved in education, as teacher and as inspector of schools. His chief fame was won as a critic of literature and society.

W. H. AUDEN (p. 291), 1907–   . After his education at Oxford, Auden taught for five years in England, and served as a noncombatant in the Spanish Civil War. He became an American citizen shortly after his emigration in 1939, and has lectured widely in America and England.

WILLIAM BLAKE (p. 112), 1757–1827. Blake's career was as an artist and engraver, and he illustrated not only his own but many other books. He was convinced that his poetry and his prophetic writings were inspired by supernatural agencies, and he provided visionary support for the American and French revolutions as the just overthrow of authority and tyranny.

ANNE BRADSTREET (p. 68), 1612?–1672. At the age of eighteen Anne Bradstreet and her husband Simon emigrated to America from England, and he was for ten years governor of the Massachusetts Bay Colony. Her poetry was first published in a pirated edition in England, under the title *The Tenth Muse Lately Sprung Up in America*.

ROBERT BRIDGES (p. 225), 1844–1930. Bridges studied at Oxford, and was for a time a practicing physician. He published a number of books of poetry and criticism, and the publication of his *Poetical Works* in 1912 was followed the next year by his appointment as poet laureate.

EMILY BRONTË (p. 182), 1818–1848. Raised in the partial seclusion of the parsonage of Haworth in Yorkshire, where her father was curate, Emily Brontë lived a rich fantasy life with her two sisters and her brother, and rarely ventured out of her home village at the edge of the moors. Besides her poetry, she is the author of the powerful novel *Wuthering Heights*.

SIR FULKE GREVILLE, LORD BROOKE (p. 34), 1554–1628. A lifelong friend of Sir Philip Sidney and a successful courtier, Greville wrote both plays and poetry. He is particularly notable for introducing Calvinist ideas into his more serious lyrics even while preserving the forms of the fashionable Petrarchan poetic tradition.

ROBERT BROWNING (p. 174), 1812–1889. Browning was privately educated, and after the friendly reception by leading literary men of his earliest poems, he turned to writing plays, which had some small success. He married in 1846 and went to live in Italy, but returned to England after the death of his wife in 1861. He wrote prodigiously during the rest of his life, and was immensely popular among the cultured.

WILLIAM CULLEN BRYANT (p. 144), 1794–1878. After practicing law for ten years, Bryant undertook a career as newspaper editor, and from 1829 onward enjoyed some fame as the liberal, crusading editor of the New York *Evening Post*.

ROBERT BURNS (p. 116), 1759–1796. Burns was the self-educated son of a Scottish farmer, and liked to promote the notion that his poetry was a natural and unlearned outpouring. He was a great popular success in his own time, despite his overt celebration of his sexual prowess.

GEORGE GORDON, LORD BYRON (p. 138), 1788–1824. Chiefly because of the heroic poses he struck, Byron enjoyed the greatest popularity of the English Romantic poets. The heir of a noble family, he was entitled to sit in the House of Lords, but in 1816 he left England in self-imposed exile. His public espousal of revolutionary causes was climaxed by his death of fever during the Greek struggle against Turkish rule.

THOMAS CAMPION (p. 42), 1567–1620. A physician and a theoretical critic, Campion was probably best known to his contemporaries as a musical composer. He wrote not only the music but also the lyrics for many of his songs.

THOMAS CAREW (p. 64), 1594?–1640. Carew was a typical Stuart courtier and was variously occupied in minor diplomatic jobs. He was well known for his wit and his licentiousness, and as a poet he regarded himself the heir of both Jonson and Donne.

EDWARD, LORD HERBERT OF CHERBURY (p. 54), 1583–1648. The elder brother of George Herbert, Lord Herbert was a diplomat, soldier, and philosopher and the author of the first purely metaphysical work by an Englishman, *De Veritate*. He is also known as the "Father of Deism" for promoting what he considered a "natural religion" as opposed to the dogmatic forms of the church.

SAMUEL TAYLOR COLERIDGE (p. 132), 1772–1834. Coleridge's medical education did not lead to a degree, and he managed to live on his journalism and on annuities bestowed upon him. He was a close friend and collaborator of Wordsworth's, but best deserves his fame for his literary criticism.

WILLIAM COLLINS (p. 108), 1721–1759. Collins attempted to establish himself as a literary figure in London, after his early years in Chichester and his education at Oxford, but his determination did not prove as great as his hopes. After inheriting enough money to live comfortably, he gave up the attempt, and his occasional fits of depression gave way to intermittent insanity.

WILLIAM COWPER (p. 109), 1731–1800. After training as a lawyer, Cowper succumbed to melancholy and delusions from which he was temporarily rescued by an Evangelical physician. Following a relapse, he remained in rural seclusion, attempting to divert himself from his depression with various domestic employments and with poetry.

HART CRANE (p. 284), 1899–1932. From a moderately well-to-do family in Ohio, Crane began writing poetry at thirteen, and left high school to go to New York and establish a literary career. He took a number of minor jobs, and managed to live on patronage and the income from his poetry. He drowned himself in the Caribbean on a return trip from Mexico, where he had gone on a Guggenheim Fellowship.

J. V. CUNNINGHAM (p. 295), 1911– . Cunningham was born in Maryland and raised in Montana and Colorado. He received B.A. and Ph.D. degrees from Stanford University, and has taught at Stanford, Chicago, and Virginia, and is currently a professor of English at Brandeis University. He has written books of criticism as well as poetry.

SAMUEL DANIEL (p. 37), 1562–1619. A minor courtier, Daniel was a champion of rhymed verse in English, and composed rhymed classical drama as well as his sonnet cycle *Delia*.

EMILY DICKINSON (p. 207), 1830–1886. One of two spinster daughters of a prominent lawyer in Amherst, Massachusetts, Emily Dickinson wrote most of her poetry between 1859 and 1865. She preferred the quiet domestic life of her home, and rarely left its precincts after she reached maturity. Only seven of her poems were published in her lifetime, and the remainder were variously edited and printed between 1890 and 1955.

JOHN DONNE (p. 49), 1572–1631. In his earlier years a Roman Catholic, Donne was ordained an Anglican priest in 1615, and from 1621 he was dean of St. Paul's Cathedral in London. His poetry ranges from satires to love lyrics to religious verse, and he is best known as the founder of the "metaphysical school" of English poetry.

MICHAEL DRAYTON (p. 37), 1563–1631. Drayton wrote a large quantity of verse of many kinds, including topographical celebrations of England

and historical and religious epistles. His most familiar work is his sonnet cycle *Idea's Mirror*.

JOHN DRYDEN (p. 75), 1631–1700. Dryden was the leading literary figure of the Restoration period, and besides his work as a poet, critic, playwright, and translator, was deeply involved in the political changes that took place during his maturity. He was appointed poet laureate in 1670, but the position was taken from him after the revolution of 1688.

T. S. ELIOT (p. 269), 1888–1965. One of the most influential critics of his time, Eliot was born in St. Louis and educated at Harvard, the Sorbonne, and Oxford. He took up permanent residence in London in 1914, and became a British subject in 1927. In England he taught school, worked in a bank, and was director of a large publishing house.

RALPH WALDO EMERSON (p. 155), 1803–1882. Emerson commenced by taking up the family profession of the ministry but resigned his church over a question of dogma. He then lectured and traveled widely, and was a leader of the New England philosophical movement called Tran scendentalism, which centered in his town of Concord. His mind be gan to fail in the 1870's, and by the time of his death he was completely senile.

WILLIAM EMPSON (p. 291), 1906– . Coming from Yorkshire, Emp son studied at Cambridge University, and lectured on English literature at universities in China and Japan. Since 1953 he has been a professor of English at Sheffield University, and has written several books of criticism.

PHILIP FRENEAU (p. 110), 1752–1832. Freneau's public career was as an editor of periodicals, and he was a staunch supporter of the cause of American independence, writing both philosophical justifications of the revolutionary ideals and satiric attacks on the British. His concerns left him little time to concentrate on his lyric and descriptive poetry.

ROBERT FROST (p. 243), 1874–1963. When his father died in 1885 Frost was taken by his mother from San Francisco, where he had been born, to her family home in Massachusetts. After a sporadic education he variously taught school and farmed in New England, and in 1912 took his family to England. He published his first books of poems there, and returned to America in 1915 after his poetry began to achieve recognition in this country. He spent the rest of his life farm ing and lecturing at several colleges and universities.

BARNABE GOOGE (p. 26), 1504–1594. In his lifetime Googe was a mem ber of both Oxford and Cambridge universities, and spent a decade in government service in Ireland. Among other accomplishments, he was one of the earliest writers of pastoral verse in English.

ROBERT GRAVES (p. 282), 1895–   . Graves is from London, and was educated at Oxford. He served as a captain in the First World War, and later taught in Cairo. Since 1929 he has made his home on Majorca, in the Mediterranean, except for brief periods of lecturing in English universities.

THOM GUNN (p. 305), 1929–   . Gunn studied at Cambridge University and at Stanford University, and has lived in Paris, Rome, and Berlin. At present he teaches at the University of California, Berkeley.

THOMAS HARDY (p. 217), 1840–1928. Hardy's early training was as an architect, and it took him from his native Dorset to London. There he commenced the writing of fiction, and continued as a novelist from the early 1870's until 1896, when hostile criticism of his *Jude the Obscure* caused him to turn exclusively to poetry. His most successful poems were written from the 1890's onward.

GEORGE HERBERT (p. 61), 1593–1633. The first public position held by Herbert was as an orator at Cambridge University, but he was ordained an Anglican priest in 1630, and lived the rest of his life in the quiet parish of Bemerton, near Salisbury. His verse is almost all of a religious nature, and was famous not only for its occasional extravagance but also for its plain style.

ROBERT HERRICK (p. 56), 1591–1674. A professed follower of Ben Jonson, Herrick spent most of his life except for a period during the Commonwealth as a country vicar in Devon. His poetry includes both sacred and secular verses.

GERARD MANLEY HOPKINS (p. 221), 1844–1889. Following his education at Oxford, Hopkins was in 1866 converted to Roman Catholicism, and in 1877 he was ordained in the Jesuit priesthood. At that time he destroyed all the poetry he had finished to that date. After serving as parish priest in a number of places, he was made professor of classics at University College, Dublin. His poems were published after his death by Robert Bridges.

A. E. HOUSMAN (p. 228), 1859–1936. Born in Shropshire and educated at Oxford, Housman was a clerk in the British Patent Office for ten years. He then turned to teaching, and lectured at University College, London, and later at Cambridge.

BEN JONSON (p. 45), 1572–1637. Like Shakespeare, Jonson was both an actor and a playwright, but exerted a more immediate influence on other writers of his generation because of his qualities as a literary critic. He consciously and deliberately modeled his plays and poems on classical drama and literature.

ELLEN KAY (p. 308), 1931–   . Ellen Kay was born in New Orleans, and received her B.A. from Mills College, California. She studied poetry writing with Yvor Winters at Stanford University, and play-writing in New York. Recently she entered an Anglican convent in New York.

JOHN KEATS (p. 146), 1795–1821. After training and certification as a physician, Keats gave up his medical career in 1816 to devote himself entirely to poetry. His last five years revealed an astounding increase in his poetic powers, but he succumbed to the family weakness to tuberculosis and died in Italy where he had gone for his health.

HENRY KING (p. 57), 1592–1669. King was educated at Oxford and was eventually elevated to the bishopric of Chichester. His friends in-cluded Ben Jonson and John Donne.

PHILIP LARKIN (p. 302), 1922–   . Larkin was born in Leicester and educated at Oxford. He has held posts in various libraries since 1943, and is now librarian at the University of Hull, Yorkshire. He has pub-lished two novels, and is the jazz correspondent for the *Daily Tele-graph*.

HENRY WADSWORTH LONGFELLOW (p. 159), 1807–1882. Following his education at Bowdoin College, Longfellow traveled in Germany and returned to become the first professor of modern languages in America, first at Bowdoin and then at Harvard. He gave up teaching in 1854 to spend his full time in writing poetry and translating.

ROBERT LOWELL (p. 296), 1917–   . Lowell is from Boston and was educated at Harvard and Kenyon College, and has taught at several American universities. During the war he spent a few months in a federal prison as a conscientious objector.

ANDREW MARVELL (p. 70), 1621–1678. During his lifetime Marvell's chief fame was as member of Parliament for Hull, and for a brief time as assistant to Milton in the Cromwell government. The bulk of his serious poetry was not published until after his death.

GEORGE MEREDITH (p. 206), 1828–1909. Meredith like Hardy is best known for his novels, and they brought him much honor in late life. He had tried several professions, including law and journalism, before he settled for a steady living as a publisher's reader. He remained at that job for thirty-five years.

JOHN MILTON (p. 66), 1608–1674. Milton was very early convinced of his vocation as a poet, and spent long years preparing himself for the task of writing his great epic *Paradise Lost*. He was a passionate Puritan, writing many pamphlets justifying the cause, and served as foreign secretary to Oliver Cromwell's government. Having become blind during his years in office, after the Restoration he lived in seclusion, writing much of his major poetry.

MARIANNE MOORE (p. 265), 1887–   . Miss Moore was born in St. Louis and educated in Pennsylvania. After teaching at a U.S. Indian school in Pennsylvania, she worked for a few years in the New York Public Library, and later edited *The Dial* magazine. Besides her poetry, she has written criticism and compiled a poetic translation of La Fontaine's *Fables*.

THOMAS NASHE (p. 41), 1567–1601. Nashe was a prolific writer on topical matters, often turning to satire and burlesque to attack his enemies and defend his friends, and he was imprisoned for a brief time for a satirical attack on the government. His picaresque adventure tale *The Unfortunate Traveller* is said to anticipate later developments in English prose fiction.

EDGAR ALLAN POE (p. 161), 1809–1849. Poe's parents, who were actors, died during his childhood, and he was raised by a family in Richmond, Virginia. His cursory education included instruction in England, at the University of Virginia, and at the Military Academy at West Point. His profession was that of editor for various publications, and he was reputed to be a drunkard.

ALEXANDER POPE (p. 87), 1688–1744. Like Dryden in the preceding generation, Pope was the most famous poet of his day, though his adherence to the Roman Catholic faith of his family prohibited his receiving a university education or any of the favors of the government. His health was never very robust, and his wit and temper made him feared and hated by the objects of his satiric poetry.

EZRA POUND (p. 263), 1885–   . After a brief career of college teaching Pound lived from 1908 in Paris, London, and Rapallo, Italy. He sponsored several authors, including T. S. Eliot and James Joyce, and helped edit a number of little magazines. His propaganda broadcasts during the Second World War, for the Fascists in Italy, led to his arrest for treason after the war, but he was declared insane and committed to an asylum. He was released in 1958, and returned to Italy.

SIR WALTER RALEGH (p. 29), 1552?–1618. Ralegh was one of the most famous courtiers of Elizabeth I, a man who served as a soldier and a leader of expeditions to America, and who wrote on a wide number of subjects in prose as well as in verse. Falsely accused of being involved in a plot against James I, he spent a long period in prison in the Tower of London before he was finally beheaded.

JOHN CROWE RANSOM (p. 268), 1888–   . A native of Tennessee, Ransom attended Vanderbilt University and Oxford University. He taught at Vanderbilt for more than twenty years, and later at Kenyon College, Ohio, and lectured widely in other colleges and universities. He has written several books of cultural and literary criticism.

EDWIN ARLINGTON ROBINSON (p. 236), 1869–1935. Raised in a small town in Maine, Robinson managed to attend Harvard for two years but had to leave because of financial difficulties after his father's death. He was for long subject to semi-impoverishment, but his life was made more easy when President Theodore Roosevelt championed his poetry, after which he worked as a government clerk until his poetry began to support him.

CHRISTINA ROSSETTI (p. 206), 1830–1894. Christina Rossetti was less publicly involved than her famous brother Dante Gabriel in the Pre-Raphaelite movement, but contributed to his magazine *The Germ*. The melancholy resignation of much of her poetry is probably traceable to long years of physical pain.

WILLIAM SHAKESPEARE (p. 38), 1564–1616. England's most famous playwright also wrote a sequence of sonnets published first in 1609 (but written sometime during the previous ten years). His plays contain a number of songs that constitute his finest lyrics.

PERCY BYSSHE SHELLEY (p. 140), 1792–1822. Shelley's atheism led to his expulsion from Oxford, and all his brief life he remained devoted to revolutionary and iconoclastic ideas. From 1815 he lived chiefly abroad in protest against English restrictiveness, and was drowned in a boating accident off the coast of Italy.

SIR PHILIP SIDNEY (p. 32), 1554–1586. In his lifetime Sidney was thought of as the ideal Renaissance courtier—a man of extensive travel and wide knowledge, a loyal soldier and diplomat, and a model writer of prose and poetry. His early death on the battlefield was the occasion for numerous eulogies extolling his perfections and mourning his promise.

EDMUND SPENSER (p. 28), 1552?–1599. Spenser's chief work, *The Faerie Queene,* failed to gain him the recognition at court that he had hoped for, and although he belonged to a notable family he was never able to achieve financial and social status. He spent much of his life in Ireland as secretary to Grey, the Lord Deputy of Ireland, a position of semi-exile from the more elegant life of the court.

WALLACE STEVENS (p. 251), 1879–1955. Stevens was born in Pennsylvania and educated at Harvard and the New York Law School. He practiced law in New York until 1916, when he joined an insurance firm in Hartford, Connecticut. He remained an executive there until his retirement. His first book of poetry was published in 1923, and he produced several volumes in the years following 1931.

SIR JOHN SUCKLING (p. 67), 1609–1642. In his day Suckling was well known for his gambling and general loose living at the court of Charles I, and he participated in a few losing campaigns during the Civil War. His death in exile in Paris may have been suicide.

HENRY HOWARD, EARL OF SURREY (p. 26), 1517?–1547. Beheaded for treason only a week before the death of Henry VIII, Surrey led the stormy life of an intriguing courtier. Despite several periods of imprisonment for his riotous and indiscreet behavior, his service to the king was notable, especially in military ventures. Surrey was the first poet to write blank verse in English.

JONATHAN SWIFT (p. 83), 1667–1745. Swift's chief fame rests on his prose satires, including *Gulliver's Travels*, and Dryden is said to have told him he would "never be a poet." Irish-born, Swift was an ordained minister in the Anglican church, and held a number of ecclesiastical positions in England and in Ireland. His last thirty years he spent chiefly in Ireland, as dean of St. Patrick's Cathedral, Dublin.

ALGERNON CHARLES SWINBURNE (p. 214), 1837–1909. Like Shelley, Swinburne consciously sought after rebelliousness and enjoyed shocking the polite reading public. His self-indulgence led to the breakdown of his health, and for the last thirty years of his life he had to resign himself to the protective care of a friend who managed all his practical affairs.

EDWARD TAYLOR (p. 82), 1644?–1729. The poetry of Taylor was not offered to the public until 1939, when portions of the manuscript poems in the Yale library were published. Taylor was born in England, but came to America in 1668, and spent his lifetime as the pastor and physician of a small town in western Massachusetts.

ALFRED, LORD TENNYSON (p. 163), 1809–1892. Tennyson left Cambridge without a degree, but he had been encouraged by his fellow students there to consider himself destined for a career in poetry. After a mixed reception to his first published verse, his fame steadily grew, and he was appointed poet laureate in 1850 after the death of Wordsworth.

CHIDIOCK TICHBORNE (p. 36), 1558?–1586. A minor courtier, Tichborne was arrested for plotting to kill Elizabeth I as part of a conspiracy to replace her with Mary, Queen of Scots. He confessed to his complicity in the plot and was executed.

HENRY VAUGHAN (p. 69), 1622–1695. Vaughan was born in Wales, and after a brief period of schooling and involvement on the Royalist side during the Civil War, he returned to the place of his birth and lived out his life as a country doctor. His poetry, much of it devoted to religious mysticism, was all published more than forty years before his death.

EDMUND WALLER (p. 65), 1606–1687. Waller was extremely wealthy, by inheritance and by marriage, and took an active part on the side of the Crown in the Civil War. He led an abortive plot to seize London for the king in 1643 and escaped execution only by betraying his associates. He was well known by his contemporaries as a smooth and polished poet, and was one of the earliest to employ heroic couplets in modern English.

WALT WHITMAN (p. 184), 1819–1892. Whitman was born on Long Island in New York, and received only sporadic education. For more than thirty years he was engaged in printing and editing, and after the Civil War, during which he worked as a male nurse in military hospitals, he was employed as a clerk by the government. A paralytic stroke in 1873 forced him into semi-retirement, and he lived out his life, revising his poetry, in Camden, New Jersey.

RICHARD WILBUR (p. 301), 1921–   . From New York City, Wilbur graduated from Amherst College and subsequently served in the U.S. Army. After the war he continued his education at Harvard, and has taught at Harvard and at Wellesley College.

WILLIAM CARLOS WILLIAMS (p. 260), 1883–1963. Williams was born in Rutherford, New Jersey, and studied medicine in America and Europe. From 1910 onward he practiced medicine in Rutherford, and published fiction, essays, and poetry.

YVOR WINTERS (p. 287), 1900–   . Winters was raised in Chicago and educated at the University of Colorado and Stanford University. He has taught English at Stanford since 1927, and is the author of several influential books of criticism.

WILLIAM WORDSWORTH (p. 119), 1770–1850. After an exuberant young manhood (which included his public support of the French Revolution and the fathering of an illegitimate daughter in France), Wordsworth settled down to rural domesticity with his sister Dorothy. He was much honored in his later years and was appointed poet laureate in 1843.

SIR THOMAS WYATT (p. 25), 1503?–1542. An eminent courtier during the reign of Henry VIII, Wyatt spent several years on the continent in the diplomatic service of the king. He was instrumental in introducing into England many of the ideas and traditions established by continental Renaissance writers, notably the Italian sonnet form.

William Butler Yeats (p. 228), 1865–1939. Yeats was born near Dublin, and attended schools there and in London. After three years studying art (his father was a painter), he turned to literature. Throughout his career he was involved in the Irish national movement, and helped found the National Theatre in Dublin, as well as serving in the Irish senate and working for the government as inspector of schools.

Index

Authors, Titles and First Lines

Titles are in italics, first lines in roman type. *A, An,* or *The* at the beginning of a title is placed at the end; in first lines, these words are indexed in their normal order. Long first lines are indexed by their first few words.